PENGUIN CANADA

STOLEN ANGELS

KATHY COOK is an internationally acclaimed journalist whose work has been published around the world, in over forty countries and in eighteen languages. In Canada, her pieces have appeared in *Reader's Digest,* the *National Post, Walrus,* and the *Ottawa Citizen.* She has won several awards including a Canadian National Magazine Award in the category of politics and public interest in 2005. This is her first book. She lives in Ottawa.

STOLEN ANGELS

THE KIDNAPPED GIRLS OF UGANDA

KATHY COOK

PENGUIN
CANADA

PENGUIN CANADA

Published by the Penguin Group

Penguin Group (Canada), 90 Eglinton Avenue East, Suite 700, Toronto, Ontario, Canada
M4P 2Y3 (a division of Pearson Canada Inc.)

Penguin Group (USA) Inc., 375 Hudson Street, New York, New York 10014, U.S.A.
Penguin Books Ltd, 80 Strand, London WC2R 0RL, England
Penguin Ireland, 25 St Stephen's Green, Dublin 2, Ireland (a division of Penguin Books Ltd)
Penguin Group (Australia), 250 Camberwell Road, Camberwell, Victoria 3124, Australia
(a division of Pearson Australia Group Pty Ltd)
Penguin Books India Pvt Ltd, 11 Community Centre, Panchsheel Park, New Delhi – 110 017,
India
Penguin Group (NZ), 67 Apollo Drive, Rosedale, North Shore 0632, New Zealand
(a division of Pearson New Zealand Ltd)
Penguin Books (South Africa) (Pty) Ltd, 24 Sturdee Avenue, Rosebank, Johannesburg 2196,
South Africa

Penguin Books Ltd, Registered Offices: 80 Strand, London WC2R 0RL, England

First published 2007

1 2 3 4 5 6 7 8 9 10 (WEB)

Canada Council   Conseil des Arts
for the Arts   du Canada

*We acknowledge the support of the Canada Council for the Arts which last
year invested $20.3 million in writing and publishing throughout Canada.*

*Nous remercions de son soutien le Conseil des Arts du Canada, qui a investi
20,3 millions de dollars l'an dernier dans les lettres et l'édition à travers le Canada.*

Manufactured in Canada.

ISBN-13: 978-0-14-305481-8
ISBN-10: 0-14-305481-3

Library and Archives Canada Cataloguing in Publication data available upon request

Visit the Penguin Group (Canada) website at **www.penguin.ca**

Special and corporate bulk purchase rates available; please see
www.penguin.ca/corporatesales or call 1-800-810-3104, ext. 477 or 474

To my husband Mike, with love.
And to Catherine and Mariam, with hope.

Suffering is the law of human beings; war is the law of the jungle. But suffering is infinitely more powerful than the law of the jungle for converting the opponent and opening his ears, which are otherwise shut, to the voice of reason. Nobody has probably drawn up more petitions or espoused more forlorn causes than I, and I have come to this fundamental conclusion that, if you want something really important to be done, you must not merely satisfy the reason, you must move the heart also.[1]

—MAHATMA GANDHI

CONTENTS

PREFACE

My first trip to Uganda took place in the summer of 2000, when *Reader's Digest* magazine asked me to research the story of a little Canadian boy who'd set out to raise money for well-drilling equipment in that impoverished country. African children, he had learned in school, were dying from drinking contaminated water. At the time my career was writing near-death adventure tales, otherwise known as "Drama in Real Life" articles, for the magazine. Medical dramas, drug-addiction dramas, animal-attack dramas, lost-in-the-wilderness dramas, all with happy endings. This was my job. Inspirational tales that educated and entertained.

After two Canadian aid agencies, Water-Can and Canadian Physicians for Aid and Relief, got behind the boy, Ryan Hreljac went on to collect enough funds so that CPAR could drill the wells. The first, now widely known as "Ryan's Well," was located near a school in the Northern Ugandan town of Lira. And so, having arrived in the country along with Ryan, his parents, and a film crew funded by the Canadian government, I headed out to visit the well. It was soon apparent to me that I was writing a fairy tale, an exotic child's story filled with ceremony and gifts and selfless altruism.

Then the executive director of CPAR-Uganda told me that only one hour north from our camp was the real story.

Gulu town was ground zero of the bizarre war—waged by children against other children—that lay behind the nation's overwhelming poverty. CPAR drove me the next day to the displaced persons' camps encircling the town. There I interviewed former child soldiers who had escaped from Northern Uganda's rebel ranks. They told gruesome and—what seemed to me at the time—incredulous stories. Their testimonies far outstripped the greatest "drama in real life" tales I had ever researched—only they didn't have a happy ending.

I didn't immediately do anything with these interviews. They were profoundly moving, but they weren't relevant to the fairy tale I was writing. They would, however, ultimately become the reason behind this book.

In the next years I returned to school to do my master's degree in journalism and moved on to other narratives. But the story came up again in 2004 when I learned that, two years after our visit, a Ugandan boy who'd been Ryan's pen pal and thirty of his fellow village children had been abducted into the rebel army ranks. The boy had managed to escape moments after his capture, fleeing first to the local CPAR office and then to Canada and Ryan's family. In the process of writing the follow-up article for *Reader's Digest,* the larger issue of this army of stolen children came flooding back to me. It struck me then that perhaps I could tell the story of these children, of this illogical war, in a more comprehensive way.

Around that time the United Nations issued a press release declaring the tragedy of Northern Uganda's child soldiers as the world's most under-reported story. By then the Lord's Resistance Army (LRA), of which an estimated 90 percent were abducted youth between ages eight and seventeen, had grown into the world's largest army of children.

I began researching the war—a war in which Uganda's popular president, Yoweri K. Museveni, had pitted his army against the LRA, although many other forces were at play. I scoured Ugandan newspaper archives, aid-agency reports, and other journalists' works. I was looking for a focal point, a drama playing out within the war that would be my way into its heart. When I began to read about the Aboke Girls I knew I'd found it.

In 1996 thirty schoolgirls had been abducted from the esteemed St. Mary's College School for Girls in Northern Uganda's Aboke village. Their plight touched the hearts of many around the world. The story of the girls' enslavement among the rebel soldiers of the Lord's Resistance Army was told on CNN, on *The Oprah Winfrey Show,* in *The New Yorker.* There were documentaries, a book. Only a few of the girls had managed to escape. But as the years passed and no more came home and the war raged on, the impact of the girls' captivity became muted by the stark reality that thousands of others suffered similar fates.

I felt the horror of these girls' lives, but not until I actually met them did I understand that there was something deeply profound in their suffering. From that moment on, the Aboke Girls touched me directly too.

STOLEN ANGELS is an account of the human will pushed to its limits. It is also a story of world politics and of Canada's role in those politics. Parts of the book were first published in *Walrus* magazine in June 2005. That article, "The Peace Wager," won a Canadian national magazine award as a work of journalism capable of affecting public policy.

The book's narrative is based on dozens of interviews and hundreds of reports and articles, and where the research is not my own I have footnoted it. I have made great efforts to go to primary sources, but on some occasions did rely on second-hand information, and so it's possible that there are some errors. Every quotation in this book is exact, although in some cases, when conversations in the Luo language were subsequently relayed to me by people without perfect command of English, I corrected the grammar. Some of what is said here will not correspond to how others recall events. In those instances where the facts are in significant dispute, I have footnoted explanations. In war there are many truths.

INTRODUCTION

In June 2006, in a secret jungle camp along the remote border of South Sudan and the Democratic Republic of Congo, the messianic Ugandan rebel leader Joseph Kony, surrounded by his army of children, gave the first press interview of his life. "I am a human being like you," the commander of the Lord's Resistance Army declared.[2] "I have eyes, a brain, and wear clothes, but they are saying we don't talk with people, we eat people. We are killers. That is not true. Why do you meet me if I am a killer?"

The children, dressed in camouflage uniforms and holding AK-47s, protected him fiercely. They also worshipped him.

Joseph Kony was Africa's most wanted man, and technically, based on the recent International Criminal Court indictments against him, also the world's most wanted. The Northern Ugandan rebel was being sought on charges of war crimes as well as crimes against humanity. These included murder, rape, slavery, inducement to rape, inducement to slavery, forced enlisting of children into the rebel ranks, and targeting civilians during military operations. Although Kony remained at large, he was the first person charged by the new court.

Kony, an uneducated, devout Catholic, claimed that a discontented God, upset at the corruption and violence of the world, was channelling through him. Following God's orders, Kony was told to take anyone who made the sign of the cross into his army, and to fight until there were none left in the world who wanted to fight. This was when the angels would come, Kony would tell his children.

He was the rebel leader in a land that now had the highest early death rate in the world, far surpassing Iraq or Darfur. His homeland—Acholiland as it is known to the locals, Northern Uganda to the international community—is an undeveloped pastoral region with villages of subsistence farmers living in mud huts with straw roofs. But all those villages were now abandoned, and 90 percent of the men over thirty-five were dead or missing. Ten percent of all early deaths were the result of people starving to death in the displaced persons' camps into which the government had forced them, allegedly for their own protection.

Some analysts called the situation a genocide. Christian groups called it unmitigated evil. It was Africa's longest ongoing war. Hardly anyone understood it.

DAYS AFTER the interview, Kony's nemesis, Ugandan president Yoweri K. Museveni, allowed a delegation of Kony's family and tribal elders to meet with Kony as a trust-building gesture meant to lead the way to peace talks.

For the first time in over a decade, Acholi elders now sat with Kony and his fellow commanders. The group also included the Catholic Archbishop of Northern Uganda, the Muslim Khadi Sheikh, a Protestant Bishop, Kony's former right-hand man Brigadier-General Kenneth Banya, who had since turned into a government informant, two of Kony's former wives, and various other elders representing the entire region of Northern Uganda.

In a simple mud hut erected in the Congo jungle, Kony and the Acholi visitors prayed and talked through the night about war and peace, justice and retribution, God and forgiveness.

Two submissive young women served the visitors tea. Watching the women, one of the delegates was certain he recognized them as the famed schoolgirls from St. Mary's in Aboke village, a school run by Comboni missionary nuns. The girls had been kidnapped ten years earlier.

The two women did not speak, but they listened for a while before disappearing into the dark African night.

PART 1

"LET US GO TO DIE
FOR OUR GIRLS"

CHAPTER 1

OCTOBER 10, 1996

"Sister, the rebels are here," the watchman whispered outside Sister Rachele Fassera's window at 2:15 A.M.[3]

Sister Rachele, forty-nine, a slight, grey-haired Italian nun, jumped out of bed and ran down the hall to Sister Alba Brulo, the Mother Superior. She had horrifying news. The two nuns ran outside their convent toward the entry gate for their adjacent school, St. Mary's School for Girls, one of Uganda's best academies. But as they approached, they saw that the gated entrance was floodlit with the torches of the rebels. Crouching under cover of a pitch-black night, the two white women, both missionary nuns of the Comboni Sisters, crept around the perimeter to the dormitories at the back of the school, where they hoped to alert the girls before the rebels found them.

But once there they saw that the rebels' torchlights already surrounded the residences. Rifle butts banged against the residence doors. "Open up! Open up! Or we'll come in and get you!" the men in camouflage military fatigues shouted.

The sisters stepped back into the banana plantation behind the school to hide. It seemed the best solution. Sister Rachele didn't think the rebels would be able to get to the girls. The dormitory doors were made of reinforced steel and the windows were protected with iron bars. Provided that none of the girls opened the door from inside, she figured the rebels would eventually move on. But if the rebels saw the nuns, they could force the keys from them.

As the night hours passed, the nuns hid behind a bush and prayed. For some of that time they heard a dull, steady pounding. Not once was there a cry or a scream. While she hid, Sister Alba thought about the day's events leading up to this attack. Two sets of families had unexpectedly arrived earlier that day and pulled their daughters from the school. Sister Alba had told them that, since midterm exams were soon starting, now wasn't a good time to remove the girls, but the parents had insisted. One family, in their haste, had almost driven through the gated door before the guard had opened it. It seemed clear to her now that some parents had already known the attack was coming, and had chosen not to warn them.

Now, THE REBELS HELD THE FIRE from their torches up against the window bars of one of the two school dormitories and peered inside. The rebels, boys mostly aged eleven to seventeen, commanded by a twenty-one-year-old leader, were hunting for virgin girls. They knew that they lived in one of these buildings. Shrouded by the darkness of their room, the 152 girls inside—aged eleven to sixteen—quietly moved off their bunk beds and climbed under their bed frames to hide. Just then, a rebel's torchlight caught the gleaming eye of a girl. "They're in here!" he shouted.

Some of the rebels rammed on the locked door, others tried to break the barred windows. After a few moments, still unable to gain entry, one yelled out: either open up or he'd throw in a grenade. Despite the threat, no one opened the door. The girls hid silently under their beds, the occasional soft trickle of water breaking the silence when one urinated on the floor in fear.

For an hour the rebels pounded with their rifle butts against the concrete wall. Finally the concrete collapsed along a window frame. A small rebel boy entered through the hole and unbolted the door, and the rest rushed in. One of the girls screamed.

A rebel hit the girl across the face with his gun and told the rest to be quiet. Then the rebel boys began pulling the girls out from under their beds. The girls, petrified, stood silently as they had their wrists bound.

Then they were led outside, where other rebels roped them together by the waists, allowing five feet between each girl. When all the girls were collected, the rebels gave each girl looted goods to carry—drugs and supplies they'd stolen from the school's infirmary, food and drink from the kitchen, clothing from the girls' luggage—then tugged on the ropes and led the girls off the school grounds, down the dirt road, and into the bush.

AT DAWN, a cloud of smoke billowed up from the courtyard. The school's truck had been blown up. Minutes later, the bells from a nearby church rang out— it was the priest, who'd been hiding, now alerting the village that the rebels were gone. In the misty haze of early morning, Sister Rachele saw ten girls running toward them in the garden. "Are you okay?" she asked.

Claudia had two huge tears dripping down her cheeks. "Sister, they took all of us!" she cried.

"Took all of you?"

The two nuns ran to the dormitories.

Nestled amid lush flower gardens in the countryside outside the village of Aboke, the school was renowned both for its academic excellence and loving environment. Some of Northern Uganda's most professional families sent their children here. Until now, the rebel activity in Uganda had been confined farther north of the school.

The nuns reached the dormitory of the older girls in Senior 4 and 5, equivalent to grades 11 and 12. Sister Rachele knocked, but all was quiet inside. "Girls, we are the sisters, are you there?"

One girl opened the door, and the students cried and laughed, overjoyed that they had all survived. When the rebels had peered in, the older girls had silently squatted down. The rebels had moved on, assuming that, with drying corn on its veranda, the building was a food storage house.

But when the group moved to the next dormitory they saw children's slippers, clothing, and books strewn about the large room. Mattresses had been flung off their beds. There was a hole in the wall, and no students were inside.

"Alba, I'll run after them," Sister Rachele said, her eyes filled with tears.

"Rachele, go," said Sister Alba, who, at sixty-two and with weak knees and high blood pressure, was less mobile. Sister Alba, the headmistress, had lived in Uganda for over thirty years. She was a soft, loving woman, overweight and all heart. Her partner at the school, Sister Rachele, thirteen years younger, was her opposite—"Iron" they called her. Strict, strong, demanding, and intelligent. She was thin and fit.

Sister Rachele ran to her room and stepped into her beige habit, white veil, and silver cross. She raced to the school office, where she grabbed all the school's money, the equivalent of US$700, to use as ransom. As she was stuffing the money into her bag, someone touched her waist. Sister Rachele turned to see tiny, short-haired Josephine, eleven, wearing only a brown sack. "Sister, I've been raped," she said.

"My God!" Sister Rachele exclaimed. She called to Sister Alba to help the distraught girl, and then left the trembling child standing alone.

Sister Rachele ran outside, where she bumped into a young teacher from the St. Mary's staff, John Bosco Ocen, a thin, short, fine-featured man who still looked like a teenager. He taught history and geography to the junior grades and lived down the road. He'd heard the rebels attacking and wanted to know what he could do to help her. "Will you come with me to find the girls?" They both knew she was asking Bosco to follow her on a suicide mission.

"Sister, let us go to die for our girls," Bosco replied without hesitation. As they walked past the weeping villagers—the rebels had abducted others during their rampage—people murmured, wondering whether this crazy man and nun would come back alive. No one dared defy Joseph Kony and his brutal child army.

Because the soldiers had looted the school's food supplies, the path they took was clearly marked by dropped bottles and empty food packages. But soon the trail led into the dense, uneven undergrowth of the forest. Their fear increased. Bosco stepped ahead of Sister Rachele. "Sister, put your feet only where I put mine," he said, following the trail into the bush. He stepped on hard earth and rocks, avoiding soft mounds of dirt. It was well known that the rebels planted land mines behind their paths to deter others from following. They walked in silence. The path, muddy and thorny, soon became treacherous. They crossed a swamp so deep that it soaked Sister Rachele to her armpits. She thought of the children trying to cross that swamp. She wondered if any of the smaller ones had drowned.

After a while they crossed a field where two women—one old, the other young—stood outside a couple of huts. "Where are you going?" they yelled.

"We're looking for the rebels together with the girls. Did they pass here?" asked Bosco.

"Yes, they passed here. And they also kidnapped my baby girl. Please let me come with you."

Bosco looked at Sister Rachele. She nodded back. Now the three travelled together, following each other's footsteps. Always Bosco first, then the young mother, then Sister Rachele. Sometimes Sister Rachele lost her footing and stepped outside Bosco's steps. She broke a twig under her foot and the group froze in fear. "Please, sister, always follow my steps," Bosco said.

After four hours, Sister Rachele looked down and saw slippers and one of the girls' identity card lying on the trail. She bent to pick up the card. Suddenly, Bosco touched her shoulder. "Sister, there," he said. The group—rebel soldiers in camouflage uniforms, several carrying AK-47 machine guns—was climbing up the next ridge.

At that moment, the rebels also saw them. They turned around and stared in silence at the nun and her two followers. Sister Rachele thought she saw a soldier wave to her, so she waved back. Bosco was the first to move.

"Let us go to die for our girls," he said for the second time as he raised his hands in the air, plastered on a smile, and walked toward the rebels.

Bosco led the way, with the mother behind and again Sister Rachele in the rear. The thirty soldiers stood in two lines waiting for them. Sister Rachele was afraid. She looked into the rebels' eyes with kindness and they looked back at her with hatred. One of the rebels asked what they wanted. Before he answered, Bosco overheard some of the young rebels commenting in Luo that they should rape the white nun in order to teach her a lesson. Earlier so brave, Bosco opened his mouth but was suddenly unable to speak. He was frozen in fear. Sister Rachele stepped forward. "I am the sister of Aboke. I would like to speak with your leader."

A man she thought to be about twenty came forward. "Why have you come—do you see any white people here?" he said. He had a fat upper lip, slightly deformed from a bullet that had once grazed him.

"I'm the sister of Aboke," Sister Rachele said again. "I've brought money."

"But we don't want money," he replied. Other rebels grabbed at Bosco and the sister, searching them. She passed a young soldier her purse. He looked at the money and then gave it back to her. She clutched her rosary beads.

"What are you doing?" the commander asked, looking at her rosary.

"I'm praying that you'll give me back the girls."

"Don't worry. I'll give you the girls," he said. Sister Rachele jumped, shocked at the words. The leader looked at the young mother, and with a sharp word and dismissive gesture, ordered her to leave them. The mother stepped away. Her daughter was to remain with the rebels. Then he gestured for Sister Rachele to follow him. "I have the rosary, too," the commander told her. "Let us pray together." In the deep woods of Northern Uganda, the rebel and the Italian nun knelt down and prayed.

Among the rebels, Sister Rachele saw many young boys, ten, eleven, and twelve years old, draped with necklaces of bullets and carrying rifles or machetes or axes. *Innocent children, abducted probably only weeks or months earlier, now dressed up like monsters,* she thought. *Their humanity stolen from them while still in childhood.* More than 80 percent of the rebels were children under eighteen, and all had been abducted and then converted through force and coercion into following the rebel way.

The path climbed again. Sister Rachele kept up with the commander. They came to a long pathway, where Sister Rachele saw a group of five girls bound in ropes walking along the road with a group of rebels. Then another group of bound girls and another group of rebels.

Then she saw Judith, fifteen, the head girl from Class 3. Judith was popular and respected by the other girls. She normally walked tall, with a slight swagger of teenage confidence. Her father was a highly respected scientist, and she was a natural leader. But now she hunched inward, sobbing, and her dress was torn open in the front. Sister Rachele thought perhaps the girl had been raped.

Sister Rachele was brought before another soldier. "Where was the parish priest when we came for you?" he said.

"He was not there. He was away."

"You may speak to your girls," he said. In Uganda, being a white woman, and a nun, granted Sister Rachele some respect. And this rebel group was part of the Lord's Resistance Army, a pseudo-Christian militia purported to follow the commands of God. Sister Rachele told the girls that they were safe and would soon be free. The captives and rebels continued hiking until they reached two huts by the Otwal railway station, where they made camp. The rebel leader wanted the girls from St. Mary's separated from the other abductees, or new recruits, that they had taken along the way.

He looked at Sister Rachele and smiled. "Now," he said, "I'll give you the girls." But first he pulled out a solar panel to charge his satellite phone and starting dialling—likely to his headquarters in South Sudan.

While he spoke on the phone, the unmistakable drone of a helicopter filled the air. The rebels sought cover and aimed their guns. The commander ordered everyone to disperse into small groups. He told Sister Rachele to take off her white veil, which could easily be spotted through their cover of green forest. The Ugandan military—the Ugandan People's Defence Force (UPDF)—were now also on their trail.

The helicopter passed overhead without seeing them below. Immediately afterward, the commander ordered everyone to run. "Let me go with my girls, they'll hinder you," Sister Rachele said. But he refused. He had no time for that now.

Sister Rachele, Bosco, and her girls all rushed along with the rebels. Fifteen minutes later a shot rang out. The pursuing Ugandan foot soldiers opened fire on the group. Sister Rachele hid with her girls as bullets whizzed over their heads. The rebels returned fire. The kidnapped girls and boys were sent ahead while the trained rebels remained in the rearguard, slowing down the pursuing soldiers. The rebels knew the woods better than the military did. This was their home.

Four more hours passed. Periodically a helicopter would fly by, forcing the group to camouflage themselves under leaves. The hunted rebels were clearly strained and nervous. Finally they came to another camp, which the rebels seemed to know well. The Ugandan military had lost them. Here Sister Rachele and Bosco found several hundred other rebels and nervous captives. Once more, the rebel chief ordered the St. Mary's girls separated from the others.

The chief sat on a chair. A woman promptly took off his shoes and put on his slippers. Sister Rachele and Bosco sat on the ground at his side. "Do you have a picture of the Virgin Mary?" he asked her.

"Unfortunately, no. But I have a crucifix," she said, and handed it to him. He looked at it, kissed it, then put it in the pocket of his shirt. The mood was becoming friendlier, almost collegial. He showed Sister Rachele his walkie-talkie, explaining that it had been taken in an attack in Karuma, a town along the Nile River. "I'm Mariano Lagira Ocaya. When we came to Aboke, if we'd found a priest, we would have done nothing," he said.

"Mariano, I'm a nun. That's worth more than a parish priest," she said to no avail. While they spoke a captive boy of about sixteen approached Sister Rachele and whispered to her: "Please tell him that I'm a seminarist." The boy hoped that Mariano's respect for the Church would somehow help his plight.

"What is he asking for?" said Mariano.

"He's a seminarist. Let him come with me," said Sister Rachele.

"Here we are all seminarists," said Mariano dismissively.

The conversation wandered. Eventually, Sister Rachele brought them back to her immediate goal. "Mariano, why don't we end the war? Our people have already suffered a lot, too much."

But Mariano shook his head. The war would continue. "We'll finish this war when President Museveni decides to rule the country by the Ten Commandments," he said.

A few minutes later, Mariano called a girl to bring over a basin of water and soap. Then he ordered Sister Rachele to wash herself. She didn't understand what he was asking of her, but he was insistent. Surprised, Sister Rachele, wanting to please Mariano, followed the girl behind a hut and stood on a mat made from banana leaves. She changed out of her habit, washed herself, then put her gown back on.

Meanwhile, several of the rebel boys seated themselves around the group of girls and started sharpening their knives, eyeing the girls in a threatening manner. The boys commented on the girls. The first they picked out from the crowd was a fat girl. Her legs were bruised and she limped. "She is useless," one said. Mariano watched as the boys asked questions. He told her to go sit on the other side. Next they picked out a girl who had come from South Sudan to study at the school. One by one, they analyzed and divided, assessing each girl and telling her to join either the group on the left or the group on the right.

The girls understood that this division was about who would be released and who would not. They all tried to get themselves chosen for the unwanted group. One held her hand as if it was paralyzed. Others limped or tried to make themselves look weak and sick. They made subtle face contortions, hoping to look ugly. Grace Grall scrunched up her dress in the middle, hoping it might make her look pregnant. The rebels asked questions of the girls: where they were from, what grade they were in, the names of their fathers, if they had any family in the government, if they wanted to go home or if they preferred to stay in the bush. Some lied, some told the truth, not knowing what answers were the least likely to make the rebels want to keep them. Some girls gave the same answers as the one before them but were sent to a different group. Eventually, most of the girls went into one group. Only the strongest and most beautiful Acholi girls, and those with parents considered high-ranking, remained in the small group.

With the girls divided, the rebels counted that they had twenty-eight girls. But they wanted thirty, so they looked again at the larger group.

Mariano pointed to Grace Grall. He'd thought he'd already selected her, he said, and told her and another girl to move into the smaller group.

When Sister Rachele returned to them, Bosco whispered nervously. "Sister, he's not giving us all the girls."

She turned around. "Mariano, are you giving me all the girls?"

He shook his head. He stooped toward the earth and with a stick wrote the number 139, the total number of the girls they'd taken from St. Mary's. "I give you 109 and keep 30 with me," he said. Sister Rachele fell to her knees before him. "Keep me instead," she begged.

Mariano said no. But he would ask Joseph Kony tomorrow, and if he agreed, then all the girls would be released. The rebel youth watching this display wondered at Mariano's respect for the nun. Several murmured that she should be killed for following them.

"Let me speak with Kony. Bring me to him," said Sister Rachele.

Mariano shook his head again. Impossible. Kony, their mystical high commander, did not receive guests. But she could write him a message. She wrote a note begging Kony to release her girls, and Mariano stuffed the note in the same pocket with her cross. "Now, go and write the names of the girls that will remain here," he said.

Sister Rachele felt she could die during that short walk to the girls. She found them divided and sitting in two groups. Mariano addressed the girls. "Jesus chose twelve apostles," he said. "We choose thirty angels." When the group of thirty girls saw Sister Rachele, they stood up and began crying and begging her to take them home as well.

Angrily, Mariano yelled a sharp order. He forbade crying. A group of soldiers pounced upon the thirty girls. The boys punched, kicked, whipped, and jumped on the screaming children.

"Jesus!" invoked Sister Rachele, shouting as loud as she could. Mariano raised his hand and the flogging stopped as quickly as it started. The terrified and now wounded girls sat back down and stopped begging for their release. Hardly able to believe the nightmare that was happening to them, Sister Rachele went among the girls and told them she'd come back for them.

"Sister, are you coming back tonight?" Charlotte, fourteen, asked.

Agatha was hyperventilating and unable to speak. Sister Rachele could hardly look at her, the terror in the Karamojong child's eyes was so palpable.

Agatha was different from the other girls. She belonged to the Karamojong tribe of northeastern Uganda, one of the few closed tribes left in Africa. Its members, who lived the same nomadic lifestyles as they would have a thousand years before, were almost untouched by the outside world. Agatha's people led a brutal existence in a desert corner of Uganda. To this day, the men still notched their arms, like a badge of honour, one knife cut for each man they'd killed during cattle raids. And in 1980, the year before Agatha's birth, her people suffered one of the worst famines in history in terms of mortality rates. About 21 percent of the population died, including 60 percent of the infants.

Some years before, Comboni missionaries had settled in Karamoja to spread the word of God to the people. Ultimately from this relationship, a Karamojong boy grew up to be a Comboni Catholic priest, and in the late 1980s was stationed in Aboke village. This priest decided to try to open the world to the Karamojong, and so he invited a few Karamojong girls to study the world at St. Mary's Aboke school. Agatha's father, who knew the priest and who wanted his daughter to have a better life, allowed her to go to this school, even though the Karamojong children did not attend school.

This was Agatha's second year here, but she suffered because she was shy. She struggled to keep up academically, and the rest of the girls considered her an anomaly—a warrior girl removed from her desert tribe.

Earlier that day, before Sister Rachele had reached them, Agatha had been raped. Perhaps it was random, but a seventeen-year-old sergeant leading her and a handful of the other girls noticed that he was out of the commanders' view. Although they were under orders not to touch the Aboke Girls—Kony wanted them brought to him as virgins—he threw Agatha down on the ground and assaulted her in front of some of her classmates. When he was done, he raised himself up, grabbed his gun, and walked onward, leaving Agatha sobbing and humiliated.

Now she was unable to communicate to Sister Rachele what had happened, what she knew would happen again.

Josephine spoke up instead. "Sister, they will rape us all tonight," she said.

Jackie Wagesa told Sister Rachele that her mother was sick. Grace Acan asked her to return with clothes for them, and then told her she had her period and asked her what she should do.

Sister Rachele couldn't fathom that she was about to leave the girls to be alone with these men. She turned around to Mariano, and with tears in her eyes knelt before him once more. "Mariano, I pray, give me all of them."

"I am not your God!" he yelled. "If you act like this, I'll give you them as corpses," he said, and walked away.

Sister Rachele followed him and apologized. He turned back to her and told her to write out the names of the girls who were remaining with him. Sister Rachele tried, but she was too distraught to write. She couldn't think clearly. Angela Afim, thirteen, a scholar among them, stepped forward. "Sister, I will write our names."

As Angela wrote out the names, Mariano called to Sister Rachele and Bosco to join him for tea and cookies with the other commanders. Sister Rachele and Bosco agreed. A few minutes later Angela Atim approached with the list. Sister Rachele looked at the paper. The names would be forever scarred into her memory:

Rebecca Kia
Jacqueline Wagesa
Grace Acan
Janet Akello
Jacqueline Alobo
Caroline Anyango
Janet Aber
Victoria Nyanjura
Susan Ejang
Agatha Longoria

Charlotte Awino
Agnes Akello
Caroline Akello
Palma Aceng
Grace Grall Akello
Pamela Adokorac
Barbara Alopo
Agnes Ocitti
Josephine Lolem
Esther Acio
Sandra Everlyn Akot
Mariam Akello
Catherine Ajok
Sylvia Alaba
Judith Enang
Jessica Anguu
Louiza Namele
Brenda Atoo
Grace Oyela
Angela Atim

While Sister Rachele read through them, Angela leaned in and whispered, "Sister, there's only twenty-nine of us. Janet hid with the other group."

Sister Rachele quickly assessed this situation. If the rebels realized they had only twenty-nine girls, Mariano might hunt down the other 109 girls and kill them all. Saving Janet put them all at risk. "Go and call her back," Sister Rachele whispered to Angela.

Angela went to Janet hiding among her classmates and told her to follow her back into the other group. Janet obediently followed Angela, whispering to the others to tell her parents to pray for her. Sister Rachele then went to Janet and hugged her tightly. "Janet, don't try this again. You are putting everyone in danger."

"Sister, I promise, I will not try to escape again."

Bosco leaned in to Sister Rachele and told her they should leave now, before the commanders changed their minds. Sister Rachele nodded.

As the last light of day began to fade, she and the thirty girls knelt together in a tight circle. Sister Rachele prayed with them, and vowed she would never give up fighting for their release. The commander had already taken her crucifix, so she handed Judith her rosary. "Judith, take care of the children," she said.

"Yes sister. I'll do it."

Sister Rachele told them not to look at them when they left.

"No, sister, we won't look at you," Judith replied. Fighting against tears, the thirty fated Catholic schoolgirls prayed together over the rosary. While they prayed, Sister Rachele and the other 109 girls walked back the way they came. Before they left, Mariano handed a ten-year-old girl to Sister Rachele from the other group of captives. He told Sister Rachele to take her back as well.

CHAPTER 2

The abduction of the girls from St. Mary's was not a random act. Joseph Kony had specifically ordered it after he'd learned that the girls in this strict, isolated Catholic school were all extremely religious, and virgins.

They were much more than that. St. Mary's School for Girls was the best school in Northern Uganda, surpassing all the boys' schools in statewide tests and competing with the most elite private schools of the southern capital of Kampala. The girls learned academics, but they also learned to be efficient farmers, good cooks, and hard workers. In Northern Uganda girls were typically shy, keeping their heads down in front of mixed company, speaking in soft whispers. But St. Mary's unleashed confident, capable, smart young women.

And among the ambitious Northern Ugandan young men, the girls of St. Mary's were those most sought-after for marriage. They were recognized for their intelligence, ability to speak and write in English, domestic talents, work ethic, farming skills, and deeply religious natures. Their husbands often took them to Kampala, where there were better jobs, or out of the country.

The graduates of St. Mary's, having qualified for scholarships to help them earn advanced degrees, held careers as doctors, diplomats, teachers, nurses, aid workers, and lawyers. They were role models to other girls.

St. Mary's School for Girls likely never would have been built without the efforts of a Roman Catholic priest.

Father John Fraser, sixty-three, a Scottish Canadian with thick glasses and a ruddy complexion, was stationed deep in the rural countryside of impoverished Malawi, fifteen hundred kilometres south of Uganda, when he heard over the radio about the abduction. In anguish, his mind turned to the school he'd fought to create, to the families he knew, and to his good friend, Sister Alba. *Such suffering they all must be enduring,* he thought.

Father John, who arrived in Uganda in 1960 as a scholarly young Comboni missionary with advanced degrees in philosophy and theology obtained in Rome, had since spent most of his adult life in Acholiland. He understood that one of the main problems in this underdeveloped region was that girls received only a primary school education. The boys who showed promise continued on to university and became professionals and community leaders. But the girls were destined for having babies, hoeing the fields, collecting firewood, and, in their destitution and dependence, accepting new women into their homes as other wives to their husbands. At that time, most of the girls in the North were married off by age thirteen to young men of twenty or older. The early marriage traumatized the girls, but the culture accepted this. It was obvious to Father John that the girls needed more education. That meant the Church needed to build more schools—the government certainly wouldn't do it. The Comboni order had already opened up one senior-grades girls' boarding school in Gulu, a town farther north. It was run by Sister Alba, but was the only one for several hundred kilometres.

None of the girls in Father John's rural parish, nestled along the north shore of the Nile River, went to school beyond grade six. So he talked to the local church council about his hopes for the Combonis to open a senior girls' school. The men weren't supportive; the local leaders wanted another advanced school for their boys. Father John explained that the girls needed a chance too.

Long before it was accepted in development work, Father John understood that educating women was the key to advancing societies. As he saw it, one school could bring up some of the girls, and then those women could be teachers and role models for the rest. Just one school could start the revolution.

His voice was heard, and in 1967 St. Mary's College School for Girls was opened in the small village of Aboke, district of Lira. The high school took in two hundred girls who had performed well in primary school. Sister Alba Brulo, who loved gardening and classical literature, moved from the Gulu school to become St. Mary's headmistress. A few years later, Sister Rachele Fassera became its deputy headmistress.

The two women, and the school, flourished. As Sister Alba would later say, she lived the life not of a spinster but of a married woman with children. God was her husband, the girls of St. Mary's were her children, and she loved them all. It was clear to Sister Alba that she was exactly where she was supposed to be. Sister Rachele, for her part, was strict with the girls, demanding much from them, but they always knew she loved them. "You can ease up later in life, not now," she'd tell them, pushing them along. She told them that they were beautiful, cherished, and capable of being anything they wanted—and then she'd send them out to hoe in the garden and collect firewood.

THE COMBONI MISSIONARY order to which Father John, Sister Rachele, and Sister Alba dedicated their lives had introduced Catholicism to Sudan, Uganda's northern neighbour, over 150 years earlier. It had marked the beginning of a new religious and political destiny for Sudan, and its southern neighbour, Uganda, that unfolds to this day.

The order was founded in the mid-1800s by Father Daniel Anthony Comboni, an Italian missionary priest ultimately destined for sainthood. Along with five other European priests he settled in an abandoned hut along the banks of the Nile River at Khartoum, today the capital of Sudan. On one side of the river lived the animist Dinka tribe, on the other the Shilluk, and both were hostile to white foreigners.

The six priests slept on wood planks, scavenged for food in the forest, and began learning the local tribal dialect while making tentative gestures to engage the locals. But the tropical humidity proved incompatible with their European immune systems, and soon they began dying. Just six weeks after setting up, their Father Superior lay near death with fever. One of his last requests to his missionaries was that they not abandon their attempt to bring the word of God to Africa. Later, over the fresh grave of his Father Superior, young Daniel Comboni, then twenty-five, cried: "O Nigrizia o morte!" Africa or death!

After eighteen months in the Sudan, however, Father Comboni was stricken with malaria and returned to Italy with the only other survivor. Shortly after this failed mission other missionaries followed, and they too died. The Catholic Church declared central Africa uninhabitable for white men and abandoned hopes of evangelizing it.

But Father Comboni did not lose hope that Christianity would be brought to central Africa; he believed it was his life's great purpose. Then, on a September morning in 1864, while he knelt praying at the Basilica of St. Peter in Rome, it came to him. He rushed home and for three days and nights wrote out his "Plan for the Regeneration of Africa."

At the time the drier coastal regions of Africa were held increasingly under a patronizing European control. But Comboni saw the Africans as intellectual equals, and asked the Church, complicit in the racism of the day, to check its superiority complex. "Let us be Catholic, really universal," he wrote in his plan, "and give Africans their rights, who are the most poor and unfortunate people of the universe." His radical concept involved setting up schools and colleges in sections of coastal Africa, then training indigenous priests and teachers who would spread the word of God, and that of the trades and secular education, to the interior. Europeans and Africans would initially work together, after which the Europeans would leave the indigenous Africans to reign.

Needing helpers, Comboni travelled across Europe lecturing on his plans. He sought financial assistance from kings and queens down to the poorest of the poor, and received much support. Preparing others to help him, he founded the Institute for African Missions in Verona and enlisted a group of priests, lay brothers, and, remarkably, sisters.

At the time, nuns were considered unsuited for foreign mission work, but Comboni argued that Africa needed them. To the Bishops of the

Vatican he declared that the time for Africa had come, and that women would lead the way. The Church was a mother, he said, giving birth and nourishment to the children of God. And it had been a woman, Mary Magdalene, the Apostle to the Apostles, who'd been chosen as the first to witness and tell the news of the Resurrection of Jesus after his death. Female missionaries would have a special motherly instinct, softer than a man's, that was necessary for Africa's nourishment. Comboni wanted women to lead religious instruction, schools, orphanages, to provide refuges for slaves, to nurse the sick, and to baptize the pagan and harem families. He even argued that priests who attempted mission work without sisters were harming themselves; that missionary nuns were a defence and a guarantee, lending credibility to the male missionary. In effect, Comboni was a pioneer for women's rights in the Catholic Church. "In Africa, a Sister is worth three priests in Europe.... The Sister in central Africa is everything. Without Sisters, mission cannot be carried out in Africa," he wrote in his plan.[4]

He knew that the risk of his recruits dying in central Africa was high—the region had lost forty-four missionaries without one success—so he preached the merits of martyrdom to his followers, reminding them that there was no honour greater than to die evangelizing for God. "Africa or Death!" became his war cry.

Eventually Father Comboni's plans made their way to the Pope, Pius IX. The Pope liked young Father Comboni's vision, including his plan for women, and asked him to lead his group of willing volunteers to Central Africa, to try yet again. So in 1872, fifteen years after his first departure, Daniel Comboni and his followers set off for Khartoum. They sailed to Cairo, acclimatized, took a steamship up the mighty Nile, and, wearing turbans like the Arabs, trotted off on camel backs into the Sahara Desert.

Khartoum was then a primary exchange point for Middle Eastern slave-trading. Comboni begged the authorities of Khartoum to outlaw slavery, and when his arguments failed to sway them he turned his missions into sanctuaries for runaway slaves. Some of those former slaves became the first Sudanese priests and nuns of modern Sudan. At the time, several European priests disapproved, asserting that Africans had neither the intellectual nor moral ability to be priests or nuns. Some intellectuals of the day even argued that Africans didn't have a human soul. Hateful rumours started by these priests circulated in Europe about Comboni's morality. But the Vatican believed in him, and Pope Pius IX silenced Comboni's detractors by ordaining him the First Bishop of Khartoum and Vicar Apostolic of Central Africa, a land mass twice the size of Europe.

As the years passed Comboni's exploits were written about in newspapers across Europe. His celebrity grew on par with that of his explorer contemporaries, David Livingstone and Henry Stanley. Wealthy Europeans donated generously to his missions. Monsignor Comboni was the adventurer-bishop who'd taken to wearing a turban, a multilingual man with a full beard, a friend to the Muslims who opened schools, hospitals, and churches across Khartoum and down into South Sudan. Within a few years his Egyptian training mission in Cairo had grown into a sanctuary for 100,000 runaway slaves.

But in the late 1870s Khartoum was hit with a long drought followed by widespread famine, then heavy rains, terrible heat, and disease. In those few years half the population of Khartoum was wiped out, and with them many of Comboni's followers, including his fellow missionaries and nuns. Comboni was devastated. "We have come to the end of our supplies and our money," he wrote home, "and we are now forced to shut the door on many people begging a little bread."

One October night in 1881, Comboni, now fifty, was caught in a fierce rainstorm while travelling to one of his rural missions. The next day he contracted a fever, and three days later, his mind lost in delirium, death seemed close. With his remaining voice he said to his followers gathered around him, "Swear that you will be faithful to your missionary vocation...." Then, when he died, the missionaries who surrounded him at his death all swore, "Africa or Death!"[5]

Comboni's followers stayed in Sudan, but their fate was a hard one. Even while Comboni was alive, Mohammed Ahmed, an Islamic fundamentalist from Egypt, had proclaimed himself the Mahdi (The Divinely

Guided One), rallied an army of supporters, and declared jihad on the infidels, the Anglo-Egyptian forces then controlling Sudan. A few months after Comboni's death the marauding Mahdi army swept across rural Sudan. Comboni's missionary priests and nuns were imprisoned and many died of starvation. A few years later, Khartoum fell to Islamic warlords. The surviving Comboni missionaries of Khartoum, who had stayed true to their leader's plea that they not abandon Africa, were imprisoned, tortured, raped, and given away as slaves. Sudan remained for fifteen years under brutal Mahdi rule, and everything Comboni created was destroyed. In Europe Comboni was forgotten, his legacy a footnote in failure.

But at the turn of the twentieth century British-Egyptian troops recaptured Sudan. Bewildered, and with nothing but the rags on their backs, the enslaved populace returned to their old homes. Among them was a Comboni priest who'd chosen to return to the old site of Comboni's missionary in Khartoum. The emaciated Dutch priest greeted the few dejected Christians who had also returned to Khartoum. He then gave mass in memory of Comboni's many martyred followers. "Africa or Death," he cried, and the seed Comboni had left behind sprouted again.

The Comboni missionaries multiplied. They rebuilt the schools and hospitals of Sudan, which were used by the people of all religions. In Sudan today, the word "Comboni" is understood as a pseudonym for "Catholic." Comboni's reputation as one of Sudan's great men, a friend and helper to the Muslims, survives to this day. And to this day, Comboni's picture—in which he wears a turban—hangs in almost every school in Sudan, most of which are now Muslim schools.

MEANWHILE, witchcraft, Christian martyrdom, and colonialism were exploding in Uganda, creating a combined power destined to reverberate far into the future. In the last years of Comboni's life, other European missionaries, Catholics from France and Protestants from England, were entering Uganda from the south. Comboni, as the prelate of all of central Africa, a land mass that included Uganda and Congo, had intended to move some of his own missionaries southward. But when England's famed journalist-explorer, Henry Stanley, wrote in the *London Daily Telegraph* in 1875 that while searching for the source of the Nile River he'd stumbled upon a tropical paradise on earth, the competing Protestant and Roman Catholic Churches of Europe rushed in ahead of him.

Stanley wrote that inside the glorious land of the Buganda kingdom (modern-day Southern Uganda) he'd found a civilized populace complete with political advisers, a national tax collection system, and a disciplined army of hundreds of thousands led by an intelligent and welcoming king. The king's court was a walled community with courtyards, music, guards, harems, servants, witch doctors, courtiers, and its own grand culture. Stanley wrote that the African king, a polygamist who led with animist sorcery, was fascinated by the idea of Christianity and was inviting European missionaries to visit him.

As a new arrival, Stanley didn't immediately appreciate the sensational brutality of King Mutesa's rule. The king portrayed himself as an animist demigod, whose power stirred awe and dread in the populace. He owned not only all the land and wealth of his kingdom, but also the bodies and souls of the living. Surrounded by a council of witch doctors, he routinely commanded human sacrifices to appease his angered gods. Executions were often intentionally cruel, and sometimes death by dismemberment was spread out over weeks. Reports from those days recorded that Mutesa executed one of his harem women (who numbered between 500 and 5000, depending on the year) almost every day.

On its face, Buganda—the dominant kingdom of the sub-Saharan region—looked civilized, but underneath, a cruel society founded on witchcraft awaited the missionaries. Knowing this, when Comboni heard of the approaching missionaries he wrote to the Vatican to stop this foolhardy advance, a warning that went unheeded. In June of 1877 the first missionaries to arrive in Buganda were Protestants from the Church Mission Society of England. Months later they were followed by the Catholic White Fathers of France. The charismatic King Mutesa generously welcomed the newcomers.

King Mutesa's kingdom gained much from his friendship with the missionaries, who in exchange for the right to preach the word of God introduced wheeled transport, plows, brick kilns, blacksmith skills, the printing press, and lanterns. From the Muslim tradesmen, who mostly wanted slaves, Mutesa exchanged his peasant people for guns and gunpowder.

In the end King Mutesa died unconverted, although a few of his four hundred royal pageboys did take up the fervour of Christianity, choosing to believe that God was neither a big snake, nor a mountain, but their one true saviour. These boys were baptized, making them Uganda's first Christian converts.

The throne transferred to King Mutesa's eldest son, King Mwanga, then sixteen. King Mwanga, an oafish youth given to excessive laughter and anger, reportedly had homosexual leanings and routinely sodomized the court's young pages. The new Christian converts in his court tried to protect these favoured boys by keeping them out of the king's sight.

As the nineteenth century drew to a close, Europe's scramble for Africa was well underway. With various countries invading Africa from all its coasts, Buganda was threatened by Germany from the south, Belgium in the west, Britain in the north, and France from the east. It wasn't long before King Mwanga decided, rightly, that the white missionaries of his court were also a threat. He outlawed Christian teachings, declared that no more whites should enter Buganda, and forbade the missionaries in his court from leaving.

The Protestant and Catholic missionaries living under house arrest at the Buganda court were horrified by the perceived evil around them. Now certain of the importance of their task, the former adversaries banded together, translating the Bible into the local language and giving secret lessons to the new Christian converts, an increasing number of whom were the king's pageboys. Secret conversions increased, with some boys and young men becoming Catholic, others Protestant, in roughly equal numbers. But when the young king discovered this he summoned all the country's executioners, stating his intention to rid his court of Christianity.

That night the Christian pageboys gathered. It was clear that the time had come to choose between God and King Mwanga, and the boys, who were between ten and eighteen and who had spent their lives indentured to the king, agreed to die for God. The next morning King Mwanga called everyone from his royal court together. "Those who do not pray, stand by me. Those who do pray, stand over there," he said. Thousands moved toward the king, but the pageboys moved to the spot the king had indicated. King Mwanga asked if they intended to defy him by remaining Christians. "Yes," they answered, knowing death would be the price. They were bound and marched fifty kilometres to Mamugongo Pyre for execution. There the boys and young men were shackled by the neck and put in huts while elaborate symbolic preparations were made. Seven days later, at dusk, the king's men, with painted black and red faces and wearing animal skins and headdresses, sang death chants from the pyre site. Some pounded tam-tams.

The boys were released from their shackles and led outside, where many in the kingdom had gathered to watch. To the onlookers the boys appeared joyous and festive, greeting each other with laughter and song. When all the boys were positioned the executioner covered them with wood and then lit the fire. The boys broke out into a recitation of the Lord's Prayer. To the amazement of onlookers, as the flames covered them and seared off their flesh, they repeated the prayer, over and over, until all were silent.

On that day, June 3, 1886, twenty-two Catholic and Protestant boys died together on the pyre in what has come to be considered the greatest act of Christian martyrdom in Africa.[6] The day is now a national holiday in Uganda. Around the court, dozens more Catholic and Protestant boys had limbs hacked off, others were disembowelled, and still others castrated. In all, forty-three Christian boys died, their interfaith martyrdom a precursor of the ecumenical dialogue and cooperation that would soon come to the divided but religious people of Uganda.

Shortly after the murders the trapped white missionaries escaped. For the next several years the Buganda kingdom fought to defend itself from invading British, French, German, and Belgian forces. A fierce political battle, grounded in the desire to exploit Africa's natural resources, soon pushed Britain and France to the brink of war. Ultimately, in 1894

Buganda fell to British colonial control. For a while King Mwanga worked as a puppet leader for the British, but when he proved difficult to control the army deposed him and made his infant son king. Meanwhile, the Protestant Church of England became the official Church of Uganda, and the quest for conversion continued.

Almost immediately after the British took over, the Protestant and Catholic missionaries returned to Buganda, where they were shocked to find a thriving Christian community. Without any priests or nuns to guide them, the people had begun baptizing themselves. The boys' murder had been intended to rid Buganda of Christianity, but instead, as has been borne out repeatedly throughout history, the martyred blood of innocents made fertile soil for Christianity's future. The people who had witnessed the boys' act shared the story far and wide. Christianity spread quickly, and fervently, across all of Southern Uganda. Miracles were attributed to the martyred boys, and in 1964 the Vatican canonized them as saints. Five years later, Pope Paul VI, standing over the pyre where the Catholic and Protestant boys had died together, declared their sacrifice so powerful that their martyrdom could form the basis of a society better than any known in modern times.

If so, that reality is yet to come.

BY THE EARLY TWENTIETH CENTURY, Protestant missionaries now living in an increasingly Christian Southern Uganda journeyed northward into remote African villages seeking more converts. But when they crossed the Nile River, marking the end of traditional Buganda and the start of Acholiland, modern-day Northern Uganda, they found a resistant people. The Acholis believed deeply in their time-tested animist gods and ancestral spirits, and so the Protestant Church, already overwhelmed with so many easy converts in the southern communities, left the rural North mostly to itself and its witchcraft.

When the Catholic Comboni missionaries walked into Northern Uganda from Sudan in 1911, they followed the plans Daniel Comboni had written out for them four decades earlier. They adopted the lifestyles of the locals, learned their language and customs, and then walked with them as equals. They lived among the poor, and established churches, schools, and hospitals. Following Comboni's words—"The missionaries will have to understand that they are stones hid under the earth, which will perhaps never come to light, but which will become part of the foundations of a vast, new building"—the missionaries began to slowly Christianize Acholiland. The churches would not be Comboni but rather indigenous, with the goal that the Combonis would leave when the churches were strong enough to sustain themselves. The hospitals and schools would help the people rise up and ultimately take fuller control of their own destinies.

Meanwhile, the British controlling the country were enlisting Northern Ugandan men as soldiers in the British-led military. The Acholi were tall and powerful people, with a legacy as fierce warriors. Working alongside British officers, the Acholi soldiers effectively kept the rest of the country obedient to Britain.

In 1962, when Uganda finally gained independence from Britain, the Acholi-dominated military took control of the entire country. But things would change forever when a non-Acholi British-trained soldier rose to power.

In 1971 a psychopathic tyrant, General Idi Amin, ousted his Acholi predecessor, Milton Obote, in a military coup. To ensure that he maintained control he resolved to kill all the Acholis in the army. Approximately 200,000 Acholi were killed. Amin also executed the educated people of Uganda, exiled Indians who then controlled Uganda's economy, sent death squads across the land, opened torture chambers, and before long destroyed the nation's economy.

All educated Acholi fled the country. The remaining Acholi soldiers and civilians ran from Kampala, the southern power centre of Uganda, and retreated north to the remote grasslands and into increasing poverty, illiteracy, and a festering resentment over their mass slaughter. They slowly returned to older customs. Many turned back to animism and sorcery.

Eight years after he came to power Idi Amin was overthrown, and the Acholis seized power again. More fighting, bloodshed, and coups followed, until the guerrilla leader Yoweri Museveni, from Western Uganda, took power in 1986 and stabilized the rest of the country.

Acholiland, however, did not settle down. The ousted Acholi soldiers from Obote's army remembered what Idi Amin had done to them when he took over. This time, when Museveni called on them to report in and surrender, they instead fled into the bush and plotted against this latest leader.

AND HERE, in the marginalized and undeveloped savannah of Northern Uganda, the inferno of hatred burned strongest. The desperate, angry people looked both to God and to their surviving pagan beliefs, the spirits in the unknown world, to help them out of the repression and horror in which they were caught.

Could Comboni have foreseen that, 115 years after his death, his introduction of Christianity to this animist land would unearth another type of stone?

Joseph Kony, an Acholi child conceived by witch doctors and converted to Catholicism by the Comboni missionaries, was now rising up as a force to be reckoned with. In the West he would have been stopped long before anything like this could have developed. But in the impoverished, war-ravaged land of central Africa, away from the glare of the world ...

CHAPTER 3

NORTHERN UGANDA, 1996

Mariano Lagira called the new recruits before him. He explained that they were now where God wanted them, with Kony's followers, and that Sister Rachele had merely been safekeeping them until this moment.

He inquired about their home lives, their siblings, and most of all their fathers, taking notes. During the interviews, a woman came with a bowl of shea nut oil. She dipped her right thumb into the oil then traced the sign of the cross on each girl's forehead, hands, mouth, and chest. "Now you are soldiers of the movement," Mariano said.

He called for one of the stolen goats to be slaughtered. In total, sixty new recruits had been found in the previous twenty-four hours. That night all the girls were ushered into a hut meant for five and told to sleep with their heads on their knees. The next morning they were divided into groups of five and sent to walk in a designated unit comprising a commander, his family of wives, subordinate soldiers, and other new recruits. The wives, who carried guns—and who had all been abducted—were told to ensure that none of the new recruits escaped.

Mariano announced the rules so that everyone understood. "If one of you escapes, the other recruits of your unit will be punished. That punishment could be death."

Five of the girls went to the camp of a sergeant, a slight, wiry man in his early twenties. He ordered them to prepare him food, telling them that they'd get a bullet if they refused his demands. He eyed them while wondering out loud if he should teach them how to service a man.

Throughout the evening the sergeant held court by his fireside, explaining how he'd been abducted eight years earlier. After all that time, he'd learned to believe in Kony. "In the end you too will submit to the will of the Lord's Resistance Army," he told the girls. He pointed to a woman, his young slave-wife whom he'd been given as a reward from Kony. She carried a gun. He told them that she had once been cut off from the rest of the rebels during a battle. She could have easily escaped, but instead she followed the rebel trail and came back to them. "You know why?" he asked, then laughed hard and long. "Because she couldn't leave me!"[7]

The girls were forbidden from singing or speaking in English. The other women watched when they relieved themselves in the bush. Each night the rebels camped, each morning they again walked, and in every village they passed they stole food and kidnapped more recruits. And although the girls were separated into units, everyone walked together.

The next morning they packed up to leave, but when he conducted a headcount Mariano scowled, realizing that Esther, a twelve-year-old girl they'd abducted farther north in the town of Gulu three days earlier, had gone missing. She had already run away the day before and been recaptured, and now Mariano once again had to send his soldiers out after her. "If you don't find her, I will kill one of the Aboke Girls," he yelled, forcing two of the girls down on the ground, preparing them for execution. New recruits always had to be convinced that escape was too risky, both for themselves and those they cared about. Minutes later Esther was pulled out from under a pile of laundry in one of the villagers' homes.

The boys grabbed her arm and dragged her kicking and screaming before Mariano. One of the boys threw her to the ground and another jumped on her chest, kicked her in the face, and broke her nose. She begged for mercy as blood ran down her nose and mouth.

Mariano told the Aboke Girls to collect sticks from the bush and then to circle around Esther. Frightened, they did as they were told. Returning to circle around her, they now had no choice but to look at the condemned girl. She stared back at them, her eyes pleading. When she tried to get up, a boy kicked her back down.

"Finish her off!" Mariano yelled. The Aboke Girls—Grace Grall, Charlotte, Angela, Agatha, Jackie, Grace Acan—stood in a circle around her. Grace Grall was forced forward. She hit Esther lightly on the legs. "Not like that!" a rebel yelled. He grabbed a stick, lifted it over his head, and pounded it down on the back of the other's head. She cried out, and tried desperately to wrestle free.

The girls cried, but then Mariano told them that whoever continued to cry would have to drink the girl's blood after she was dead. Then he lined them up and one by one forced each girl to give Esther a forceful blow to the head or neck. When they didn't hit her hard enough, he made them hit her again. Finally, one of their blows sent Esther into convulsions, and then she stopped moving. She was dead.

The girls walked away, silently, their innocence stolen forever. At that moment, their ties to the old lives at St. Mary's were suddenly cut. Now they were murderers. Each felt guilty, for instead of choosing to die themselves, they had followed orders to kill a child.

But the lesson wasn't over. Mariano called another girl before them. She wasn't much older than they were. He ordered her to disrobe. Her entire body was covered with scars and open gashes, the signs of countless whippings. The girls prayed silently in their heads. Mariano called the wounds her "better scars" because they had improved her behaviour and her demonstrated enthusiasm for life with the rebels.

"You Aboke Girls are really big-headed and undisciplined. You sit on chairs as if you are not women, lazy as if you are not young girls, sitting beside the granary as if you are competing with men!" he yelled. "I am going to show you my true colours now."[8]

He told them that each was sentenced to fifty strokes of the cane, and he forbade them from crying or shaking during the beating. He said that even if the Holy Spirit told him that they should be released, he'd kill them all anyway. "Do you hear me?" he yelled.

"Yes," the girls answered obediently.

He said they were guilty of not alerting the rebels when Esther had run away. The girls were instructed that if they flinched, moved, or cried during the caning, they'd be whipped twice as long. He sent two young rebels to make whips from vine branches. The girls lay down on their stomachs and the whippings began. Palma and Agatha couldn't handle the pain and instinctively moved their hands to cover their buttocks.[9] That earned them a second round of lashings. Afterward, the bloodied girls were paraded before the commanders, humiliated and beaten down.

For the next week the rebel units moved together through the bushes, raiding for more recruits and looting whenever they happened upon homes.

Then, one morning, the Aboke Girls were taken to bathe in the river. They were brought back to Mariano, who had drawn a large circle in the orange dirt and carved it up into triangular sections. Around the centre point he drew another tiny circle and placed an egg inside it.

He ordered the girls to remove their blouses and to stand topless inside their individual triangles. Mariano was joined by a designated holy man, who moved into the small circle and picked up the egg. He also held a container of oil and a jar of white powder made from ash and water.

Other rebels circled around singing hymns while the holy man moved among the girls, drawing a heart and a cross on their chests, foreheads, hands, backs, and breasts. Each of the rebels had undergone a similar initiation ritual. The girls were told to pass the egg between each other, and if the egg fell, it was the spirit declaring that this person desired to escape. The holy man explained that the rituals protected them from attacks and disease by binding them to the Holy Spirit.

But first, the Spirit demanded a test. For the next three days the girls remained bare-chested and unbathed. If they disbelieved and desired to escape, the marks on their bodies would vanish in this time. The girls never knew what would happen to them if this occurred, but each was careful not to let their marks fade away.

Two days later the topless girls passed another group of rebels by a riverbank. As they walked by the boy soldiers laughed and commented at their exposed breasts.

On the third day their markings were inspected and all passed the test. The girls bathed early in the morning, put on new dresses provided by the rebel women, and kneeled barefoot before Mariano in the compound. Mariano led a series of prayers, which the Aboke Girls recited back to him. Afterward they sang hymns together, celebrating their baptism into this new world where Joseph Kony was their saviour.

AS THE WEEKS PASSED and interactions between the rebels and the Aboke Girls increased, one of the girls revealed to a rebel that one of the sergeants had raped Agatha. It was a serious charge: Kony wanted the girls to be the child-bearers for his top commanders, and he wanted them to arrive pure. His soldiers had risked their lives travelling so far south for these girls, and they weren't to be simply used for pleasure. So, after Mariano received confirmation from Agatha about the rape, he sentenced the guilty sergeant to two hundred strokes for violating Article 9 of Kony's Commandments, which stipulated that no fighter could take a woman inside the Lord's Resistance Army who didn't belong to him.

The sergeant was beaten in front of them all. Afterward, Mariano called Kony over the satellite radio and asked if there should be a further punishment. Death, the LRA leader ordered. The bloodied seventeen-year-old boy who had broken the rules of the rebels was unceremoniously bayonetted and his body thrown in the bushes.

Agatha and the others now knew that they wouldn't be raped by any other rebels.

Eventually the days merged together. The girls walked through the bush, carrying loads, watching fresh abductions, sleeping under trees, in fields, or in abandoned huts, and praying whenever they could.

On October 20, 1996, the tenth day of their abduction, Ugandan radio aired an appeal from Pope John Paul II to release the Aboke Girls. The military radio station played the message over and over. "Thirty girls are now in the hands of their abductors while their families and the Catholic community are in anguish over their fate," the Pope said. "I appeal to the conscience of those responsible to bring this brutal kidnapping to an end: respect the lives and dignity of these young people. In the name of God, I ask for their immediate liberation."

In the hills outside Gulu, an enraged Mariano threw down his radio and called for the Aboke Girls to appear before him. He was livid. He asked what was so special about them that the Pope would try to help them when he hadn't for the others. Charlotte, Grace Grall, Grace Acan, Agatha, Agnes, Janet, Jackie, Sylvia, Judith, Angela—all of them—stood silent before him, looking down at the ground.

"From now on you are soldiers of the movement. I will never let you go!" he yelled. He ordered boy soldiers to throw the girls to the ground. They lay on their stomachs, and while the boys lashed into their backsides, twenty times, the girls prayed to God for strength.

This time, not one of them flinched.

CHAPTER 4

LRA BASE CAMP, SOUTH SUDAN

Joseph Kony, tall, lean, and dressed in white, walked majestically through his camp in South Sudan, around firepits, across clotheslines, all the while gazing into the eyes of the frightened children. Following behind and beside him were several dozen adult guards. Kony stopped before a boy whose demeanour had somehow disturbed him. The child quivered as Kony, who emitted the aura of someone capable of seeing into a person's soul, looked down at the child and frowned. Kony told his guards to grab the child, remarking to all that the Holy Spirit had peered into the child's soul and identified him as a traitor.

Kony sentenced the boy to death. His lieutenants dragged the boy to the execution field, where a group of new recruits involved in military training would kill him.[10] Kony continued on his walk, gazing into yet more souls, and eventually he identified another young soldier who needed to die.

He made his way to his camp's sick bay, looking in on the sick and wounded receiving medical attention. He sent some to the Juba Hospital, forty kilometres north and run by the Sudanese government.

With his daily rounds completed, Kony returned to his house in the centre of the camp. The steel building, protected by an iron roof, was surrounded by mud-and-straw huts that housed thousands of rebels. Next to Kony's home he kept his wives and children together in a large grass building. He visited them often, sitting with his growing family by the hearth fire and playing with his children. Several of his wives were fond of him. He complimented their cooking, was often polite, and told them interesting stories. Sometimes he even helped change diapers. His wives, although all abducted, tried to please him, and many competed with each other for his affections.

Kony's libido was legendary. He had over thirty wives, most of whom had been virgins before marriage, and had boasted of his intentions to have a thousand wives one day, like the biblical King Solomon. Kony believed his purpose on Earth was to create a new, pure race, born inside the LRA camp, unexposed to the evil of the outside world.

Each night Kony visited his wives and selected one to come back to sleep with him. In the morning that wife would bring him water for washing. She'd arrange his dreadlocks, clean his house, and wash his clothes before returning to her own home to join the others.

Since 1994, when Kony's rebel group had contacted the Sudanese government offering to assist them in their own civil war, he had received a monthly salary, food, and arms from the Khartoum-based Islamic government. This helped him fight Yoweri Museveni's Ugandan army, but in exchange his troops also spent a significant portion of their time fighting the Sudan People's Liberation Army (SPLA), the South Sudanese rebels who opposed the Khartoum regime. Kony's camp was located between the Sudanese government forces and the rebels, as a buffer. He never fought in battles himself. Most of Kony's days were spent inside the camp, sitting by the radio and waiting for reports from the field. He had a television, and when he could, he liked to watch old western movies with his wives and children.

Kony forbade his soldiers from communicating with outsiders, unless he gave them special permission, and insisted that they sever their family ties. Kony was more than a guerrilla fighter. He was a cult leader who had created his own religion by merging traditional animism with Catholic, Protestant, and Muslim teachings, and who demanded that those around him be loyal disciples. Each night he recited prayers that mixed Protestantism and Catholicism. Some days he and his other commanders knelt and faced Mecca to pray. He adopted Islam's Friday, not Christianity's Sunday, as his Sabbath day. One of his core teachings was designed to solidify his grip on his young soldiers: they were taught that if they tried to leave, the Ugandans would kill them. The children belonged with Kony; he was their protector. This was their destiny, and they must not think otherwise. He told them that it was sinful to worry. They had to have faith.

Joseph Kony was an enigma, a shadowy character who'd managed to create such an illusion around him that even some educated people in Northern Uganda believed he was a spirit, or many spirits, using a human body to facilitate its purpose. Rumours circulated that he'd replaced his physical body five times. Some of the children who escaped later swore that they'd watched him mutate from old to young before their eyes.

Details of Kony's early life are sketchy, but it is known that he was born into a family of witch doctors in 1961 at Agwengtina Parish in the Odek subcounty of Gulu. Kony's first cousin on his mother's side was Alice Lakwena, the most famous witch doctor of Eastern Africa, known as the Holy Spirit Priestess. After Museveni seized control of Uganda, and his soldiers arrived in Gulu and began stealing from the already impoverished people, she led thousands of her Acholi followers into rebellion against him. They were desperate, and so chose to believe her claims that her spiritual powers and rituals of purification would protect them from the army's bullets. She managed some surprising early military victories, but ultimately, most of her unarmed followers were killed after attacking Museveni's army in 1987. She escaped to Kenya.

Some of Kony's witch-doctoring family renounced witchcraft in the 1970s and converted to Catholicism. Kony's father studied Catholicism and worked as a lay preacher, assisting the priest in his town. For a short time the young Kony was an altar boy. Sometimes he assisted the Italian Comboni priests when they served mass. Some remember that he also led the youth in evening prayers at Odek Catholic Parish, where he recited the rosary to his peers.

Kony was a poor student who dropped out after the seventh grade. He was quiet, didn't study much, didn't brush his hair or tuck in his shirt. He walked barefoot to school, and yet was favoured by the girls.

He was also a leader on the soccer field, where the schoolboys would kick around oranges instead of real soccer balls.

After dropping out of school, the teenage Kony built himself a grass hut next to the family homestead. He spent several unremarkable years tending his garden down by the river. He had ten brothers and sisters. They all struggled with abject poverty; the family's cows, which had constituted their wealth (like most other families around them), had been stolen by marauding underpaid soldiers. Simple survival was a great daily effort.

In 1987, at age twenty-six, Kony believed that a spirit entered his body for the first time.[11] For several days the afflicted Kony could not speak. Local witch doctors joined together to exorcise the demon, but they could not. His family killed chickens as a sacrifice then moved up to goats and even cows, but nothing helped. Those around him assumed Kony was going mad.

One day Kony gathered food for sustenance, walked up a hill, and sat down. For two weeks he prayed to God. As he would later recount time and again to his followers, that was when the spirit revealed itself. He explained that a dark cloud formed above him and it poured rain everywhere, but somehow he did not get wet. "Today you will become a fighter," the spirit told him. "You are going to fight in the name of the Almighty God. Go and teach the word of God and distribute medicine to the sick."[12]

Kony returned from the hill and preached what the spirit had told him. In his first speech, given while he appeared possessed, he declared to the startled peasant farmers around that God had asked him to liberate humanity from suffering and disease. His eyes bulging and face contorting under possession, Kony declared that healing alone was pointless when the healed were only killed in battle. So God had demanded that he fight to destroy all who wanted to fight, until there were none left who desired war. In his possessed form Kony explained that he was not here to overthrow a government, but to destroy evil forces in the world. He would also destroy all forms of witchcraft and sorcery, which were the ways of the devil. And he explained that his coming first to the Acholi did not mean he honoured them, but rather that they were the vehicle for him to bring peace to the world.

Kony claimed that the second coming of Christ was channelling through him.

To many who heard him, Kony was just another in a long line of those in Northern Uganda who claimed supernatural powers. But in a land of little education, and much death and suffering, his spirit possession was, at least, interesting. For some, who looked anywhere for an answer to their problems, his spirit possession even offered some hope.

For months Kony's ravings persisted. He returned to the hill to seek advice, and this time the spirit voice told him, "Go and organize your men to fight. Anybody who knows the name of God is your soldier. Anybody who makes the Sign of the Cross, you capture and train in the name of God. He will become your fighter."[13]

Soon afterward, Kony disappeared into the bush with seven followers, some of whom were likely his younger brothers and one a female cousin.[14]

Several psychologists familiar with Kony's actions have theorized that he likely suffered from dissociative identity disorder, also known as multiple personality disorder. The condition is characterized by the "switching" of identities when under stress. The person with multiple personalities generally has a complex inner world, with some personalities interacting with each other while other subpersonalities remain unaware of these competing personas. The person might address himself as "he" or "we," and will typically suffer from large blocks of lost time, or amnesia. Psychiatry has found that the condition is caused by overwhelming stress, an abusive childhood that included a lack of nurturing, an innate ability to separate one's memories and perceptions from conscious awareness, and abnormal psychological development. Sufferers typically feel detached from life and are controlling of themselves and those around them.

No one can know for sure what Kony may have suffered from. What is known is that back in 1987, shortly after Museveni took military control of Uganda, Kony united with the unemployed soldiers of defeated rebel groups. He also partnered with, and then betrayed, an anti-Museveni rebel group known as the Uganda National Liberation Army. He built up the rest of his army by abducting recruits—quickly realizing that boys between eleven and sixteen were the best candidates—and giving them two choices: to submit to him, or to die.

Those who entered Kony's group soon understood that they were under the command of a man who exercised absolute control—who argued that "God can confirm that I am an embodiment and the personification of the Holy Spirit."[15] The reality was that those who entered his army could not leave. And Kony's discipline was fierce.

By April 1988 he felt ready to take on President Museveni. Kony sent a letter to Museveni's brigade commander working along the Sudan border calling on all soldiers to defect to him and threatening those who refused with annihilation. The letter reportedly said "The time had come, when the world would see no more soldiers, but holy angels everywhere," and was signed "Commander Abraham."

Guerrilla tactics mixed with religious speeches became Kony's dominant method of control. He stressed that the end of the world was at hand and that the year 2000 would never arrive—the saviour was on its way. He declared that he was taking children, the only innocents left, to rescue them from the old world, deemed too corrupt for God to save.

By 1996 Kony's army of abducted had grown to six thousand strong, although 90 percent of those were children under the age of seventeen. By the standards of the armies surrounding him, his was a small group, still in the infancy of what it was about to become: the world's largest child army.

And soon the St. Mary's schoolgirls would join him.

FOR THE NEXT two months the Aboke Girls walked with their captors, moving through the bushes and jungles and grasslands of Northern Uganda, camping out behind the Comboni-operated St. Mary's Lacor Hospital for a while, watching as the rebels battled periodically with Ugandan soldiers and terrorized the surrounding villagers who fled into the hospital grounds for safety. Finally they crossed the unprotected border into Sudan. They walked seventy kilometres northward through a no man's land of starving Dinka plains and into Arab–Sudanese-controlled territory, crossing checkpoints before finally arriving at Aru Camp to meet their new master.

CHAPTER 5

The orange dirt turned pale and the land appeared drier. The elephant and spear grass turned to dried shrubs and thistle trees. The hundreds of abducted children were sick from two months of walking barefoot in the bush. Blisters had opened and raw skin now covered the bottoms of their swollen feet. Sores oozed with infections. Among them, the Aboke Girls now numbered only twenty-three. Seven of the girls had found the will, and the opportunity, to run away before crossing into Sudan, where they all knew escape would be almost impossible. Some were able to flee amid the confusion when the Ugandan military attacked the rebels outside Gulu. Others fled when the rebels crossed the roads. A few ran away together, others on their own. But each girl who escaped made it to safety.

The remaining Aboke Girls assumed that the missing girls were dead. But those seven girls—Barbara Alopo, Agnes Ocitti, Josephine Lolem, Esther Acio, Sandra Everlyn Akot, Caroline Akello, and Pamela Adokorac—had all succeeded in avoiding the fate that awaited the others.

The rebels no longer feared crossing roads, and passed through Sudanese-government military checkpoints without incident. Other soldiers passed on the road, waving. In the distance Grace Grall saw hundreds of tiny mud huts closely aligned, and she understood from the rebels that they'd arrived. As they limped closer, hundreds of young rebels, most appearing to be about her age, ran to the road and clapped, enthusiastically welcoming the new recruits. What was this strange Sudanese land they'd just crossed into?

SUDAN MEANS "land of the black people." It is Africa's largest country. It cuts across the predominantly black Christian south of Africa and the Muslim Arab north, bordering Egypt on the north and Libya on the northwest, Eritrea and Ethiopia to the east, Uganda to the south, the Democratic Republic of Congo on the southwest, and Chad to the west. The Sahara Desert cuts across all of northern Sudan. Both of the major tributaries of the world's longest river, the White Nile, south to north, and the Blue Nile, east to west, flow through Sudan. They join in its capital, Khartoum, before continuing north to Egypt and into the Mediterranean Sea. Many paleontologists now believe that the Nile is the true birthplace of the human race—that the first incarnation of humankind built homes along its banks.

Sudan gained its independence from British-Egyptian colonial control in 1956. Two-thirds of its population of approximately thirty million now lived in the dry land of the Arab Muslim north. About six million lived in South Sudan, mostly Christians and animists belonging to the Dinka or Nuer tribes. The Dinka were ancestrally linked, as extended family, to the Acholi people of Northern Uganda.

In the early 1970s American companies discovered large oil reserves in central and southern Sudan, and, in theory, the country should have been quite wealthy by now. Instead, a civil war had raged for more than fifteen years—beginning shortly after Chevron Oil began attempting to draw out oil from the reserves located just south of the divide between northern and southern Sudan.

Now, South Sudan was destroyed. An estimated two million people had been killed from the effects of the war since it began in 1983, almost a million of them from starvation after being forced from their homes, and more than four million people—basically the entire region—were displaced.

The core problem lay in a 1972 peace deal, drawn up before oil was discovered, between the black African South Sudanese and the more powerful Arab Muslim North Sudanese. The deal gave the southern regional government ownership of any revenue from minerals found in southern land. The northern federal government in Khartoum, realizing that this concession would play out badly for them now that oil had been discovered in the South, chose to redraw the map of Sudan, slightly changing the boundaries of the South and North, reclaiming the new oil-rich central territory, and making deals with American oil companies.

Angry South Sudanese had protested violently, but the Khartoum government, then the sixth-largest recipient of military aid from president Jimmy Carter's Cold War–engaged United States and confident of ongoing U.S. support, refused negotiations and opted to take military control of the areas around the well-drilling machines owned by U.S. Chevron Oil.

Khartoum also sent a sergeant in their army, Museveni's old university friend John Garang, to appease the southerners. But Garang had other plans, and instead of quelling the revolt he joined the disparate rebel groups together under his own new rebel umbrella group, the Sudan People's Liberation Army (SPLA). Garang was an intellectual leader who sought a secular and socialist south. While demanding economic concessions, he focused rebel attacks on the foreign oil-drilling operations being set up in the central-south. Khartoum, with its oil reserves and future prosperity in jeopardy, responded with a military crackdown by imposing Islamic shariah law on the entire country, Muslim or not; until that time the South had been exempted from the laws of Islam. And so, by 1983, the civil war between the Arab North and the black African South that had been settled a decade earlier was formally on again. This time, however, the goal was oil wealth.[16]

In the first years of the rebellion, Garang's new army successfully destroyed all Western oil projects operating in South Sudan. Each time the Sudanese government attempted to secure the oil fields, the rebels attacked again. Exasperated, and after Omar Al-Bashir's government took over Sudan in a coup in 1989, Chevron Oil finally wrote off its interests in Sudan and sold its $1 billion investment for a token $25 million to a Sudanese firm. That firm was quickly transferred into private Canadian hands when a small Canadian company called Arakis Energy took over this problematic but potential gold mine of an oil concession.[17]

Meanwhile, as the Cold War ended and as Sudan's oil proved too difficult to explore under the continuing civil war, the U.S. lost interest in Sudan. In 1991, when Sudan opposed the American invasion of Iraq, George Bush Sr. shut off all support to Sudan and the two countries moved swiftly from friendship to overt enmity.

Adversaries of the United States and Israel moved to Sudan, including Carlos the Jackal (the world's most wanted terrorist in the 1970s and 1980s, now imprisoned in France) and Osama bin Laden, who moved there from Afghanistan in 1991, where he strengthened his Al Qaeda terrorist organization until 1996, when he was exiled. During his years in Sudan bin Laden maintained a home in Khartoum and a home in the countryside. He also reportedly started several businesses, from construction to the farming of sunflowers.

The U.S. cut diplomatic ties with Sudan. And yet the increasing hostility between the two countries was ignored by Canada's Arakis Energy. During this period the Canadian oil company executives, determined to succeed, worked closely with the Sudanese government to get oil out of the ground and to the international market. The rebels of the South were equally determined to prevent it. By then, all South Sudanese lived in "protected" displaced persons' camps, aligned either to the SPLA or to the government militia forces.[18]

Sudan was a mess, and South Sudan was the most destitute, godforsaken, despairing, and dangerous place on the planet, especially for women. Here, life expectancy was just thirty-six years, and only one in a hundred girls completed primary school.

It was inside this hell, in a military base at the front line of the war, that the Aboke Girls found their new home.

AT THE LRA BASE CAMP the rebels motioned for the new female recruits to move into the middle of camp, where rebel women tended to their swollen and infected feet. The boys went to another corner of the camp. They were informed that Kony was having an operation and was not available to greet them personally.

But two days later a bell sounded and the commanders, evidently flushed with excitement, jumped to attention. Everyone in the camp left their tasks and assembled in the prayer field. The top commanders walked onto the field first, wearing white robes. The LRA rank and file shouted and clapped excitedly. There was a fervour in the air. A tall, thin man in military uniform and with a large cross hanging from his neck walked to the front, flanked by layers of guards.

Grace Grall, who'd thought Joseph Kony would be ugly, wondered who this attractive man might be, with his broad smile, brown skin, and kind eyes. Joseph Kony introduced himself, welcomed them, and told them to forget the past. His voice resonated across the field. He was expressive, first slowing his words and then speeding up. He whispered, then shouted. His commanders looked at him with awe. The army appeared to be filled with true believers. Grace thought he seemed like a bishop, and she clapped along with the others.

Finally he turned his attention to the girls of Aboke. Kony told them they were his prized girls, hand-selected by God. The nuns of St. Mary's had been keeping them for him, educating smart girls in preparation for their new lives with him. They would teach the others, and bear strong, intelligent children who would grow up to lead the world.

He looked over the girls and chose four for himself, including the sweet-faced Jackie Wagesa, the lightest coloured and the youngest of the girls. He also chose Sylvia, Mariam, and Catherine.

All the Aboke Girls were then brought into a thatched hut. Brigadier-General Nyeko Tolbert welcomed them and introduced himself as the personnel manager. He said that Joseph Kony had directed him to divide them up among their new husbands. He told them theirs was an impor-tant duty—to help their husband in his military activities, and to satisfy all his personal needs.

While he assessed the girls, other rebels collected small stones, wrapped them in leather, and tied them to each girl's wrists. The girls looked around, and noticed that everyone in the camp had this leather packet on their wrists. None of them had the courage to ask what the stones were for, but later it was explained that the spirits used the rocks to protect them in battle.

General Tolbert assessed each girl one by one—and in a system designed to keep the commanders from competing over the same girl, he distributed them. It was only Kony who got to pick his favourites. Kenneth Banya received Grace Acan. Sam Kolo, Kony's trusted adviser, received two Aboke Girls. Grace Grall went to Lieutenant Lakati, a man in his forties who already had three wives. Charlotte Awino and Jessica Anguu both went to Raska Lukwiya. Angela Atim and Louiza Namele to Commander George Omona. Vincent Otti took two. General Tolbert, who had five wives already, kept Palma Achieng for himself. Janet Akello went to Colonel Charles Otim, a wounded commander with one leg, and Agatha Longoria, the Karamojong girl who'd been raped, was given to a senior commander in his fifties.

After all the Aboke Girls were distributed among the LRA's top command, the remaining abducted girls were given to the lower-ranking officers. Some of the junior officers, who had done well in battle, received their first wife. The young men crowded around the field, filled with anticipation, hoping to be among the rewarded. Most of the girls had little idea what was happening.

The youngest girls, considered pure, always went to the most trusted military officers. Some of the older ones, adult women abducted not for military duty but to be domestic slaves, went to the lower-ranking soldiers, or to the sick soldiers, those already suspected of having HIV and other diseases.

When General Tolbert finished dividing the girls, wedding prayers, religious anointings with water, and marriage instructions followed. And then most of the soldiers took their new young brides back to their mud huts and raped them.

Several of the girls always resisted, and these girls were beaten until they succumbed. Some of the men had killed their previous wives, and the girls married off to these men understood that disobedience was not an option. Certainly, there were young men, abducted from good homes, who wanted only companionship. But generally these boys did not climb the ranks. And besides, a monitoring system was in place inside the camps. Joseph Kony expected men to have sex with their women, because the Holy Spirit had told him that these special new children, born inside the LRA, would be the ones who would eventually lead the world to peace and salvation.

WHEN PALMA FIRST found herself alone with General Tolbert, he questioned her. He wanted to know her age, her home village, the name of her parents, and when she'd had her first period. When she told him she hadn't had her period yet, he looked at her with disappointment.

"You're a bit young," he mumbled.[19] LRA rules stated that no man was to have intercourse with a girl who hadn't yet passed into womanhood. The rules stipulated that she was his "tin-tin," or adolescent daughter who would one day become his wife. Tolbert told Palma to stay with his other wives, all of whom were aged twelve to seventeen. Two of them had one child each. None of them liked her, and within days of her arrival began beating her daily.

Meanwhile, Agatha Longoria, staying in a family just next to Tolbert's group, soon realized that the grey-haired man she'd been given to was secretly kind. He never beat her, or otherwise touched her—perhaps aware that she'd been raped en route, and that not enough time had gone by to know if she was HIV positive. He was also educated, and each night he sat around their camp's hearth fire and told his wives and children about the world. Agatha was his only wife who also knew of the world, and because she'd just been in school, he asked her to tell them stories about it. He had several children from his other wives, but Agatha could tell that it was she whom he liked to talk to.

Sometimes his other wives beat her when he was out fighting the South Sudan rebels, the SPLA. Agatha tried to complain to her husband about them, but he explained that they were uneducated and jealous, and that her best option was not to quarrel back.

Then there was Janet Akello, whose father was an engineer in Lira and whose happy, loving family had prayed together daily. Now she'd been given to twenty-five-year-old Charles Otim, who had four other wives and a missing leg. He'd been abducted at seventeen, in 1989, and as one of the first into the LRA was now a colonel who had learned what was required of him to stay alive. That was why he forced Janet to kill, with a stick, a sickly ten-year-old boy who had just tried to escape from Otim's group. After the boy lay dead in front of her, her new husband warned that if she attempted to escape she would meet the same fate. The memory of that boy now haunted Janet. Every night she prayed for forgiveness.

In the next camp over from her was Grace Grall, staying in Lakati's camp, which consisted of several mud huts and a central fire. When she first arrived Lakati had looked over his new wife, assessed her body, then told her she'd become a soldier soon, and as such must learn to survive on her own. He walked away and thereafter pretended she didn't exist.

In the daytime Grace Grall fetched water and tended crops. With the other wives she did housework, cleaning, and cooking. She collected termites for the nightly meal. She cut ten bundles of grass a day, which were then sold to the Sudanese government. If she returned to camp at night a bundle short, she was beaten. Two of her co-wives were commanders themselves, although subservient to Lakati's orders. They despised Grace immediately, and threatened that one day they would take her to the bush and murder her, and that no one would know what had happened. Grace learned to stay quiet around them.

Her biggest problem was Lakati. After a week of ignoring her, he called for her one night. *What does he want?* Grace wondered, entering his tent. "I am going to take you as a wife," he said.

"What do you mean?" she whispered, trembling before him. It was hard for her to speak.

"If you refuse, I will kill you."

Meanwhile, the girls with Kony[20] soon realized that he was a busy man. He had dozens of wives, perhaps a hundred children, and an army to lead. He didn't have the time to focus on them, and so being within the fold of the Kony family actually gave the girls some protection. They were the first-wives of the LRA, and unlike the wives of the rank and file, they did not engage in active battle as soldiers.

Some of the girls in Kony's camp saw that the Aboke Girls appeared paralyzed by misery. Their sad faces betrayed them. So the girls, co-wives, tried to help by telling the newcomers to face the reality and not to think too much about it—that negative thoughts alone could kill them.

FOR THE NEXT DAYS and weeks the Aboke Girls struggled to adapt to their new concubine families and sexual obligations. Although the girls lived in adjacent camps they were forbidden to communicate with and even to look at one another. Even when they all gathered together on the prayer field they couldn't stand close together. The rebels knew that in the early days, before new recruits' wills were broken, any interaction with those they had known beforehand would likely involve escape plans.

So the girls were now divided, left to suffer and survive on their own. Each soon learned that for whatever reason—by decree, jealousy, or both—each Aboke Girl was hated by her co-wives. The girls could not ask questions, and nothing was explained.

Grace Grall was heartbroken by the reality of it. She'd had such dreams for her future, and had overcome such hardship to get to St. Mary's. But now she saw that her life would be spent bent over in the fields with children strapped to her back and with a polygamous, sadistically cruel husband twice her age. Her destiny was to be a slave.

She'd been born in 1981 in a traditional earthen hut in a small village in northeastern Uganda. Grace's father hadn't bothered to marry her teenage mother before having children with her, and so her maternal grandparents were always after him to pay them the expected dowry of five cows as proof of marriage. But instead of delivering the cows, Grace's father left her mother and their three children and moved to the town of Lira, looking for better work than what a village life could offer. Soon he opened a small grocery store, married another woman, and began having more children. Sometimes he visited his old family home, and when he did he stayed with Grace's mother. Such were the ways of many Ugandan men.

When the time came for Grace to go to school, her father declined to pay for her. But his own brother, Grace's uncle—a farmer poorer than her father—found it in his heart to pay her way—about 40,000 shillings, or $25, a year.

Grace was an excellent student, quickly becoming fluent in English. Stories from outside her world had made her restless to experience life beyond the village. The shy girl who kept her head lowered around adults soon had a fantasy life of going to college. She knew she was expected to do as other girls in her village did: to find a husband and follow her mother's footsteps, tending the fields of maize, sorghum, and potatoes with yet another newborn baby strapped to her back, worrying about either the rain or the heat and the health of her children. But her fantasy grew stronger by the day.

Instead of making friends, she spent all her spare time studying, hoping somehow that she'd get one of the few scholarships for the northern children and find herself a different destiny. But just as she started junior high school her uncle died in a car accident. With him went her school fees. Grace had no choice but to drop out and become, like most of the girls around her, an assistant to her mother in the fields.

But after a year passed, Grace's father, his business prospering and perhaps wanting to reward his eldest daughter for her hard work, arrived unexpectedly at her mother's home and told Grace that he'd found a place for her at St. Mary's.

Dreams and hope returned to Grace. At Aboke she made friends for the first time in her life. But now, all that struggle for education had led here.[21]

After a few weeks inside Sudan living with her new family, Grace Grall was sent for two weeks' training at Brigadier-General Kenneth Banya's military training camp. Grace Acan, who was Grace Grall's friend, was now married to Banya, although she didn't see Grace Acan there.

With dozens of other new recruits, Grace Grall arrived at the training field feeling pleased to be away from her new family. An underling to Banya gave her and the others an AK-47 machine gun and trained her how to load and dismantle this and other guns. She was also taught to parade. She learned to shoot on the job, raiding South Sudanese Dinka villages for food. The Dinka civilians were armed and starving, and they always fought to protect their food, so she got plenty of practice while stealing.

CHAPTER 6

Kenneth Banya, Kony's right-hand man, considered himself smart, educated, and moral, and yet a series of events had corrupted all his ambition and left him here, stuck inside a rebel group that was growing increasingly brutal.[22] So it was with several of Kony's close leaders: intelligent men who worked alongside one of the cruellest men in the world, doing his bidding and excelling at it. Such was the insanity of evil. Sometimes a single choice was enough to lead one down a trail where there was no turning back. All further decisions were simply a reaction to that first fateful choice to step down the wrong road.

But this was wartime, and rules of honour differed here. And since he was at the top now—training, strategizing, making alliances—if it all played out Banya could one day leave the bush and return as a valiant leader, a freedom fighter for his Acholi people, and the deaths of all these children and civilians could be washed away from his mind as he made up for it with great actions in the future. Besides, he'd tell himself, it was wartime and he didn't have a choice.

Born in May 1945 in a small village outside Lira, Banya grew into an ambitious man. At a time when most Ugandans were illiterate, he'd finished high school in Gulu in 1969 with top marks. He studied industrial chemistry in 1970 before being recruited by the government air force. He was sent to Tel Aviv where he learned to fly a plane. Seven years of study followed in the U.S.S.R., where he became a flight engineer and learned how to organize an army. Banya returned to Uganda during

Idi Amin's reign, but Amin was killing Acholi soldiers en masse, so he ran away to Tanzania, where he met the young rebel leader Yoweri Museveni and banded together with his rebel forces. In 1979 they invaded Uganda and overthrew Amin.

Museveni had then been an angry young scholar filled with anti-colonialist thoughts. In the 1960s he studied economics and political science at Tanzania's University of Dar es Salaam, then a hotbed of Marxist socialism, and forged alliances with other young revolutionaries interested in uplifting the black man from colonial oppression. Classmate John Garang, who went on to become the guerrilla leader of South Sudan's SPLA, was one of his best friends.

During this time Museveni believed that violence had rehabilitative capabilities. He wrote his bachelor thesis on "Fanon's Theory of Violence: Its Verification in Liberated Mozambique." For research he took guerrilla warfare training with Mozambique's rebels. In his thesis he wrote:

> But not only is violence the only effective instrument of bringing about the real overthrow of colonial rules, it is also a laxative, a purgative, an agent for creating new men. In the course of this violent struggle, all the psychic complexes, arising out of the colonial situation, dissolve, disappear in thin air. The native kills the settler and sees that the settler has got the same skin as the native.[23]

He argued that killing itself transformed the oppressed personality into a freed one. He was a philosophical leader, an African equivalent of Cuba's Che Guevara.

Shortly after university he tested his philosophy on the battlefield, and after helping lead the rebellion against Idi Amin, was rewarded with the position of minister of state for defence. Kenneth Banya guarded him. Museveni was then Uganda's youngest minister.

Museveni ran for president the next year, against Milton Obote—an Acholi who'd been president before Idi Amin took over—and a democratic candidate, Dr. Paul Ssemongere, who was widely popular and running on a campaign of true democracy. It appeared likely that Ssemongere actually won, but Obote stole the election and used the military to seize control of the country. Outraged, Museveni took to the bush to plot another revolution. He hid in central Uganda, in the Luwero Triangle, where he created an alliance with the thousands of Rwandan Tutsi refugees then living in Uganda. One of those was Paul Kagame, now president of Rwanda. They joined forces and for five years war raged in the Luwero Triangle. Mass atrocities took place, never fully understood or investigated, and 300,000 died, mostly civilians. In 1985 Obote's own army revolted against him and called for Museveni to form a new government with them. But Museveni continued his onslaught, with his rebel ragtag army made up of thousands of children taking Kampala on January 25, 1986. Throughout this time, Banya was an officer in the government.

When Museveni seized power, Kenneth Banya retreated to his family homestead in Northern Uganda, where he farmed and tended the oxen while assessing his next move. He was forty-one and tired of war and had stayed out of the last year of the fighting. In fact, he'd secured a letter from the district commissioner absolving him of any responsibility—an insurance policy in case Museveni's forces didn't believe him. Banya hoped for a good government job once things stabilized, for he'd never had anything personal against Museveni and hoped he'd remember him as the man who'd once been his guard.

Banya was married to an Acholi woman, and by 1987 they had five children. She and the children had already left the instability of Uganda for London. If he couldn't get a good job with Museveni and bring them back, he might have joined them there.

But in October 1987 rebels showed up at his doorstep and abducted him. It was 5 P.M., and he'd been drinking crude waragi alcohol with his brother and a friend. He asked why they were taking him. "You are a soldier, we are fighting, so you cannot stay at home."[24] Banya protested, but the armed men told him that if he didn't go willingly they'd force his family to join them. Banya went willingly. He was marched northward. When they reached Latanya village the rebels regrouped with other members of their unit, and here Banya learned that Joseph Kony's young army had decided to target the senior soldiers in the area in order to use their military skills. Together the former high-ranking soldiers were taken to Kony at a secret camp along the Sudan border, where Kony slaughtered a bull for a celebration feast and merrily welcomed the senior men to his ranks.[25]

Kony said he needed his recruits trained, and he looked to Banya for advice. So Banya drew up a suggested military structure for Kony's new rebel group. Banya made himself a brigade commander, and knowing how to keep himself out of the line of fire, his brigade's purpose was to train the recruits, not to fight.

And so it was that Banya formed a secret training ground in the no man's land of South Sudan. The man who spoke fluent English, Russian, Luo, Arabic, Luganda, Kiswahili, Langi, Alur, and Jaluo now worked on the recruits.[26]

His trained and indoctrinated children quickly turned into highly effective combatants. Advances in automatic weapons meant that the guns were light enough for the children to handle. The children also needed less food, rarely questioned orders, and looked for approval by pleasing those above them. Their small size made them difficult targets for the opposing soldiers, and their bravery in battle was often unparalleled. As well, opposing soldiers were often reluctant to kill child soldiers.

Banya never returned to Northern Uganda, and so he told himself he could never defect even if he'd wanted to. On one side there was Kony's wrath, on the other, Museveni's. Fate had intervened in his plans, and now he waged war against what the West considered one of the greatest African leaders, Uganda's president Yoweri K. Museveni. With all doors closed, he made the most of where he was.

Recently, that had meant receiving a beautiful, cultured, obedient, educated young wife to add to his five other wives. Aboke Girl Grace Acan, eldest daughter of Consy Ogwal and a respected Acholi government man, had joined his growing family.

AFTER COMPLETING two weeks of military training, Grace Grall became a private. She slept with an AK-47 machine gun tied to her and sometimes spent the night lying in a trench on guard duty.

Her relationship with her co-wives continued to degenerate. They routinely forbade her from eating. Their hatred seemed to be related to her position as an Aboke Girl, and Grace began to suspect that they'd been ordered to be cruel to her.

Lakati too seemed to hate her, never offering her a kind word or gesture while using her body as he willed. He beat her every day. "Aboke Girls are stupid," he'd say, striking her. Sometimes, sadistically, he'd starve her for days while forcing her to cook for everyone else. He had a guard watch her to see if she so much as licked her fingers. Grace, her stomach cramped in hunger, restrained herself. But at times the guard would lie and report on her for eating. Then Lakati would order her to get a stick and he'd whip her. Grace soon shrivelled into a skeletal frame. It wasn't long before she was thinking about suicide.

All the Aboke Girls were suffering similar fates, but they couldn't discuss their troubles with each other. Because they were forbidden from communicating among themselves, the only chance the increasingly isolated girls had was when they collected water, two kilometres outside the camp, and bumped into each other.

One day, on her walk to the water hole, Grace came upon Judith, their former elected head girl back at St. Mary's. There were no guards with them as their location, with Sudan army camps on one side and the war's front line against John Garang's SPLA rebels on the other, was its own cell. "I'm going to escape," Judith said. She too had lost a lot of weight, and like Grace, had been trained to fight.

"Don't—if you try you might be killed," Grace said, and suggested she wait until they were in Uganda. Kony had told them they'd soon be ready to attack the army there.

Judith continued on, carrying two jerry cans of water, passing the bloated bodies of the dead: many of the youngest ones in the camp were dying from malnutrition and diarrhea. Their bodies were discarded out here, left for the animals.

Another time Grace met tiny Jackie Wagesa, who was still staying with Kony as his premenstrual daughter. "I think my mother is dead,"

Jackie said. Her mother had been wasting away with an undefined illness, likely AIDS.

Grace told her that although she didn't know, her sense was that Jackie's mother was still alive. Then Grace added, "If you don't see me again, I'm dead, or I escaped." Grace was considering her options. Any attempt at escape would be fraught with difficulty, and if caught she'd be tortured to death. Suicide seemed easier.

The girls knew they couldn't be seen together, so they moved on quickly from these brief exchanges, often departing with a prayer for each other.

SOON AFTER completing basic military training, Grace Grall and Judith were sent on short trips with other soldiers, marching into Northern Uganda for surprise raids and disciplinary actions. Instead of fighting the Ugandan military, though, Kony repeatedly ordered them to find any rebels who had deserted him.

One day a young rebel soldier escaped with his gun. Grace and her fellow soldiers went to his village where they found him hiding with his family. They retrieved the gun, tied up the boy, and then rounded up his family and neighbours. The commander explained that since these people had failed in their duty to inform the rebels of the deserter's whereabouts, they would be killed as a warning message to others. Kony had cited the Old Testament when he'd explained the need to punish the community. He'd told his followers that the lips of those who spoke evil should be removed, arms that had sinned should be cut off, and eyes that had seen that which they should not should be plucked out.

Because Grace was still a junior rebel, she was told that for emotional strength training she could not look away. She watched, without crying or flinching, as the boy's feet, then arms and legs were cut off. Then she watched in numb detachment as everyone else was hacked to death amid their futile screams for mercy.

On Christmas Day the rebels celebrated with food and songs and laughter. New Year's Day was another day of celebration. But on January 3, 1997, Kony ordered the camp to gather at the prayer field. Here Kony raged with fury and ordered that a brigade would leave the next day for

Kitgum to punish its people. "Nobody in Kitgum should be left alive!" he shouted.

From the other rebels Grace learned what had happened. An Acholi hunter following his game had stumbled upon an LRA arms cache at the base of a mountain in Lamwo village. Instead of leaving well enough alone, he reported his find to the military in Kitgum and they removed ten trucks loaded with the LRA's artillery. As well, a group of Kony's new recruits had recently escaped from the LRA, and Kitgum had welcomed the children back.

"Those old enough to differentiate between good and bad should all be killed, even the old ones … They don't listen to what I say!" Kony yelled.[27] He raved that, since he was delivering a new Acholi generation, he could kill everyone in Acholiland and line their heads on the road for others to see.

Kony moved on to the cleansing ceremony, preparing the fighters for battle. He shouted out prayers, asking God to give them the power to defeat their enemy. Commanders poured water over the heads of those beneath them in rank. Everyone clapped, their stone amulets clanging together on their wrists. "The problems we are facing will end in heaven, where God is," they shouted.[28]

The next day the group moved into Kitgum, three kilometres from the Sudan border. Over the following five days they killed and raped and burned everyone who couldn't outrun them, leaving 412 civilians dead. The rebels lined dismembered heads along the road. Tens of thousands of terrified Acholi ran with their belongings on their backs and camped out at a local school and a motel close to the military barracks. On the sixth day, despite having been only a few kilometres down the road the entire time, the military finally arrived to protect the people. The Ugandan rebels retreated across the border into Sudan.[29]

GRACE GRALL walked with her fellow soldiers through the parched land of Sudan, a gun on her arm. With no rain having fallen in months, the grass was dead and wilted. Thistle bushes covered the land. Although some of them carried jerry cans of water, the supply was restricted to commanders and none dared to attempt to steal any despite their desperate dehydration. Some of the children begged to drink each other's urine. Engaged in power struggles themselves, some of the boys refused to pass their urine in cups, instead forcing the recipients to their knees.

The marching continued, miles on end without water, the midday sun scorching down. Grace Grall's dry throat cracked from the inside when she attempted to speak. Her lips were swollen and dried hard with blood. Her tongue was thick and dry. The stabbing pain was growing unbearable. She'd seen others kill themselves during these long marches, their dry throats being the final emotional straw, and now she too had had enough. She turned her machine gun on herself, but before she pulled the trigger, another rebel hit her. "Why should you shoot yourself? You just die," he said. She staggered back to her feet, her resolve gone.

Hours passed, and the group came upon an abandoned village. Here, Grace noticed a mudhole in a garden. She dug into the wet dirt and watched anxiously as water seeped to the surface. She slaked it up. Just then gunfire erupted around her—an ambush by the SPLA. She ran ahead, leaving the others to defend themselves. With everyone occupied in the gunfight, she searched the deserted village and found a bushel bag of peanuts that a Dinka civilian had left behind. She greedily stuffed handfuls in her mouth. Minutes later a commander found her. "Why are you eating my peanuts?" he yelled.

She gave him the bag and watched him fill his jerry can with the peanuts until a pop sound stopped him. His eyes went wide and he clenched his stomach, where he'd been shot. Grace peered out at an armed man she assumed was the owner of the peanuts. She turned and ran. A bullet whizzed past, and then gunfire broke out all around her. Grace grabbed her gun and started firing. It was yet another ambush.

When it was over, Grace collected the dead commander's gun and the peanuts still at his side. She followed her group as they continued marching through the bush. As the hours passed, now loaded down and still dehydrated, she grew faint. She grabbed a papaya stem and cracked it in half. Inside was a liquid that relieves thirst but further dehydrates the body. Grace knew this, but still she sucked on it.

Within minutes the brown earth turned white and the world hazed over. Grace collapsed. Because they didn't want to leave a trail for Garang's army to find, some of the rebels dragged her off the path, removed her uniform for another to wear, and buried her in a shallow grave before moving on.

Darkness crept over the arid land. The stars shone above. The animals took to their hiding spots; crickets chirped in the grass. Then, in the middle of the night, clouds moved together and it rained for the first time in weeks. After a while the water dripping on Grace's face awakened her. Opening her eyes, she panicked. *Where's my gun?* she thought, reaching down for it, fearing a beating if she'd lost it. The earth around her stopped her movement. Grace dug herself out from the grave, clambering over the other bodies who'd shared her resting spot, and realized that she was the only survivor.

She called out. No one answered. Grace sat there, wondering what she should do: she was alone in Sudan, in enemy territory and without a gun or clothes, and was too weak to attempt the unknown journey through the woods and plains to Uganda. She looked up to the stars and almost laughed at the irony of it. Her first time alone since her abduction, and yet if she wanted to live she had no choice. She stood up and followed the footprints back to the rebels.

When she walked into their camp, a sad, skeletal sight, naked and covered in dirt, a female commander laughed. "Sister must be praying very hard—she has resurrected one of her girls!" she said. Someone brought her water and the commander threw her clothes back at her, saying, "Be on standby."

Judith looked at Grace, but didn't dare welcome her back.

CHAPTER 7

LRA Base Camp, South Sudan, April 1997

The LRA had been receiving military assistance and food from the Sudanese government since 1994 in retaliation for President Museveni's support of the South Sudan rebels, the SPLA. Museveni claimed that he provided Garang's rebels only with political support, but this was widely known not to be true.

Now, backed with expensive military equipment from unnamed Western donors, the Ugandan government chose to invade Sudan. In a joint offensive, Ugandan and SPLA forces swept northward from the Ugandan border through Sudan's southern provinces of Equatoria and Bahr El Ghazal, capturing Sudanese army garrisons from Yei to Tonj towns. They took thousands of prisoners of war, including at least a thousand members of West Bank Nile Front, another Ugandan rebel group supported by the Sudanese government. The combined forces now moved toward the LRA camp.

One early April morning, Grace Grall noticed the commanders running around and looking agitated. After Kony called an assembly she walked to the prayer grounds with the others. Surrounded by his personal guards, Kony strode to the front. "The Holy Spirit has spoken to me," he began. The spirit had told him that seven hundred Ugandan soldiers had crossed into Sudan and that they were joining the SPLA and advancing toward them. He selected a brigade of 250 soldiers, led by Mariano Lagira, to go forth to fight the approaching force. Everyone else was on standby.

Grace Grall returned to her family home with her husband. Even though she'd chosen life when she awakened from her shallow grave, she knew she would soon kill herself. Her suffering in these last months had brought her very close to God, and she believed He'd understand. To die now in battle was not an upsetting prospect.

As the day passed without the return of soldiers, tension grew in the camp. A second group was sent forward. A few hours later wounded soldiers staggered into the camp, speaking of great losses and an impending assault.

The commanders panicked. The Sudanese camp next door was evacuated. Kony jumped into his dark green pickup truck and sped down the road toward Juba, a stronghold of the Sudanese army. His pregnant wives and children, crammed into a lorry, followed just metres behind him. Grace watched a mortar explode into the lorry before it could leave the camp. It blasted apart, killing several of the women and children inside.[30] Everyone started running. Gunfire and bombs descended into the camp.

But Grace stood still, clutching her gun, as the tanks rolled in and crushed huts. Instead of fighting, she sat down against a tree in the middle of the battlefield. Bombs exploded around her. Bullets zipped past. People screamed and moaned. Most of the rebels had fled, but one group stayed behind to slow the enemy advance, fighting back from the surrounding trenches. A commander yelled at her to shoot her rifle but she ignored him. *"You wanted to die,"* she told herself, *"but maybe this is your day to go home."*

After a while Grace was alone, but for the groans of the wounded around her. The battle continued in the woods beyond. Day turned to dusk and then to night. The sounds of the battle grew more distant.[31]

Hoping to sleep in the bush, she stood up and tied her saucepans to her back, wrapped her AK-47 around her chest, and piled her luggage on her head. She clambered over the bodies, noticing many young ones. A mortar exploded behind her, smashing the saucepans off her back. She fell to the ground. After a moment, she raised herself up and checked to see if she was still alive. Satisfied, she untied the luggage from her body, keeping only her gun, and ran into the bush to hide. She settled in and soon drifted to sleep.

Hours later soldiers walked through the camp speaking Kiswahili—a language that identified them as SPLA to the few injured rebels who remained. A seventeen-year-old girl who'd been collecting water when the troops attacked was hiding in the trenches. When a soldier saw her he started yelling, but then another soldier looked at her and said, "If she's a girl she might be one of the Aboke Girls."[32] The girl was overjoyed when she heard the words—she knew it meant that, even though she wasn't an Aboke Girl, they would free her. They grabbed her and took her to the Ugandan soldiers.

But Grace Grall hadn't woken up, and when she did, she was alone. For three days she stayed hidden in the grass, sleeping, eating soil and leaves to ward off hunger, and waiting for the sounds of battle to end. There was no water to be found. On the third day she decided it was time to make her way back to Uganda. If she accidentally crossed the path of the LRA, she would say she'd been looking for them.

Along the way she met a lost group of boys and girls she recognized from base camp, who said they were going to Juba. They invited her to join them, but she refused. One asked where she was planning to go, and she explained that she was heading to Uganda because she saw others going there. It was a lie.

"You are very stupid. Where is this girl from?" a young boy said.

"She's from Aboke," one of the girls said. Everyone in the group had a gun, and without a rebel commander to lead them, they jockeyed for power.

"Aboke Girls are very stupid. They're making us suffer. Kill her," the boy said, raising his gun at her.

Another girl stopped him. "No. She's already so skinny, she'll just die on the way." They left her behind and continued toward Juba.

A few minutes later eight of the girls came back for Grace and encouraged her to join them. Instead, Grace took charge and began to lead the group toward Uganda; they followed her as though she were a commander. Some understood that they were escaping together, others thought they were simply trying to find the rest of the brigade. Some were older, others younger. No one trusted anyone in the group.

When they reached a river and Grace said they had to cross it, a few became angry, drawing their guns and claiming that it was her plan to kill them. But Grace sat down at the riverbank and invited them to eat soil and drink water together before they killed her. The dirt, she knew, would temporarily lessen their hunger pains. The other girls complied, but the conversation quickly turned back to how they were going to kill her.

"You can't kill me. I'd rather drown in the water," Grace said, jumping into the river even though she couldn't swim. She flailed in the water but soon found her footing, crossing at a shallow section. The others followed her route, and they all made it across. To Grace it was a miracle.

Once on the other side, she said "Let's throw away our guns." It felt almost as if the words had come directly from God; Grace hadn't known she could be so strong. Again the girls thought it was a trap, and again they threatened to kill her. Grace held firm, though, explaining that the Dinka would kill them if they saw their guns. And once more they conceded, throwing the guns under a thorn bush and continuing on through the hostile land.

Minutes later Grace saw a mud hut with naked children playing outside. She shouted out greetings, but as soon as the children heard her they ran inside. A family of Dinkas then ran from the hut and into the protection of the nearby bushes behind their home. Some carried guns.

"We have to flee," a girl said.

Grace shook her head. "When we flee, these people will shoot us. It is time to surrender. If we die, it's fine. It's God's will."

The girls laughed. "You are completely mad!" one said.

Grace turned with a hard face to her peers. "If you run, I'm going to scream that you are the ones who abducted me, so that they only kill you." She raised her hands in the air and walked toward the homestead. "We are not bad people!" she shouted in English. The girls followed, shouting in Luo. But it was no use. The Dinka didn't understand either language.

The Dinka men walked out of the bushes, guns drawn, and searched the girls for weapons. They shouted incomprehensibly and waved accusatory fingers in their faces. Grace knew they blamed them for attacking their villages and stealing food from the starving. The men tied the girls' hands behind their backs, blindfolded them, and positioned them in a line. When the men stepped back and their rifles clicked, Grace knew they'd just been sentenced to death by firing squad.

"We were abducted from Uganda!" she yelled. "Some of us were taken from school! We have come to you for help!" None of the other girls spoke. She was the only one who knew English, and Luo had proven useless. "You are going to kill us, but we came to you for help!"

Out of the hut stepped an old man brandishing a sharp hoe and shouting to the men. He walked up to Grace and pulled down her blindfold. Grace tensed her body, believing he was about to cut her to pieces. "Repeat what you said," he said in English.

She repeated her story. The man turned and spoke in the tribal dialect to his relatives. The other men put their guns down and walked under a shade tree, where they sat in heated discussion. The women directed Grace and the other girls to another shade tree, giving them water and porridge that they wolfed down hungrily. Finally the old man returned to Grace and told her that he'd take her group to the nearest SPLA camp for them to decide.

They were a sorry sight: a frail old Dinka man leading nine tied-up Ugandan girls down a dirt trail. En route they met a group of SPLA soldiers. The old man and the soldiers soon began yelling at one another, but after a moment the soldiers let them pass. The old man told Grace that the soldiers had called her and her friends useless and wanted to kill them, but that he'd replied he was a Christian and as such did not want the girls killed in front of him. It was up to their commander to decide, he'd added.

At the SPLA camp the old man brought the girls to the commander. Watching the scene, Grace could tell the old man was defending her. The commander, a huge man with facial scars, listened to the story then turned and smiled at them.

The scarred man brought Grace to his high commander, John Garang. Garang offered her tea and then announced in flawless English that he'd be taking them to General Salim Saleh, Museveni's half-brother, who was leading the Ugandan assault.

They drove in a convoy through South Sudan and into Kony's abandoned camp, Aru—where their men scanned the remains for intelligence—and then continued on to General Saleh.

General Saleh looked at Grace. "Where do you come from?" he asked, having heard that, unlike the others, she spoke fluent English. She was too frightened to respond. "Are you from Aboke?"

She nodded, and he smiled. He told her he'd been looking for her, and would take her to Uganda.

They drove to the Kitgum base, where a helicopter airlifted her to Gulu. Meanwhile, two other Aboke Girls had been rescued during the same military operation and returned to their families.

In Gulu, Grace's father picked her up and brought her to her mother's home in the village. Upon seeing Grace her mother fell to the ground, sobbing, unable to speak. But Grace felt nothing inside. She left without hugging her mother, and told her father that she wanted to go back to St. Mary's school in Aboke. She didn't feel safe in the village.

Her father instead brought her to Lira to stay with his new wife and children. He didn't ask Grace a single question about her six months in the bush. Perhaps he was trying to respect her dignity by allowing her to keep to herself what he knew would have been stories of defilement and abuse. The reality of these stories would have rendered Grace an outcast, a girl tarnished and no longer valued for marriage by any of the more educated or prosperous in their society. Consequently, they simply pretended that it hadn't happened.

But Grace's stepmother didn't pretend, nor did she like Grace's being in the house. "You're Kony's wife," she'd whisper hatefully.

Sometimes Grace overheard her stepmother arguing that the family's money shouldn't go to Grace's education. When she was alone with Grace, she would tell her that she was no longer fit for school and should instead find a husband to pay her way. "Your dad should not pay your school fees. He is my husband. You should get your own."[33] Of course, her status now as a former rebel-wife meant that no status-conscious Ugandan man would want her. Not only would he fear her past as a murderous rebel and question her ability to now nurture children, he'd also worry about the unknown diseases she might carry. Influenced by their deeply religious upbringings, most Ugandan men looked for purity and innocence in their partners.

To Grace this didn't much matter. She had no intention of being with a man again in her life.

Grace's father ignored his wife's complaints and provided the small tuition to return Grace to St. Mary's. Within a week of her rescue she was back at the school.

Sister Alba and Sister Rachele welcomed Grace joyfully, drawing her in with hugs and kisses. She accepted these but did not offer much affection in return. Surrounding the school now was a twelve-foot-high concrete fence topped with razor-wire. Sister Alba had seen to that. Sister Alba led Grace to her new bunkbed in her old dorm room. Grace noticed that the hole in the wall had been filled in with concrete.

Grace was given some new dresses and a sweater. The nuns took her for an AIDS test, which came back negative. And suddenly there she was, as if in a time warp, sitting in Senior 2—grade ten—learning from John Bosco. She was just a normal schoolgirl again, although she no longer spoke to anyone.

Grace had always been a quiet girl, uncertain of her ability to speak up when others talked to her, but now she was silent, almost completely unable to respond to others. Deep down she knew something evil was inside her. She followed orders, ate, worked, and did her homework. But the hatred she felt for herself, and others, was growing.

PART 2

"IN THE ABSENCE OF THE CHILDREN"

CHAPTER 8

LIRA, NORTHERN UGANDA, OCTOBER 10, 1996

"They've taken all the girls from St. Mary's!" a neighbour yelled as she pounded on Angelina Atyam's door. Angelina jumped out of bed and the two ran down the street screaming, looking for a vehicle to take them to St. Mary's. Another parent with a child in the school was standing out on the road. One of their neighbours offered to drive them the fifteen kilometres to St. Mary's, and off they went.

It was 7 A.M. when Angelina ran into St. Mary's looking for her daughter Charlotte. As she ran she noticed children's clothing, notebooks, and empty wrappings from biscuits littered across the soccer field. Charlotte's dormitory room was a mess, and empty.

Angelina Atyam, thirty-nine, was one of St. Mary's first graduates. She'd gone on to Germany to train as a nurse and then found work as the matron of a tiny village hospital Father John Fraser had built near Masindi Falls. She and Father John worked closely together during the difficult end years of Idi Amin's rule in the late 1970s, when the poverty was so great that some no longer had clothes to wear, and none had salt or sugar to add to their food. Back then, with so many women dying in childbirth, Father John proposed to Angelina that they open a maternity clinic—and its eventual launch was one of the most satisfying moments of her life. Later, when Angelina moved to Lira with her husband, she opened a private midwife business out of her home. When it was time, she sent her eldest daughter, Charlotte Awino, to St. Mary's school in Aboke.

Charlotte was precious to Angelina. She was the type of child who noticed when her mother was sick or tired. At those times Charlotte would ask Angelina if she'd like a cup of tea, the steaming teacup already in her hand on offer.

Angelina stepped back outside and noticed men sitting on the ground, openly weeping. She'd never seen such a thing; African men didn't cry. Women rolled on the ground sobbing. Sister Alba was in tears. Angelina joined them.

Among the parents was Consy Ogwal, thirty-two, whose eldest daughter, Grace Acan, was missing. Consy's husband, who worked in government, had given her the news hours earlier before bursting out in sobs. Consy, like Angelina, had never seen a man cry before, and shocked, couldn't ask him more. Instead she ran toward town.

Consy found other parents wandering on the street, and they told her about the abductions and the Lord's Resistance Army rebels, which until now, they'd all thought, had caused problems only in the far-north communities bordering Sudan.

Consy felt numb and was unable to cry. Consy had been so proud when Grace Acan was admitted to St. Mary's. Consy quit school after finishing primary seven because her family hadn't had the money to keep her going, and she had wanted her beautiful daughter to have more choices than she'd had, for Consy had married at sixteen and started having babies right away. Now, without a certificate of education, she couldn't find work and was dependent financially on her husband.

By mid-morning the African extended family system had kicked in. The school was filled with hundreds of people waiting desperately for news.

None came for twenty-four hours. Then the parents, gathered again at St. Mary's, heard word that Sister Rachele was returning with most, but not all, of the girls. Each parent looked down the road, waiting and hoping that their daughters would be coming back to them. Finally, the trucks appeared. Watching the arriving truckloads of girls, Angelina Atyam met the eyes of her niece. The girl looked away and Angelina had her answer. Charlotte wasn't coming home. The world stood still, the moment of horror complete, enveloping, overwhelming. It felt to Angelina like an out-of-body experience.

Sister Rachele walked past the parents. The nun was a pathetic sight, covered in mud and scratches, her eyes etched red with pain. She disappeared into a room to talk to Sister Alba, then returned and taped a list naming the thirty missing girls on the notice board at the entrance of the school. The parents whose daughters hadn't returned ran to the board. Angelina saw Charlotte's name.

She stepped away, lost her footing, and fell to the ground. Her numb disbelief gave way and she began screaming in a guttural tone.

Consy Ogwal's husband told her he was certain the rebels would keep their daughter, who was strikingly pretty, with big eyes and a smile that melted hearts. Grace Acan was obedient, strong, and trusting. Consy now saw that Grace was third on the list. She turned and started walking back to town. It took her a moment to understand what this meant, and then her mind pictured her daughter moving with the rebels, being taken as a slave or a wife. Being abused. Consy wondered if she'd ever learn what had happened to Grace. The life of her eldest child flashed through her mind. She remembered Grace as a baby, Grace first walking, her first words. She saw Grace's laughing face when she used to chase the chickens in their yard. She thought of the dreams they used to talk about together, how Grace could grow up to be anything she wanted to become. It all raced through her and overwhelmed her senses. She shouted to the sky: "God, what have you done?" and then the world hazed over. She fell to the ground, unconscious. A stranger prayed over her, counselling her, and finally Consy opened her eyes and found the strength to stand again.

Nearby was the quiet Florence Lacor, who had rushed down from Gulu, 150 kilometres north of the school. Her daughter was Angela, the child who'd written her classmates' names for Sister Rachele. A friend of Angela's who'd been released recognized Angela's sad, soft eyes in Florence's own. "Angela remained," she said, hugging Florence.

"It's okay," she said, pulling free of the girl and falling to her knees to pray. A single mother with four children, Florence, as a born-again

Christian, was certain Jesus was there for her. She got up off her knees and walked to get a ride back to Lira, then another up to Gulu. She didn't say goodbye to the other grieving parents. Her faith told her that a degree of patience was in order before God brought Angela home.

Alfred Olum, an unemployed factory worker, now scanned the list. That morning he and his wife, Isabella, a teacher, had learned of the abduction on the radio in their home in Kampala. Isabella, still mourning the sudden death of their three-year-old daughter months earlier, was in shock. It was Alfred who took the next bus up to Lira. And now he saw his beautiful daughter's name, Louiza.

Ben Pere, an extroverted former military officer in Obote's regime, who was known to them all, saw that both of his daughters, Jacqueline and Susan, were on the list. Emmanuel Orongo, a Kampala banker who'd been in Lira attending his mother's funeral, now saw his eldest daughter's name. Brenda Atoo, his pride and joy, used to cry if she got less than 90 percent on a test. She'd planned to be a scientist, and had graduated as the top girl in her primary school. He was so proud of her.

Now, both men sobbed with the women.

As the day wore on, parents collected daughters, hugging them with declarations of love and heartfelt regret for not having protected them. The school was closed indefinitely, and all remaining students were sent home.

When the light of day began to fade, the nuns told the parents it wasn't safe to stay at the school. They went home and cried, and all but Florence returned early the next day to sit in the schoolground, now devoid of students, and wait.

They sat together, grief-stricken, waiting for the police, or the military, or the president, to show up. And while they waited they cried and prayed and shouted in anger. Days passed and they rallied to do something other than cry. Ben Pere led the parents into Sister Rachele's office and told her that they'd decided to follow the rebels themselves. They'd lost some days, but thought they could still track them down.

"No. If you go as parents they will kill you," Sister Rachele said.

"But you went, sister, and they didn't kill you," Angelina pointed out.

Sister Rachele didn't reply. Her mind was reeling; she was still trying to think what she could do for the girls. She was sick with grief, and with guilt. After a few moments she asked the parents to give her a little more time so that she could talk to both the rebels and the army before they also got involved. They agreed, and Sister Rachele drove to Gulu, hoping to speak to the Northern Uganda army commander.

FOUR DAYS after the abduction a military helicopter touched down at St. Mary's. Angelina Atyam watched as the men climbed out. *Afraid of the roads, where they might run into the people who have my daughter,* she thought bitterly. Although the school had been closed to students, the parents still met there every day. Angelina walked into Sister Alba's office to confront the Ugandan soldiers now filling the headmistress's office. She saw ten men in camouflage uniforms, boots, and with sticks and guns. She flew into a rage and leaned across the table at the head intelligence officer. "How come all these gadgets you put on do not protect us!" she shouted. A bodyguard grabbed her and angrily pushed her back. Judith's father, Dr. Otim, whispered to her to control herself.

But Angelina kept yelling at the military men. "You're not here when we need you. Why are you here now?" Then she broke down and cried. She knew they weren't going to help them.

She was right. As the weeks went by, the Aboke Girls' parents continued to ache with grief. The Ugandan military, overburdened, had abandoned them, leaving them to deal with their grief as if their daughters were dead, not kidnapped. The guilt the parents felt, for underestimating the danger their girls had been in and leaving them to be kidnapped by a group of terrorist rapists, was overwhelming. And so they did the only thing they could do. They joined together to establish an investigative and activist network they called, with understatement, the Concerned Parents Association.

The parents used all their contacts. Some had family in the government, others had family abroad. One of those contacts led them to the highest office at the Vatican.

Several parents also had family in the more remote northern areas, in Gulu, Pader, and Kitgum. They went up to the villages and began talking to other parents. What they found shocked them: thousands of parents had children who'd been abducted by the rebels. These parents were suffering just as they were, and it was the first they'd heard of it.

"Why did you keep quiet all this time? Why didn't you talk?" Angelina asked one group. The Kampala newspaper hadn't mentioned anything of this, nor had the government-run radio in the area. If they had known, they would have protected their daughters.

The parents, mostly subsistence farmers, said they feared that the rebels would come and kill them all if they spoke up. The rebels had already threatened them, and had already killed some of the parents who'd tried to confront them.

Now UNDERSTANDING the sheer magnitude of the abductions, the Aboke Girls' parents returned to Lira and congregated at Angelina's little house. It was here, with its simple concrete walls, crocheted blankets, and images of Jesus on the walls, that she ran her midwife business. The parents decided that they would no longer live in fear of the rebels, and that they must speak out on behalf of the suffering thousands.

It was a simple decision. But it was one that would eventually lead to their daughters' fame—and to the Aboke Girls' central strategic significance in the war.

The parents carried out elections for their association. The popular Ben Pere, who'd lost two daughters to the rebels and still had strong military connections from his days as an officer, was elected chairperson. Angelina Atyam became the deputy and the treasurer.

Emmanuel Orongo also joined them. Two weeks after his daughter's abduction, when he'd returned to his banker's job in Kampala, he discovered he'd been fired for his absence. He didn't care. It was impossible for him to focus on anything other than getting his daughter back. Angelina dropped all her pregnant clients, similarly unable to concentrate on anything else. The parents met at her home every day, sometimes two or three times a day. The meetings began and ended with prayers. And every Saturday the parents congregated at Lira's Catholic cathedral for a full day of prayers and fasting for their children.

They raised as much money as they could. Parents brought 500 shillings (30 cents); some who could afford more gave 5,000 shillings ($3); some just 200 shillings. With that money, some of them travelled in an overloaded bus to Kitgum in order to knock on the military doors there. Other times they took the bus down to Kampala and visited members of Parliament, military officers, and other authorities, hoping to persuade the government to venture into the bush and get their girls back.

The parents also wrote letters to foreign governments and individuals, asking for help. A few governments responded with sympathy. The British High Commissioner wrote that what the North needed was development. "Who are we going to develop in the absence of the children?" Angelina scoffed to the others. His indifference to their stolen children left them cold, but at least he'd responded. Most did not.

They brainstormed, looking for ideas. Someone thought they could try to contact the rebels over the radio. Some thought the local politicians were too corrupt, that they'd merely use the case for personal profit if they could. Others thought the answer lay with the president of Sudan, and that they should work those connections. Someone suggested they go to the witch doctor for help, upsetting the more staunch Catholics in the group.

CHAPTER 9

Kitgum, Northern Uganda, February 1997

"Why does Museveni want to be a monster?" the Anglican Bishop of Kitgum, Macleord Baker Ochola II, shouted from his pulpit in Uganda's northernmost province. More than four hundred of his people had just been massacred by Kony's forces. "If he feels he still has some more days to rule, he should listen or follow what God wants and not what he desires," he continued. Although it was the rebels who terrorized the people, it was Museveni's army who stood by and left them unprotected. "God does not want his people to live in a state of fear in their country!"[34]

Bishop Ochola understood this fear. His daughter had been gang-raped by the rebels years earlier and had killed herself the next day. At the time he'd been in Canada, completing theological studies in Saskatchewan.

"Praise the Lord," people shouted, placing their hands to the sky. "Hallelujah!"

Thousands listened at the church service in honour of the massacred. Bishop Ochola cried out that his people were devastated. It had taken the military five days to come to the rescue, even though their forces were just a few kilometres away. Most of Kitgum understood the message: Museveni's military would not protect them.

Bishop Ochola led one of the largest and fastest-growing Christian congregations in the world; spread out over sixteen thousand square kilometres, it comprised twenty-six parishes, with five archdeacons, and thirty-one priests. He presided over what some Anglican analysts call the most ardently Christian location on the planet. Almost all his people were first- and second-generation Christians.[35] They were also among the world's poorest, but their land was fertile, and as he told them, they were rich in spirit.

"Talking peace with the rebels does not mean the government is weak or defeated," Bishop Ochola shouted. He argued that peace talks were the best way to help the innocent, defenceless people of Acholiland. And because most of the rebels were boys and girls abducted from the villages, the government should grant them pardons to encourage an end to the conflict.

The government had maintained a policy in the North that anyone who spoke to the rebels was considered a collaborator and subject to imprisonment, or worse. The policy fiercely divided the people and prevented any type of dialogue that might help find a way to end the war.

After the mass, Bishop Ochola drove to the nearby Catholic Comboni House. He asked the priests to invite the Catholics of Kitgum to come together with his Anglican people to pray for the end of the war. Father Carlos Rodriguez, a Spanish Comboni missionary, agreed to participate. Bishop Ochola then asked the Muslim leader, who, also overwhelmed by the people's suffering, agreed.

A week later, a two-thousand-strong interfaith group showed up to pray together outside the Kitgum Hospital where the Lamwo Massacre survivors were infirmed. Bishop Ochola called for forgiveness. He preached that they were united as humans. The Muslim Imam gave his people a similar message, as did the Catholic priests. And in a peculiar sight, never before seen in Uganda, Catholics, Protestants, and Muslims all prayed together. Some prayed with their hands on the ground, some with their hands in the air, and some with their hands clasped together.

NOT FAR AWAY, Sister Rachele, Angelina Atyam, and Ben Pere sat in the military's Gulu office. An officer was telling them that intelligence reports suggested the girls were now all in Kony's camp in Aru, Sudan.

"Are the children all alive and in good health?" Angelina asked.[36] Being from Lira, which was farther south, the parents had not been directly affected by these new displaced persons' camps, which were becoming the new homes for the people of the far north.

The officer coughed nervously, then explained that their well-being depended on which commander they had been given to. He chose to be honest, and said that all the girls had been given to commanders as wives. "We know that at least one has been given to Kony," he added.

With tears dropping from her cheeks, Sister Rachele asked him to rescue the children in Sudan. The officer shook his head and said Sudan was a different country; the Ugandan military could not cross the border. Sudan and Uganda had suspended diplomatic relations a year earlier over the issue of each supporting the other's rebel armies. If the Ugandan military tracked Kony to his base camp they risked starting an all-out war with Sudan, and Uganda was not prepared for that.

Ben Pere jumped up and demanded that the international community come and confront them. The officer suggested they speak to international organizations about that, adding that he dealt only with the military option.

"It's not the answer," Sister Rachele whispered.

"To avoid any further abductions, the only solution is the military option," he countered.

The parents left the officer and moved into the jail behind. Two LRA commanders had recently been caught, one of whom had apparently been involved in kidnapping their girls. When they found him—a teenager with a wild look and uncombed hair—he immediately recognized Sister Rachele from the bush.

The boy was sullen and defiant, but as they continued speaking to him he opened up and answered their questions. Angelina asked him if the girls were allowed to decide which men they were given to. The boy said they were given by order.

Ben Pere was a traditional man who understood that early and polygamous marriages sometimes occurred in their culture. He desperately wanted to believe someone was caring for his daughters, perhaps these new husbands. He asked if they took the girls for reasons other than sex. The boy said sex was the only reason. The parents were devastated.

After they left Gulu, Ben Pere, Angelina Atyam, and Sister Rachele headed down to Kampala, where they met with President Museveni in his government office. Museveni welcomed them in graciously, and Ben Pere and Angelina asked if he would help them.

Ben Pere stepped forward and told the president that they knew of the high-level meeting between Uganda and Sudan taking place the following day under Iran's mediation. He asked if they could be there to present their case. Museveni picked up his phone and reserved four more seats in his helicopter.

The next day the group arrived at Sambiya Lodge in Murchison Park, a wildlife area along the Nile River at the border of North and South Uganda. The foreign affairs ministers of Iran, Malawi, and Uganda were already there, as well as Sudan's undersecretary for foreign affairs. All were there to help Sudan and Uganda work through their disagreements. After introductions, Ben Pere told the delegates about the abduction of all their daughters. Angelina tried to speak but could only cry, so in her place Dr. Frank Olyet, another parent of a stolen Aboke Girl, explained the context of the war, stressing that its main victims were the children. The listening delegates frowned and looked physically pained.

The Malawian foreign minister broke the long silence that followed, offering words about how African culture respects children. The Iranian minister promised to bring up the issue in mediation, scheduled for later that day. Finally, Sudan's representative said he knew nothing about this incident and would inform his government.

The parents thanked the delegates and left the room to allow the negotiations between these rival countries to continue in private.

CHAPTER 10

Several weeks later a military jeep turned down the dirt path that led to St. Mary's school in Aboke. Sister Rachele rushed to the vehicle from the dining hall and was shocked to see the Ugandan intelligence officer who'd first told her about her girls being handed out as sex-slave wives. He looked pleased with himself as he told her that they had received permission from Sudan to collect the girls. He wanted to know if she and Ben Pere would come identify them in Kony's camp, adding that they'd leave tomorrow for Sudan.

"Alba, I'm going to Sudan!" Sister Rachele shouted. "I'm going to get the girls!"[37]

After the officer left she drove to Lira to inform Ben Pere. Listening to Sister Rachele's news, Ben Pere grew nervous. Anxiously, he turned his mind to organizational matters. They needed to bring pictures of the missing girls, he said, and a list of the commanders to whom they were married off. Back at St. Mary's, they found Grace Grall and she supplied the commanders' names.

There was a short delay, but a few days later Sister Rachele and Ben Pere, accompanied by a group of Ugandan military officers, flew to Nairobi and then boarded another plane to Khartoum. Sister Rachele felt she was living a dream as she passed over the mountains of South Sudan, knowing her girls were somewhere below her.

Khartoum greeted Sister Rachele and Ben Pere with a whoosh of hot, humid air. Sudan was even hotter than Uganda. A security guard walked them to the VIP lounge, where a man in a long white robe and turban welcomed them. It was late at night now, and so they were taken to their rooms at the Hotel Meridien in Khartoum.

With the Ugandans on Sudanese soil, President Omar Al-Bashir's political adviser called a retired German politician, Rudolf Decker, and asked him to help ensure that the mediation process worked. Decker, who'd been involved in mediation efforts with Uganda and Sudan before and was accepted by both Al-Bashir and Uganda's Museveni, got on a plane to Khartoum the next morning.

Two days later, as the entourage waited for final permission to head to Kony's camp, Sister Rachele was given a boat lunch on the Nile River hosted by the chief of the Sudanese intelligence service, Dr. Gutbi El-Mahadi. As they floated down the Nile he assured her that the Sudanese government was taking the case of the abducted Aboke Girls very seriously. "To us Muslims, this is a moral and religious matter. We would not like to mix it up with political issues,"[38] he said. He predicted a happy outcome for Sister Rachele from this visit, as had Al-Bashir when he'd told them earlier, "God willing, you will go back with the children." Sister Rachele believed that God was paving the way for them.

But later that afternoon, back at the hotel, the director-general of Uganda's secret service handed her a report from Ugandan intelligence that said Kony and his commanders were now removing weapons and uniforms from his camps in advance of the visit, and that Kony had forbidden communication between the Sudanese army and the LRA during the visit. Furthermore, the director-general's secret sources had reported that the Aboke Girls were being transferred to another camp, which they would not be allowed to visit. The report stated that this was a top-secret plan being kept from the Sudanese military in Juba for fear they might pass the information to their superiors in Khartoum, who in turn might instruct the delegation to visit Kony's other camps. The secret report concluded that the visit was being stage-managed by the LRA.

Fear swept through Sister Rachele. "What are you going to do with this?"

The chief of intelligence said he'd personally deliver the report to President Al-Bashir the next day, and insisted that a high-ranking Sudanese officer, with enough authority to authorize surprise checks on Kony's camps, would accompany their team into the camps.

Early the next morning the group was brought to President Al-Bashir's office. Al-Bashir stressed that the Aboke Girls' case was a moral issue for him and his government, and that he wanted them released. The chief of intelligence then handed the secret report to the president, who betrayed no emotion as he read it. Al-Bashir said that he'd send a security officer to assist.

After the meeting adjourned, a second intelligence report came suggesting that the Aboke Girls would be moved to the front line on the assumption that the delegation wouldn't risk their lives to head there. The report stated that a female commander called Margaret would be the only one allowed to answer their questions. It was also established that Kony was in Khartoum, not at his camps.

A short while later, the call came in that they were to head out with Decker, which made Sister Rachele feel better. But Decker himself was growing uneasy. It wasn't until he was on the plane to Juba that he realized none of his trusted contacts were accompanying them and that he'd met this security officer only one day earlier.

The group arrived at the airport, where an old Boeing was being loaded with bags of wheat and many soldiers. Sister Rachele, refusing an offer to sit up front, got into the belly of the plane, where she sat on top of wheat sacks. Decker sat in the passenger seat. After takeoff, he asked the captain if it was a risky flight.

The captain told him that only the last descent into Juba was dangerous, explaining that because the rebels had surface-to-air missiles with a range of four thousand metres, they would fly at maximum height above Juba and then land in a spiralling nosedive. Noticing Decker's frown, the captain assured him that he did this all the time.

A few hours later they spiralled to a safe landing. "Welcome to Juba," a Sudanese colonel greeted them. He led them to an entourage of three jeeps, with armed soldiers posted in the back.

Juba was a dilapidated mix of ruins, shanty huts, and potholed roads.

A sign at the central roundabout pointed to the "Belgian Congo," which hadn't existed in thirty-seven years. They were dropped off at Hotel El Salam, a small guest house, where the front clerk informed them that their rooms weren't ready. Sudanese government soldiers stood around watching a television set in the lobby. So instead of checking in, the group headed directly out to Kony's camp.

They stopped at a military checkpoint at a marker along the road called Mile 15. Then, along the junction of the Nimule and Torit roads, they came upon the LRA camp for pregnant and breast-feeding soldiers, which was hidden just inside the bush. The group got out of their three jeeps and marched on foot into the bush a short distance until they reached a group of huts. They were deserted, except for some old men.

The old men said the women were out looking for firewood. The Sudanese colonel told him to go collect them. Meanwhile, Sister Rachele looked through the huts, but they were empty.

After a few minutes some teenage girls and young women in sundresses stepped out of the bush—all either pregnant or with young children strapped to their backs or suckling on their breasts. They sat down on the ground and stared silently at the visitors.

"Have you seen the Aboke Girls?" Sister Rachele asked. "Do you know where they are?"

They yelled at her to leave them alone, that they had fled from Museveni's death squads and were refugees now. They shouted out that she'd followed them to Sudan to kill them.

"Girls ..." Sister Rachele tried, but they continued shouting at her, arguing that they never wanted to go back to Museveni's Uganda.

Sister Rachele wondered what was happening. It was as if the girls were acting. Recalling the secret report, she turned to the loudest speaker, a woman in her thirties. "Are you Margaret?" she said. The woman's expression turned to surprise and the Sudanese officers gestured for her to leave the group.

"Please, tell me if our girls are here," Sister Rachele said to the remaining girls, but they refused to say another word now that Margaret was gone.

The group left the girls alone and returned to their jeeps. One of the

Sudanese remarked that if they found one Aboke Girl, they'd find them all. The grouped bumped along the Nimule road, passing several road checks and little villages before reaching a stick in the road that read Mile 34, Kony's headquarters. Just off the road they found the camp of a hundred houses, but it was abandoned. Another six miles and they would reach the war's front line, with opposing troops on either side. And so they continued up the road, stopping at a Sudanese army camp and inquiring about the safety of the road ahead. The colonel reported that everything was quiet at the front.

When they reached Mile 39 seven shots were fired in the air by a guard along the road announcing their arrival. Sister Rachele now realized that the LRA camp and the Sudanese army camp bordered each other. The Sudanese camp was on the north, the Juba side, and Kony's camp was on the south—with only a stick in the road marking the separation point. It was obvious to her that Kony's camp of thousands of children was the buffer separating the Sudanese government forces from the southern rebels. The next camp after Kony's was at Mile 40, and was the front camp for Garang's rebels.

Suddenly they were surrounded by LRA soldiers carrying modern machine guns and walkie-talkies and staring at them unhappily. The colonel said he wanted to talk to their superiors, but the men refused. "They are far away."

Another Sudanese officer explained that they were there on behalf of President Al-Bashir to collect the Aboke Girls.

"I don't know anything about the Aboke Girls," a rebel said.

But before long a commander emerged from the bush. Sister Rachele noticed that Ben Pere was suddenly trembling. "Hello, Vincent Otti," Pere said to the ugly man who had deep vertical wrinkles on either side of his mouth. Ben Pere spoke in Lango, their mutual first language. Otti gave his hand and Ben Pere shook it, with the bitter knowledge that, according to the list of commanders Grace Grall had given them, this horrible man, known to them all as the Butcher of Atiak, was now his son-in-law. (Atiak, in Gulu district, was Otti's home village, where in 1995 three hundred people had been hacked and stabbed to death in the

LRA's first large attack on civilians. The same number of LRA troops had surrounded the trading centre, then announced: "You Acholi have refused to support us. We shall now teach you a lesson." Survivors reported that Otti led the massacre.)[39] Twelve years earlier Ben Pere and Vincent Otti had served together in the same squadron in Obote's government army. Now, Ben Pere felt he wanted to kill Otti, or for Otti to kill him; that either way, one of them needed to die.

"I heard that my daughter is married to you," Ben Pere said. Sister Rachele, instantly perceiving what was happening, attempted to take control of the conversation. She showed the Sudanese colonel Otti's name on her list. The colonel addressed Otti: "According to our information, one of the Aboke Girls is in your possession," he said, showing him a picture of Jacqueline, Ben Pere's elder daughter.[40]

Otti claimed that he didn't have the girl, but Sister Rachele informed the colonel that she'd been told Otti did indeed have her. Vincent Otti turned away. Ben Pere could tell he felt ashamed of himself.

The colonel asked Otti if there were any women in the camp. Otti said they did have women, but not the ones they were looking for. He ordered his soldiers to rally the girls, and the boys disappeared into the bushes.

When they were alone for a moment, Decker pleaded with Otti for his cooperation and help.

Decker later wrote down Otti's response. Otti looked beyond Decker, seemingly searching for words, then said: "I am like a trained dog. When I am sent somewhere, I'll go. When I am called back, I come back. Do you understand?"[41]

Moments later, groups of female fighters, barefooted, wearing dresses, and carrying guns, stepped out of the bush. About fifty girls between ages fourteen and eighteen stood in three lines before Sister Rachele, fear and anguish marking their faces.

The Sudanese colonel told them to identify themselves. Sister Rachele moved closer to each girl, hoping they might whisper something, but they responded only with frightened eyes and silence.

Sister Rachele felt their terror, and the menacing stares of the surrounding male rebels. *Slaves,* she thought, looking at them. If these girls stepped out of line, surely somebody would die. Ben Pere and Sister Rachele both wept at the sight of them.

"May I pray with them?" Sister Rachele finally said. Vincent Otti agreed.

She started the Lord's Prayer and the girls joined in unison, in a choir of despair. The voices of the girls grew louder as each pulled strength from the prayer. "Amen," Sister Rachele whispered, and she turned and walked back to the jeeps. She felt as she had months earlier when she'd left her thirty girls behind.

The group drove away, drained, hungry, and discouraged. When they passed the abandoned camp at Mile 34 again, Ben Pere commented that there were chickens running around and laundry hanging out to dry. The Sudanese colonel suggested they could make a surprise visit to that camp early the next morning. The group agreed it was worth a try, and decided not to utter a word to anyone else of their plan.

That night they visited the army barracks in Juba and a compound on the east bank of the Nile where male LRA soldiers also stayed, but the soldiers all pretended that they spoke only Arabic.[42]

At 7 A.M. the next morning their truck pulled into Kony's camp at Mile 34. The camp was bustling with morning activities, and their sudden arrival caused a panic of disruption. Children ran everywhere, hiding. Overwhelmed, Sister Rachele jumped out of the jeep and ran after the children, looking through the crowd for an Aboke Girl face. The Sudanese colonel ran after her. Then an armed teenage boy ran up and ordered her to stop. He suggested they sit. "We have not come to sit, we have come to collect the Aboke Girls," the Sudanese colonel replied.

"How dare you talk to me like that!" the boy yelled, stalling them as the Aboke Girls were secretly herded into a nearby hut and told to keep quiet.

Sister Rachele was shocked by the lack of respect given to Juba's security chief, and wondered what that meant. "Please," she said. "I am the sister from Aboke." She reminded him that rebel chief Mariano Lagira Ocaya had given some of her girls back earlier, and asked for his help.

The boy relaxed, seemingly appreciating the nun's presence and her polite manners, and agreed that they could look around. But just then

Ben Pere stepped out of one of the huts with a thirteen-year-old girl, Monica, and two other young girls. "This girl says that our girls are here!" he shouted, holding onto Monica. He explained that at first they'd said they weren't allowed to talk to him, but that when he promised to take them back to Uganda the girl had revealed the truth.

Tension filled the air. The rebels turned hostile; they kicked at Ben Pere. The terrified girls looked down, probably praying for their lives. The Sudanese colonel stepped forward, now furious with Ben Pere. "How dare you make such a promise," he said slowly, emphasizing the gravity of the charge.

Ben Pere turned to Sister Rachele. "But their lives are in danger," he pleaded. "We can take them with us, can't we?"

Decker asked the Sudanese if they could take these girls, but the Sudanese said their assignment was only for the St. Mary's schoolgirls from Aboke village.

Sister Rachele, sweeping past the angry rebels before her, ran to some rebels on the other side of the road and begged to speak to Mariano Lagira Ocaya. "He gave me the 109 girls. Please, let me talk to him!"

But the mood in the camp had grown increasingly hostile, and it was clearly time to leave before they were all killed. The Sudanese colonel rushed them all into their truck, driving off amid insults and curses from the rebels.

FROM ONE of the nearby huts, the Aboke Girls clustered together and watched through the cracks in the door while Sister Rachele and the outsiders left. Ben Pere's younger daughter, Susan, sobbed and cried out for her "daddy" as she watched her father leave.

Moments later an assembly was called. Monica, the girl who had spoken to Ben Pere, was brought into the centre of camp. The Aboke Girls were released from the hut and gathered with the others. With all assembled, a commander yelled at Monica for speaking to the outsiders. The girl kept her head down and tried to apologize, but it did not matter. The commander smashed a log into her face, and once she had fallen, stabbed her to death.[43]

CHAPTER 11

In March of 1997 Angelina Atyam and Ben Pere arrived at the United Nations in New York City. Human Rights Watch was doing everything it could to tell the story of Northern Uganda's abducted children to the world, and part of that involved bringing these parents over to knock on doors at the UN.

Angelina was hopeful that one well-placed Acholi man might be able to assist them. Olara Otunnu, likely Uganda's most educated expatriate, was the UN's undersecretary general for Children in Conflict. He was also a practising lawyer, a law professor, president of the International Peace Academy, and served on the boards of the Carnegie Commission on Preventing Deadly Conflict and the International Crisis Group.[44]

Seeing the Acholi delegation at the door, Olara Otunnu welcomed them in. The meeting went on for three hours. Otunnu listened and talked, and Angelina pleaded and cried for him to help get their children back.

Otunnu found it hard when people from his homeland came to talk to him about the suffering of these children. In other places—Sri Lanka, the Balkans, Sierra Leone—he and other connected people could sometimes help by talking to the main players. But in Uganda's case he felt that Museveni, a longtime enemy of his, actually wanted the war to continue. The ongoing unrest in the North benefited Museveni politically in that it allowed him to keep a firm military control over the entire country. It also justified his need for high military spending in the eyes of donor countries that provided most of Uganda's funding. As long as the war continued, Western arguments that he allow multiple political parties and a true democracy could be effectively countered by the reality that Uganda was at war. And, unfortunately for these parents, the United States was solidly behind Museveni, who as a strong African ally represented a strategic benefit.

"The politics of this is such that, horrible though the situation is, I cannot give you the impression that the international community will come to your assistance, because they are firmly on Museveni's side, and whatever Mr. Museveni says, that is what they will support," said Otunnu. "If he says give me more arms to fight, they'll give him more arms. If he says give me time, I'm negotiating, they'll say, have time.

"I don't want to give you the impression the United Nations will do something miraculous," he continued, "because they won't. The United Nations will follow the big powers, and the big powers are firmly in support of Museveni."

Angelina grew bitter listening to him, but Otunnu believed she should know the truth as he saw it. He knew that the UN ambassadors and their staff would listen, would reassure, would promise to look into it. They might even issue a statement, but nothing else. The parents were on their own. Angelina wanted to scream at him, *"How many children? How long should we wait?!"* But instead she and the delegation said goodbye to Otunnu and went knocking on more doors. And, as Otunnu had predicted, they did not find the help they were looking for.

Human Rights Watch also used some of its media connections to arrange for Angelina to appear on CNN. As she told the world the story of her abducted daughter, Charlotte, Angelina was emotive, descriptive, and the camera loved her.

A WEEK LATER Angelina returned to her family in Lira. There, a secret source, a rebel collaborator, brought her a note from the Lord's Resistance Army commander Mariano Lagira, the man who had stolen her daughter. The note said that Mariano wanted to meet her at a secret rendezvous point.

A flood of emotions made her tremble with anger, fear, anticipation, and longing. Angelina already knew that the LRA might kill or torture her daughter in order to punish her for speaking out. But it was clear in her mind that speaking out without fear was the right thing to do, and that her great challenge was to willingly risk her daughter's life. As she told others, their lives were in God's hands. And now she would go to the LRA.

Angelina quietly took herself to a home in the outskirts of Gulu. In this secret location she found two rebels; the one with the fat and distorted upper lip from a bullet wound was Mariano Lagira. He greeted her and then asked the name of her daughter, as if he wasn't certain who she was.

"You already know her. You know her so well you cannot tell me a lie that you don't know her!" Angelina burst out. "If you're going to go and kill her, then kill her."

Mariano shook his head. He had a different plan. "We could give you your daughter if you stop talking about children who have been taken, calling them abducted." Her heart quickened at the idea of Charlotte coming back to her. How she'd prayed for this. "They weren't abducted," Mariano continued, "they were rescued from Museveni's rule." The children were where they belonged, he told her.

Angelina's mind spun. She and the other parents had spent months building a new community spirit, and she'd agreed to speak for them. If she accepted this offer, she'd be abandoning them all. The community would be destroyed. To her, Charlotte had become all the missing children, and they had become Charlotte. She felt sick inside, but understood she couldn't do it.

"I can't take one child; I need the rest. Because as concerned parents, we're a family," she told Mariano. "I cannot take mine alone and leave the rest. The minimum I could take is if you give me all the Aboke Girls."

"We cannot do that," he said.

She asked him to go back and to think about it. She didn't hate the rebels; they were her people. But if they wanted to fight, they should recruit the willing, those eighteeen and over who wanted to fight.

When Angelina went home and told her family about what had happened, her two eldest daughters were furious with her for sacrificing Charlotte for the others.[45] Night after night she thought bitterly about the choice Mariano had given her. She couldn't sleep. She couldn't eat. She wondered if her actions were causing Charlotte to be tortured. Or perhaps she'd be the last of any child released, held to spite Angelina's activism. The memory of Charlotte dominated her. She could no longer be happy. She would try not to talk about it all the time with her other children, or her husband, but the pain never left her. At every meal she included an empty chair for Charlotte. She frequently washed all of Charlotte's clothes and hung them out to dry. Her husband would sometimes yell at her. "Do you know she's dead?" Angelina would yell back.[46]

ONE DAY Father John Fraser arrived at Angelina Atyam's house for a surprise visit, checking in to see if he could help her in some way. Since the Comboni Mission philosophy maintained that priests should be moved every so often so that the locals wouldn't grow dependent on them, and since Father John was near retirement, he'd been moved from Malawi to Kitchener, Ontario, so that he could be near his family. Now he was visiting Uganda for a month to check up on the people he'd left in the early 1990s.

Angelina welcomed her old friend and parish priest to her living room, where they had tea and talked. He noticed how tired her eyes were and that she'd lost a lot of weight.

"This is not the Uganda you knew. It's very strange. The love is no longer there," she told him. Nobody in Uganda cared about them, she said. That was why she was travelling everywhere, speaking out on behalf of the other parents.[47]

"If somebody talked loud, during the Idi Amin regime, maybe some people wouldn't have died," she added. She saw the same cycle of cowardice now and couldn't understand how it was still happening.

It brought back their years together working at the maternity hospital in Apache's Masindi Falls. They were all so poor back then, but the people had loved one another. They talked about those days.

"Apache was so different," Father John said.

"And now there's even more problems in the North, but no love," she said. "This is an evil that is something new."

Father John told her he was surprised that people in responsible positions weren't doing more about the problem. But Angelina explained that the international community had other priorities, and that meanwhile they were trying everything they could. The parents, she said, had already agreed to give up their need for justice if it could bring peace; they just wanted the children back. "Last Saturday I heard that forty rebels were killed," she went on. "I said to the journalist, you find out if any of them were under eighteen. If they are, don't write them down as 'rebels killed'; they are 'children killed.' This is a crime against children. But they called it 'Government troops have given a bloody nose to the rebels'!"

"Those are expressions journalists use," Father John said, trying to soothe her anger. He was no stranger to the peril of polarized views, or to the horrors of war. The middle of eight children, he'd been born in 1934 into the industrial slums of Glasgow, Scotland. In a city divided by conflict between the majority Protestants and minority Catholics, parents would disown children for marrying those of the wrong faith. But John's family was secretly interfaith: his mother was a Protestant who'd converted to Catholicism when she married, and his paternal grandmother had been Jewish. He'd grown up knowing that religion could be misused to foster hatred and division.

It was as a teenager that he'd begun to dream of a missionary's life in Africa; life in the factories of Glasgow hadn't excited his formidable imagination. When he visited the local priest to ask for a recommendation letter to allow him into seminary school, the priest asked if he even went to church. "Sometimes," John had said. But when he said he wanted to become a missionary priest in Africa, the priest had laughed and remarked, "Well, they take anybody." He wrote up the letter and soon afterward John was off to seminary school in London, and then the Vatican, before setting sail for Africa those many years ago.

He stayed through all the wars and bloody coups. When Idi Amin controlled Uganda in the 1970s, turning it into the poorest country in the world and exiling all foreigners, Father John had defied Vatican orders and remained with the Northern Ugandan people. Throughout those years he secretly transported members of his parish to the safety of the Kenyan border.

Now Father John told Angelina that the story of the abducted children hadn't made the news in North America. He thought perhaps the West didn't know about it. Angelina stood up, visibly angry, and opened a desk in her dining room. She pulled out the New York–based Human Rights Watch aid-agency document, *Scars of Death,* and handed him the hundred-page report documenting the abductions. The West might have missed her appearance on CNN, but not this.

She felt abandoned by the world—by the governments, the media, and even the Church. She said she didn't need donations, but wanted to see that others cared.

Then Angelina told him that a tension had been growing between her and Sister Rachele, and that she didn't know how to make it better. She could see it in Sister Rachele's eyes every time they met. Angelina knew it had to do with Sister Rachele's parting vow to the girls that she would never stop looking for them. Whenever the nun saw Angelina it came as a painful reminder that she had more work to do.

Father John said he'd go visit Sister Alba and Sister Rachele at St. Mary's, and off he went, driving along the bumpy orange dirt road and arriving at the guarded gates of the school.

Sister Rachele sat outside under a palm tree, wearing her habit and a large silver cross, and told Father John she was filled with hope these days that the girls were coming home at any moment. In the last months she'd travelled far on behalf of the girls. She had talked about them with UN Secretary-General Kofi Annan, Nelson Mandela, Hillary Clinton, the Pope, Museveni, and Sudan's Al-Bashir. Everyone—Uganda, Sudan, the NGOs, the LRA representatives based in Nairobi and London—had been cooperating in securing the release of the girls, she said. The United Nations had also just passed a resolution that condemned the abduction of children and their use as soldiers and called for the children's immediate release. She told him that all the countries had approved it, and that this she considered a miracle. Now she was expecting the reality.

Sister Rachele told him that she knew everyone cared. Everyone had told her that the problem must be solved, and she refused to believe their words were only lip service. "I see the solution; it is simple," she said. "Let us talk to each other and settle our differences and bring home the children."

In the end Sister Rachele told Father John that she didn't understand why the girls weren't yet back. She added that although they prayed a lot, perhaps they all had to pray even more.

CHAPTER 12

Up in Gulu, Florence Lacor had been hiding alone in her hut and doing nothing but praying. Shortly after Angela's abduction, Florence had sent her three other children to live with her brother, in the safety of Kampala, and so was left alone with her thoughts and prayers.

But her precious daughter Angela had been gone almost a year, and all this praying, day and night, hadn't yet brought her back. Florence's faith in God was unwavering, and she refused to think Angela wasn't coming back, so as the months went by and Angela didn't return she'd begun to believe that God was expecting more from her. Florence then forced herself to leave her home and applied to work as a counsellor with war-affected children.

World Vision, the Christian nongovernmental charitable organization, had set up a rehabilitation centre in Gulu for former child soldiers and was looking for staff. Perhaps because the World Vision people knew about Angela, as well as the fact that Florence had volunteered for the NGO a year before Angela's abduction and that she spoke fluent English, she was hired.

Florence also hoped that by counselling other children from the LRA she'd be able to understand Angela better when she returned. In truth, everything she felt, everything she cared about, had to do with her daughter. Now spending her days with the children who'd returned from Joseph Kony, Florence began to learn how they suffered and how they survived. This meant that she did understand Angela better.

Understanding the reality, no matter how hard it was, was better than letting her mind race with all the possibilities of how her stolen daughter might be living.

Florence soon realized that although outsiders often focused on the abduction, the forced killings, and the maimings, the psychology of the children's suffering was much deeper than those few horrific acts. It was their fear and powerlessness that hurt them the most. She learned that it was the girls and women who bore the greatest suffering inside the LRA. They'd be given to a man who might have ten wives, and he usually treated his women worse than dogs, using their bodies when he wanted and then throwing them back outside without offering even a scrap of kindness. He'd threaten them too: "I can kill you because you're nothing to me." It was no wonder that when the girls and women returned they were all so bitter. The treatment they endured from the men hurt even more than being forced to kill one another.

Each night after work Florence returned to her little hut and thought about the life her daughter must be living. Nightmares filled her sleep. Sometimes, in the middle of the night or early in the morning, when she drifted between sleeping and waking, voices came to her. One night they told her to pray for Angela, revealing to her that Angela was in imminent danger because her feet were swelling and she could not walk. Florence knew that the children who grew too tired to walk were killed by the others. Suddenly awake and terrified for her daughter's life, she climbed out of bed and knelt down on the concrete floor, praying for God to heal her daughter's feet and to give her encouragement to keep walking.

Another time a voice told her that danger was approaching for Angela—that some of the rebels wanted to kill her. Florence again knelt down and prayed, believing in the supernatural reality of the voice.

One special night Angela visited her mother in a dream. "Mommy, I cannot continue," she said.

"No, you have to pray, trust in God, have hope," Florence responded.

"I can't."

Florence held her. "Please, don't give up. God is with you. God will not abandon you. Please pray." And Angela prayed slowly. "Continue."

Angela's prayers increased. "Okay, always continue to pray," Florence told her daughter. She woke up then, but she could still feel Angela in her arms.

Sometimes at night there'd be shooting and bombing outside, just a few kilometres away, and she'd think Angela was being shot at. When it rained, she'd think of Angela exposed, with nothing to cover her. But still, she trusted. There was nothing else Florence could do, and to not trust would surely kill her. And so she prayed, believing that every bullet from every gun was directed by God, and that God still had mercy upon Angela.

And then each morning she would climb out of bed, make herself an egg, some fruit, tea, and a sweet biscuit, and walk to the World Vision Rehabilitation Centre to greet the children good morning. Sometimes she worked nights, and then she'd see the children having nightmares. Some always shouted out at night, and afterward she'd ask them what was happening, but they wouldn't know. Occasionally a child, usually one of the boys, would wake at night and tear out of bed, his arms holding an imaginary gun as if chasing someone away. She would gently ask the child what had happened, but he never remembered.

As time went by, Florence learned that invariably, once the children shared their experiences, a pain lifted in them. She saw a lot of healing taking place between the time the withdrawn children first returned from the bush to when, after a while, they could laugh and talk and cry.

Sometimes when a child finally opened up, they'd tell her that another child in the centre, or now back in the community, had been the one who abducted them or otherwise abused them. And so she'd bring the two together, and the one who committed the crime against the other would ask to be forgiven. The children usually gave their forgiveness, and afterward she could see that both began to heal. She'd see them smiling, sometimes interacting with one another.

All the advances soothed her spirit, but still Florence would not speak of Angela. She would not ask any of the children if they knew of her daughter; she did not even want them to know she had a daughter inside the LRA ranks. Her co-workers quickly learned that Florence's daughter was not a topic for discussion, and so were careful not to betray her secret. But every time the children spoke she strained to overhear their conversations, hoping to hear her daughter's name.

Meanwhile, as the children opened up, she'd ask them everything. How they were abducted, how they felt, what it felt like to kill another, or to be given to a man, to be beaten up when they tried to say no. She tried to learn what affected them the most. Each child was different, but there was one constant: they did not talk about the things that affected them the most. So sometimes she had them draw pictures and would ask the children to explain them. Usually they drew pictures of something terrible. Those drawings provided clues that she would work with later on.

Each night she would return to her home alone. As time went by, she recognized herself in the children. Her nightmares, her inability to say the name "Angela," her avoidance of even those she trusted.

And so, at night in bed, she began to turn her therapy on herself. She was always patient with the children, and encouraged them to act happy. She knew that in order for them to talk they first needed to relax, to let their guard down. So she asked herself, *How do I relax?,* and then decided that she too must act as though she was a happy, jolly person.

Another problem was that she thought about Angela incessantly. It was too hard on her, and so she decided that in her nightly prayers she would pray for other children as well. It started with prayers for a particular child at the centre, then moved to prayers for all the children at the centre, and sometimes prayers for herself. Eventually she began praying for all the children in the bush, and finally, for all the commanders too.

One evening her forgiveness was complete. She knelt again at the foot of her bed and spoke out loud. "I say Lord, I forgive Kony. I forgive Otti, I forgive the rebel leaders, I forgive them with all my heart. I forgive those who have abducted my daughter. I forgive them, and I set them free, and I pray Lord that you'll open a door where there is no door, and they will all come out of the bush."[48]

BACK IN THE FOOD HALL at St. Mary's, a girl ahead of Grace Grall in the line for food bumped her, and Grace's books fell. *I wish I had a gun,* she thought, then caught herself, shocked by her inner voice, her inner evil. Sometimes, when girls giggled and whispered together while she was trying to sleep, Grace would think how she'd discipline them if they were in the bush. If she had a gun. But then she'd be horrified at herself. Why was she so cruel? What demon was inside of her?

Sometimes at night she told herself that she should have chosen death instead of committing the crimes she had. That God had been testing her and she had failed. She was now a sinner with the stains of innocent blood smeared all over her. And then she'd cry. Through her tears she prayed, begging God for forgiveness. Grace cried herself to sleep each night, sobbing into her pillow so that no one else would hear.

Between classes she sometimes hid in the toilet stall to cry. Through her tears, she prayed to God to release her friends. But then the sobs could change to anger, and she'd think how much she hated people, even those around her, her innocent classmates who knew nothing of the horror she'd lived through.

Then one evening her anger took over. While Grace and others were studying in the dormitory, a girl switched off the central light, then flicked it on, and then off, and on, and off. "Stop that!" one of Grace's friends yelled, another kidnapped Aboke Girl, who like Grace had escaped from the rebels, although before crossing into Sudan.

"You rebels!" the girl by the light switch yelled back. Grace saw red. She ran up to the girl, knocked her down, and struck her again and again. The other girls screamed and soon a teacher ran in and pulled Grace off the child.

Sister Rachele called Grace into her office. They talked for a while about her time in the bush, and Sister Rachele asked her to be strong, to turn away when people said hurtful things, and to know that she was loved by Sister Rachele and Sister Alba.

Ashamed, Grace apologized to the girl, who accepted her apology.

One day Sister Alba called Grace into her office. She knew that this closed-off child needed extra love, and so she talked to her, telling the story of her own life, about her parents and the crowded backyards of Rome, about her favourite characters in books, about gardening and the beauty of flowers. Grace listened, but said little in return. Sister Alba began calling on Grace to come visit her every few days. Grace didn't understand why she had to sit there with her, but she listened closely while Sister Alba read passages aloud to her from the books she was reading and poems that touched her. Their meetings soon became special for both of them as a bond grew between the two. They spent many hours together. And slowly, something gave way in Grace. She felt that Sister Alba loved her, and so it was. She opened up and told Sister Alba how she was feeling, and what she had experienced in the camps. Sister Alba listened and understood.

Grace soon began to improve in school. Almost all the other girls now gave her space to heal, and were kind to her. Sometimes her fellow classmates, showing her a quiet love and acceptance, spontaneously took her hand while they walked between classes. The other girls included her in study sessions. They saw that Sister Alba cherished Grace, and so they too overcame some of their earlier trepidation toward her and gave her extra love.

As time went by, Grace was able to forgive herself. She stopped crying as often, and she realized that she was again able to concentrate in class. Still, she was far from feeling okay. She still questioned herself, and deep down felt that she did not deserve to still be alive.

MEANWHILE, Alfred Olum of Kampala, Louiza Namale's father, couldn't sit back and do nothing, pretending that life was normal. He told himself that while Angelina Atyam and Sister Rachele travelled the world, he'd traverse the city of Kampala, demanding to be heard.

He bought himself a white, long-sleeved T-shirt, and on the front of the shirt, in bright-red block letters, he carefully painted the words SUDAN RELEASE ABOKE GIRLS NOW. On the back he wrote KONY RETURN ABOKE GIRLS NOW.

Every day he protested in front of different embassies across Kampala, walking back and forth showing everyone the big red letters on his white shirt. Eventually, a group from the Netherlands invited him in to talk. They said they'd inquire about the girls and wished him luck. He didn't hear more. So Alfred moved his T-shirt campaign to the Libyan embassy, reasoning that Colonel Muammar Gaddafi, the new good-guy of the Arabic world, might want to help him get his daughter back. After a few days of protesting on the street, he asked for time with Gaddafi's top aide in Uganda and was thrilled when the man invited him in. But after listening to Alfred, the aide asked, "Are these children Muslim?"

"They are Christian," Alfred responded.

"That's too bad," the man said. Alfred felt sick. But he continued on.

For a while he focused on the South African embassy, demanding to talk to the ambassador. The ambassador was always too busy, but he did send a message to Alfred telling him that he was aware of the situation.

Alfred kept on pushing. One morning, over tea and an egg, he read in the newspaper that former U.S. president Jimmy Carter was coming to Kampala for a conference. "Why don't I also go and talk to these people," he told his wife, Isabella, before she went to her teaching job. He exchanged his T-shirt for a pressed shirt and tie, reasoning that for an American president he should wear his best. The T-shirt was more to shame the Arabs.

Alfred peered inside the seminar hall and spotted the white-haired former president talking to Ugandan men and white foreigners, all well dressed. Jimmy Carter and his wife now ran the Carter Center, a powerful NGO devoted to helping the world find peace and health.

Alfred waited until the conference broke for coffee. Amid the confusion of people milling about, he walked up to Carter without being stopped by security guards. Although Carter was surrounded by a group of dignitaries, Alfred was able to move into the circle and greet him. Carter greeted him back, smiling and shaking his hand. The group around Carter likely thought Alfred was one of them, another aid worker or a politician. But then Alfred began to speak about what had happened to his daughter and the other girls in Aboke. Alfred trembled in pain as he told the story. Carter listened intently, and because he listened, no one stopped Alfred from speaking. After several minutes Carter excused himself, explaining that the meetings were starting again, but before he left he told Alfred that he'd already heard of the Aboke

Girls. He also promised him that he'd come back to Uganda and take up the issue of the stolen children.

Alfred returned home to tell his wife the good news—that maybe this old American president was their answer to getting Louiza back—but Isabella was deeply depressed and couldn't share his joy. Her husband had stopped working and was obsessed with finding a way of getting Louiza back, leaving Isabella as the family's sole breadwinner on a paltry teaching salary of forty dollars a month. Both her younger daughters had recently died from disease, and she'd been unable to afford an autopsy to tell her why. And nightmares tortured her. Each night she quarrelled with an apparition of Louiza, who appeared suddenly before her in a soldier's uniform. They'd have a wonderful hug, then Louiza would turn to leave.

"Don't go!" Isabella always begged.

"Yes, I have to. They'll kill me," Louiza responded.

Isabella would swear to protect her, but Louiza said they'd kill her too. Then Louiza would disappear. Isabella would wake drenched in sweat.

CHAPTER 13

UGANDA, MAY 1997

The Northern Uganda to which Grace Grall had returned was different from the one she'd left. Gulu had seen civilians killed and tortured on a daily basis over the past year, and over a thousand children had been abducted. The transition from rebel unrest to outright war had begun.

When President Museveni opened Uganda's Parliament on May 2, 1997, he was defiant. "Religious leaders and some politicians are asking me to compromise with Satan," he said, referring to Bishop Ochola's words. "But I do not think the victims of the devilish acts of Kony will forgive me if I agree to negotiate peace with these bandits."[49]

Museveni called Kony and the rebel leaders parasites of society who were fighting to live a lavish lifestyle they couldn't afford. He said that if he didn't punish Kony's bandits, others might be encouraged to loot. "When will our society ever settle down to develop? In any case these criminals have not only looted, but have also murdered thousands," he told Parliament.[50]

Museveni's Parliamentary Sessional Committee on Defence and Foreign Affairs had recently recommended that the government continue to battle the rebels to defeat. A minority report, which claimed to reflect the majority view of Ugandans, suggested mediation and peace talks, but it did not win Museveni's favour.[51] He believed that showing overwhelming power on the battlefield was the best way to achieve lasting peace. The enemy had to be destroyed. If he negotiated, other would-be rebel groups might think he was weak and try the same thing.

As part of his new military offensive, Museveni replaced the army commander in the North, whom he'd judged too lenient on the Acholi people. General James Kazini, Museveni's nephew, and General Salim Saleh, his half-brother, were now in control of the Ugandan army's anti-rebel operation in the North.

General Kazini was determined to defeat the rebellion. His new military strategy was evidently based on the assumption that the population supported the rebels, and that if the rebels were left without civilian support, it would be easy to destroy them.[52]

The reality, however, was more complicated. The people did not support Kony, but they wanted their children back alive, and so this meant that some who had family inside the LRA would act as collaborators. Others simply feared the rebels and would do as asked. Generally, the people of Acholiland felt that neither Museveni, who'd come to power himself as a rebel leader, nor the Kony rebels were there for them. Back in the late 1980s and early 90s Museveni's troops had committed many crimes against Acholi civilians, and the Ugandan soldiers had stolen with impunity from them. The reality was that the Acholi people feared all soldiers, rebel or otherwise, and Museveni's new government had yet to offer anything to help them.

Now, to remove the people from the rebels, Kazini, operating on Saleh's orders, sent his Ugandan soldiers from village to village, ordering the locals to move off their homelands. Typically, the military stormed the villages at dawn and insisted that the people flee immediately to a section of land near the military barracks. In other villages, the people were given two to seven days' notice and told to congregate at the market trading centres, close to military posts. Anyone who remained in their homes would be considered a rebel.

Tens of thousands of Acholi farmers were quickly moved into centres without any health, sanitation, food, or other assistance. Within days of arrival many realized that they were without not only food but also any obvious means of getting it. Almost immediately, children began dying.

Some villagers defied the Ugandan orders, and so the military came with rocket launchers attached to the backs of trucks, declared them all rebels, and fired into them.[53] Other villages were bombed from the air.

To appease foreign governments watching and financially supporting Uganda, the military officially denied using force and insisted that the people voluntarily ran to the displaced persons' camps for protection.[54] The people of Gulu resented Saleh for forcing them out of their homes, an act that, according to the Geneva Conventions on Warfare, constituted a war crime. Most of the property left behind was stolen, both by rebels and Ugandan soldiers. People who tried to return to their homes found them burned down. There was no safe haven.

Soon after the people were off their land, Saleh began a commercial farming business in the area. People in the camps whispered to each other that the government's policy of forcing them into camps was in reality a calculated move to steal their land.[55]

THE ANGLICAN BISHOP of Kitgum, Bishop Ochola, was suffering an unbearable pain. Two months earlier, his wife, Winnifred, had been killed in Kitgum when the vehicle she was travelling in struck a land mine planted by the rebels. She'd been his best friend, the mother of his four children, and Bishop Ochola felt as though lightning had ripped him in two. His children now cried all day, and he didn't know how to soothe them. Feeling he couldn't take it any more, he turned to God and asked for help. It didn't take long before he understood why he had to suffer so much: experience was the best teacher, and now he truly understood suffering. To him, God was sending a clear message: *You have to dedicate your life to work for peace so that other people won't suffer as you do.*

Bishop Ochola now wanted to bring the religions together—to do more than pray. He wanted them to work to break the impasse by pushing together for peace and reconciliation between the many tribes in Uganda. He thought that if the religious leaders could demonstrate true leadership and overcome their divisions, perhaps the people would follow. Perhaps then the country could unite and heal, not just in the North, but in all of Uganda.

The Bishop invited all the religious leaders to visit him in Kitgum to talk about his concept of the Acholi Religious Leaders Peace Initiative. He told the group that a big part of the problem was that Northern Uganda had no real leaders left. After Idi Amin's reign ended, some Acholi leaders had returned from exile, but since Northern Uganda remained a war zone, the educated and connected Acholi moved either to Kampala or abroad. Although Museveni's one-party system had tried to bring Acholis into his government, the few who'd been accepted were seen by other Acholis as being morally compromised. The people simply didn't trust any of them, and in the end the people of Northern Uganda had no real voice. Bishop Ochola believed that the churches and mosques could work together to fill that void. Ninety percent of Northern Ugandans were actively religious; most were of various Christian denominations and about 10 percent were Muslim. But the people of different religions tended to ignore each other. It was time for this to change.

Included in the small group was Father Carlos Rodriguez Soto, a Spanish Comboni priest who enthusiastically backed Bishop Ochola's idea. A hard-nosed, serious man, Father Carlos was the only non-Ugandan on the team. He had arrived in Gulu in 1984, when he was twenty-four, and become fluent in Luo. But when the northern war broke out in 1987 he was sent back to Spain, where the Combonis trained him in journalism and used him as the editor and writer for their mission magazine. He'd returned in 1994 and had been in Uganda in 1995 when one thousand children were abducted from Kitgum, but no one had said anything then. He'd known Sister Rachele back then too, and had considered her a quiet person, even dull, but now he recognized her as a hero and understood that he was guilty of not having done enough for the captured children. He could make up for that now by putting his training to use and becoming the eyes and ears of the war. He knew that as a white European he had certain protections that a black Ugandan priest might not: whereas the LRA might kill a Ugandan priest speaking out against them, they seemed to leave the foreign missionaries alone. The Ugandan government too was very protective of what messages could be told—a Ugandan trying to report on the war might end up declared a rebel collaborator, or treasonous, or a spy; he could go missing and there'd be no outcry. But an attack on Father Carlos would be international news, something Museveni's government learned after they'd abused an Italian Comboni priest ten years earlier.

It was clear to everyone in the North that honest information was missing in this war. Given the risks to local journalists who tried to report truthfully, and the fact that no international journalists bothered coming to Northern Uganda to tell the story, Father Carlos decided that his role was to document the atrocities of the war so that the truth could eventually emerge. He immediately set his journalistic mind to documenting crimes, interviewing victims, and taking corroborating photos.

The lack of technology was a challenge: Father Carlos had to use an old manual typewriter he kept in his room, typing on carbon paper to make backup copies. There were still no telephones in Kitgum; nor had cellular phone coverage reached the area. And despite being the North's largest city and central meeting point, Gulu had just one public phone line and no photocopier or fax machine in the area. The only way the religious leaders could communicate with one another was through public CB radio calls and through letters that took a long time to be delivered. Added to this was the fact that the Comboni priests had almost no money. Although given a home and food, they were without salaries and on their own for funding.

But Father Carlos continued his investigations. At night he'd type up summaries—"To the attention of Ambassador _____, His Excellency of _____"—then stuff the notes in envelopes, stamp them, and drop the letters off in the mail that was periodically collected. He had to believe that someone out there would help them if only they knew the truth of the horror in forgotten Acholiland.

Father Carlos and Bishop Ochola also opened a new organization, the Joint Justice and Peace Committee, from which they sent out messages to the army proposing peaceful approaches to end the war. They advocated amnesty for the LRA soldiers, almost all of whom had started out as abducted civilians. They also recommended dialogue with the rebels—dialogue that Museveni had outlawed as an act of treason. These early proposals, however, were simply ignored.

CHAPTER 14

DECEMBER 10, 1997

In a display of American support for Uganda—and corresponding antagonism toward Sudan—U.S. Secretary of State Madeleine Albright flew to Uganda for a meeting with President Yoweri Museveni and South Sudan's rebel leader John Garang, along with his three top generals. Afterward she joined Museveni at a press conference. A month earlier in Washington Albright had announced sweeping new economic sanctions against the government of Sudan. All Sudanese assets in the United States were now blocked, and American individuals and companies were barred from dealing with the country.

Now, talking to the international press, Albright said that she admired Museveni's work and was very encouraged to see the advances Uganda had made—its strong economic growth, its vigorous and independent press, its dramatic progress toward national reconciliation. She explained that Washington was seeking to isolate Khartoum's leaders. Then Museveni opened the floor to questions.

The first reporter asked Museveni what he'd like the United States to do to assist Uganda in coping with the problems in Northern Uganda. "When you have got fire then you need fire brigade," he responded. His army was building up its forces along the border with Sudan, intending to help the SPLA "liberate" South Sudan from the Khartoum regime. Museveni thanked the United States for its financial support of the Ugandan army, and seemed to ask for more. "We always discuss with our friends, the Americans, how to put out terrorism fire. They have got a lot of experience in the various places, and I'm sure we can benefit from that experience."

The next reporter asked Secretary of State Albright what she thought of Museveni's insistence against allowing multi-party democracy. Albright responded, "Well, first of all, let me say that we believe that the progress made in Uganda under President Museveni has been remarkable. We admire the work that he has done, and look forward to working with him in the future. I think that one of the messages that the United States always has as we travel around is that every country's human rights record can be improved, and that is true here also. We talked about this very briefly...."[56]

Some Ugandan intellectuals were dismayed to hear Albright supporting what they perceived as a continuation of war in this wounded country, and wondered why she'd reinforce the lie that Uganda was making strong progress. Uganda was one of the poorest countries in the world, with one of the lowest life expectancies. Museveni had been in power for eleven years and had received a billion dollars in development loans from the West, and yet the country wasn't doing as well as it had in 1970, before Idi Amin destroyed it.

Ugandan intellectuals sometimes spoke of this deception when they travelled outside the country. To them, the answer was the same as it had always been: first, the West took tens of millions into slavery; then they colonized Africa for their own advantage; then they helped fight the Cold War by propping up African dictators who could be bought. And now their free-market economics was forcing open African economies, their bankers and businessmen keeping Africa down while extracting trillions of dollars in profits for the West. And all the while the West told lies that Africa, and especially Uganda, was a success story. But voices like this had been crying out for years about the criminal way their countries were being ripped out from under them through the World Bank and International Monetary Fund's Structural Adjustment Plan. And those voices were largely ignored in a world opinion that didn't know enough, or care enough, about African politics to judge.

AFTER ALBRIGHT'S SPEECH she flew to Gulu and arrived at St. Mary's Lacor Hospital, established by the Combonis and run by Dr. Piero Corti of Italy and his late Canadian wife, Dr. Lucille Teasdale. St. Mary's was now one of East Africa's best hospitals. Largely unprotected, it operated in the middle of the Northern Ugandan war zone—a beacon of hope radiating humanity in this darkened and destitute place. Coming events would only expand its role.

Dr. Corti led Albright around the facility. They walked through the surgery rooms, the children's ward, the malnourished infants' corridor, the acute injury ward where LRA rebels lay next to Ugandan soldiers. They traversed the open areas, where she saw patients lying on the ground with their families, to the far right corner of the hospital where fifteen hundred villagers, too afraid to sleep in their homes, had formed an unofficial displaced persons' camp.

After the tour Albright spoke to the hospital staff. "This has been a very moving visit for me and I am honoured that you would show me around, doctor." She looked to Dr. Corti, who smiled back. "I have seen here what Eleanor Roosevelt has said is the 'damnable duality of the human nature.' In each of us there is the possibility to be a beast, but also the possibility to reach for the stars." She then committed a two-million dollar endowment fund to the hospital and dedicated her visit to the memory of Corti's wife, surgeon Lucille Teasdale, who had died of AIDS in 1996 after contracting it from a soldier she was operating on.[57]

The facility had begun as a simple medical dispensary that the Combonis had converted into a thirty-bed hospital. Dr. Corti, having discovered it in the late 1950s, resolved to turn the little infirmary into a world-class hospital in the forgotten heartland of Africa, where so many people continued to die from easily treated maladies because they lacked basic medical care. He also decided to follow the Comboni model of empowering the local people and train Africans to be its nurses and doctors.

That first year he brought in four planeloads of donated medical equipment. Within months, medical interns from Kampala were coming up to train at the new hospital under the direction of Piero and

Lucille. The couple remained through the insecurity of war, committed to the people who needed them most. As the years passed, Lacor Hospital, as it became known, endured rebel attacks, mortar fire, death threats, and a host of other complications. It opened research labs, hosted foreign doctors and researchers, partnered with Italian hospitals, and gained some international fame. The hospital now served two thousand people a day, with 450 beds for overnight patients. Its patients were the poorest of the poor in Africa; some 80 percent of them were children and women. Beyond its medical services, the hospital offered the people hope. It employed them, accepted others as volunteers, and kept their loved ones alive.

A few days after Albright's visit, Sudan's minister of culture and information went on national radio to declare that Albright's actions had revealed U.S. aggression against his country. "This shows the United States is against any free national direction in all Arab, Islamic and African countries. We affirm to the traitors and agents of America who have sold themselves to Satan that the brave and heroic Sudanese people will foil all their plots."[58]

CHAPTER 15

KONY'S CAMP, SOUTH SUDAN

Living inside Kony's camp, but not as one of his wives, Judith Enang, the head girl from St. Mary's entrusted by Sister Rachele to take care of her classmates, had more access to the outside world than the other Aboke Girls. She was also the only one to have made a friend.

Catarina, a senior from Gulu Secondary School, was married to Sam, a man with one eye. Both Sam and Judith's husband, Lieutenant-Colonel Kapeco, were guards of Kony's, so they all stayed together in Kony's quarters. Because Catarina wasn't an Aboke Girl, Judith was free to interact with her. The girls grew to love each other. While they collected firewood and scavenged for food together in the bush, they exchanged stories from books they'd read, recited old school lessons, and whispered in English.

New recruits were not permitted to speak English. Because most rebels didn't understand it, they feared it served as a cover for escape plans. And as the language of Ugandan schools, it also reminded many of the rebel boys of their own ignorance. Yet the girls dared to whisper it together, practising for their futures.

Over time, Judith and Catarina became friendly with the Arab Sudanese officer who came regularly to speak to Kony. Sometimes he spoke English to them and they responded in kind—a fact that some of the guards noticed.

Judith, who'd never forgotten her promise to Sister Rachele to take care of the girls, was trying to devise a group escape plan. She'd told various Aboke Girls as much when she saw them in their trips to collect water, hoping to encourage and prepare them. With Grace Grall and two others having been rescued during the April 1997 joint Ugandan-SPLA military assault against Kony, the girls now numbered twenty. As their leader, Judith represented the remaining Aboke Girls' best hope for escape, and they were waiting for her to figure out how.

The reason for what happened next remains unclear. Some of the Aboke Girls say that while Kony was away Judith, the Arab Sudanese officer, and another conspired to facilitate the Aboke Girls' escape. Other witnesses say that it stemmed from the jealousy and resentment of the Aboke Girls and their preferred status in the camp, and that Judith simply received the punishment meant for them all. All agree, though, that Judith should never have spoken in English.

This much is known: one day in late December 1997, a few days before the New Year began, the guards told Kony that Judith and Catarina were planning an escape. One guard also lied that Judith was having sexual relations with the Arab. Judith and Catarina were seized and their arms were tied behind their backs. Then they were locked in a room while a meeting took place among the commanders.

It was decided that the two girls should be beaten but not killed. Then one of the commanders declared that Judith needed to be executed. He argued that despite their efforts to keep close tabs on them, the number of Aboke Girls was dwindling. The girls' wills hadn't been broken; their education made them more determined and willing to risk escape than the less-educated children. And their parents' and Sister Rachele's unrelenting advocacy had meant that, while the world ignored the others, an international outcry had gone out for the Aboke Girls. This fact, along with their preferential treatment as wives of the LRA top command, was causing confusion and resentment within the lower LRA ranks. It was time, the commander said, to increase the suffering of the Aboke Girls. They should beat Judith, their former leader, to death, so that the rest of the girls would be too afraid to escape. And since they were going to kill Judith, they should also kill her co-conspirator.

The commanders voted on it. Judith's husband, Lieutenant-Colonel Kapeco, didn't want her killed. But in the end both girls were sentenced to die.

Kapeco moved away from the execution site, retreating in silence as Judith and Catarina were beaten and whipped with chains and sticks by strong young men. A boy slashed into Judith with a machete, slicing her arm and leg to the bone. Writhing and bloodied, the girls were thrown in a pit for the night. In the morning Catarina was missing; while the guards were sleeping she had climbed out and run to a nearby village.

The rebels found Catarina, brought her back to camp, and beat her to death.

A few hours later, Grace Acan, Consy's missing daughter, walked to the pit and looked down at Judith lying bloodied on the earth. Grace had known Judith all her life. They'd been raised almost as sisters; their mothers were best friends and lived across the street from each other in Lira. Judith looked up and saw Grace standing above her. "Grace, please help me," Judith cried softly. Grace didn't know if there was anything she could do. Then her husband, Kenneth Banya, looked over and saw her at the pit. "You are going there to help your friend because you are also a culprit and want to escape!" he yelled.[59] Grace stepped away and returned to Banya's hearth fire. All she could offer now were her prayers.

The other girls were frightened too and didn't respond to Judith's cries. The next evening one of the girls saw two men approach with torches. They picked up Judith and dragged her to the bush. A short while later they came back on their own.

The next day several husbands of the Aboke Girls brought their wives to see Judith crucified to a tree. She called out to them, but they could not help her and were led back to their homes.

A week later a group of children out fetching water found Judith dead against the tree, where she'd been left to die from animals and the elements. Because Judith's body wasn't yet decomposing despite the tropical heat, the children whispered that she'd lived for days before God took her.

Shortly after Judith's execution, Joseph Kony told the camp that the new punishment for a guard who allowed an Aboke Girl to escape was automatic death.

THE MONTHS PASSED in a routine of rebel camp life. Each morning the children jogged around the camp perimeter, some carrying guns, others boulders, singing soldier and prayer songs. After these military exercises, most of the children spent their days farming, digging in the fields, and collecting firewood and water.

Although the Sudanese government provided them with bags of maize flour, the supplied and gardened food wasn't enough for them all. Boys aged seven and eight, taken too young to be of much use to the rebels, were the first to die from hunger, diarrhea, and disease. The youngest ones, without the discipline to go willingly hungry, were also more likely to try to steal food from the commanders, punishment for which was death.

Kony would periodically gather them all on the prayer field. He would lecture on God, politics, and the rules of the Holy Spirit within him. There were many rules to follow. Menstruating girls were not allowed on the prayer field or to touch cooking utensils. Stones could not be used when making fires, as the angel spirits might cause the stones to explode. The spirits also forbade cigarettes and alcohol. Although teenage boys and girls often worked and fought alongside one another, no free relationships were allowed. If an unmarried boy and girl were caught together, the punishment was public execution. New rules came and went depending on the spirit inside Kony. Sometimes he told them the spirit had directed that soldiers could not sleep with their wives before battle, other times he directed them all to fast. Occasionally he instructed that abductees be released.

During these talks to his troops, Kony would begin to speak evocatively of various spirits as he sat on his metal chair, dipping his finger in a cup of water and making the sign of the cross. He liked to wear his white robes and rosary at these times. When a spirit took him, his face changed and his eyes grew large.

He would talk about battles and prophesied their outcomes. He told his followers that the world would change dramatically in the year 2000, and that when the war ended some of them would return to Acholiland, where there would be nothing left, no homes or family, and that the white people would rule Acholiland as they rebuilt it.

Kony would also talk of spirits channelling through him and leading the war effort. He told his young followers that the spirit Juma Oris was still the highest spirit, but that he was assisted by many others. A female Sudanese spirit called Silly Silindi was the operation commander and leader of the female soldiers of the army. Silly Silindi spoke in English in a soft, high-pitched voice.

The spirit Ing Chu was Chinese and controlled the bullets fired by Museveni's army, ensuring that they hit only the sinful members of Kony's army—those who dreamed of escape, or disbelieved, or had secretly sinned. Ing Chu also at times commanded an imaginary battalion of jeeps that would assist the child soldiers. Then there was El wel Best, another Asian spirit, who helped plan battle tactics. Silver Koni, a spirit from the Democratic Republic of Congo, also controlled bullets. King Bruce, an American G.I. spirit, made stones explode like grenades. Sometimes Major Bianca showed up, an American woman who was responsible for the base camp and would sometimes conduct intelligence missions. Jim Brickey, another American spirit, was a black man who, like Major Bianca, conducted intelligence operations. But Jim Brickey, who also went by the name Who Are You?, sometimes switched sides and worked for Museveni when he was punishing Kony's soldiers for their undisclosed sins. Another was a spirit doctor who worked as the chief medical officer. There were many more.

Sometimes Kony spoke of the mystery that would end the war. "Nobody knows how this war will end. It will die out slowly," he told them. "One day, people will discover that the war is not there. They will be afraid to go home because they will fear that the violence will flare up again. But they will be waiting for nothing."[60]

Another time he told his followers that some of them would defect to the government and turn their guns against him. Kenneth Banya was shocked by what happened next. Kony pointed to him and said: "This man will be captured alive but the government will not do anything to him. He will pass through many bullets but he will not be wounded."[61]

SINCE JUDITH'S MURDER, the Aboke Girls now all remained exclusively in Sudan. Their role was to work as labourers in the fields, to collect firewood, to cook and clean for their husbands and the other rebels. Some worked as nurses, others as teachers.

Some of the girls' lives with their husbands and co-wives got easier. Palma Achieng's ongoing abuse at the hands of Alice, the older wife of her husband, Brigadier-General Tolbert, had come to an end. For years Alice had beaten and starved her, but in 1998 the other co-wives rose up against Alice and reported her cruelty to Tolbert, telling him that they feared Palma would die. The co-wives, teenagers like herself, had also apologized to Palma, explaining that they'd helped Alice abuse her out of jealousy. They had worried that the pretty, educated Palma would soon become Tolbert's favourite wife.

But that had been before, when Palma was still Tolbert's virginal child-bride. A few months earlier Palma had had her first period. For a while she fended off Tolbert's advances, but one night he came to her sleeping spot next to the other wives, put a pistol to her temple, and told her that if she refused he'd kill her. So she went to his sleeping room and became his wife. Afterward the other wives somehow weren't so threatened by Palma, perhaps because an equilibrium had been established.

Tolbert had punished Alice after learning of Palma's mistreatment, and soon Palma began building a quiet friendship with her other co-wives. But Alice's resentment and fury grew, giving her the courage to escape from the LRA. Her flight was short-lived, however; she was recaptured and brought back into Tolbert's fold. She was beaten along with two female friends who knew of her escape plans but hadn't reported her. One of those friends died in the beating. After that Alice and Tolbert didn't get along and he sent her to become the wife of a different man.[62]

During this time, Palma, Grace Acan, and Charlotte were trained as nurses by an English-speaking doctor in Juba and a Gulu doctor now based in the camp. The Aboke Girls removed bullets from injured soldiers, sewed up torn flesh, and cleaned infected wounds.

PART 3

"WHO IS ENDOWED WITH REASON AND CONSCIENCE?"

CHAPTER 16

Angelina Atyam continued speaking out for the missing children, and was soon back in New York City. It was December 10, 1998, and the United Nations was celebrating the fiftieth anniversary of the Universal Declaration of Human Rights by awarding its Human Rights prize, as it had done every five years since 1968. Among its recipients were Eleanor Roosevelt, Nelson Mandela, and Dr. Martin Luther King Jr. Today Angelina Atyam was receiving that honour.

Yet she felt sick about it. To Angelina she had done nothing other than leave her daughter in a vulnerable situation. Surely others in the world had done things that had results, she told herself. Still, here she was in New York, standing with Secretary-General Kofi Annan on the stage at the United Nations theatre in front of a formally dressed audience of thousands. When Annan gave her the plaque and shook her hand, she told him, "This should be given to some people who have done great jobs, good things."

"Angelina, take this and remember the work has just begun," he said quietly.

Her daughter was now trapped in an increasingly complicated world dynamic. A few months earlier, on August 7, 1998, Al Qaeda had blown up the U.S. embassies in Nairobi and Dar es Salaam. Intelligence reports suggested that another planned attack, on the American embassy in Kampala, had been foiled. Osama bin Laden had claimed responsibility and declared that more Americans would die.

Weeks after the attacks the U.S. government had bombed targets in Afghanistan and fired eighteen cruise missiles into a pharmaceutical plant that produced all the malaria medication for Sudan and half its other medicines. Madeleine Albright had stated that, according to U.S. intelligence, the plant was also manufacturing chemical weapons—an allegation that most Western analysts would later call untrue. Tensions were escalating, and none of this played well for the prospects of the successful return of the Aboke Girls.

Above Angelina Atyam and Kofi Annan a banner read: ALL HUMAN BEINGS ARE BORN FREE AND EQUAL IN DIGNITY AND RIGHTS. THEY ARE ENDOWED WITH REASON AND CONSCIENCE AND SHOULD ACT TOWARDS ONE ANOTHER IN A SPIRIT OF BROTHERHOOD. Angelina accepted the award, thinking she'd cry. As she moved aside Jimmy Carter took the stage, accepting the same award for his longstanding humanitarian work through the Carter Center.

MEANWHILE, the other Aboke Girls' parents struggled to cope with their loss and the knowledge of their daughters' continued suffering at the hands of the LRA.

In Gulu, Florence Lacor, Angela Atim's mother, persevered in a life devoid of family. Sometimes her children would call her at the World Vision Rehabilitation Centre from her brother's home in Kampala. They'd ask if she'd heard about Angela. "I heard she's still there, you pray for her and she'll come back," Florence would say. Then they would change topics, and soon there was awkward silence. With the war having ripped apart their family, Florence felt she had little to share with her children. And with money so tight, she never visited them. Still, Angela's abduction didn't hurt Florence now as much as it had. Her faith in God was unwavering, and after managing to forgive the rebels, her soul was more at ease.

One day Florence facilitated a group talk at the centre with children who had recently escaped. She listened to a boy who seemed to know a lot about the rebels, and for the first time since the abduction two years earlier, she said, "Do you know about the Aboke Girls? Do you know what's happened to them?"

The boy, filled with bravado before the group, told her how they were once going to kill them all.

"What happened?" she asked, careful to sound disinterested.

"We beat them instead. The commander said, 'If they do it again we'll kill them.'" Florence nodded and changed the subject.

She didn't yet know that Angela was married off to the same man who had also taken Louiza, Alfred and Isabella's daughter. If there was any consolation for Angela and Louiza, at least they could live together as co-wives. Florence would have known more if she'd been willing to keep in touch with the parents of the Concerned Parents Association, but sharing in their grief was too difficult for her. To Florence, the struggle of faith was between her and Angela and God.

Soon it was lunchtime, and she and the children ate poshe and beans with their fingers.

STRESS HAS A WAY of eating into people, and for some of the other Ugandan parents, racked with guilt for not having protected their children, the stress was killing them. Ben Pere, chairperson of the Concerned Parents Association, had died shortly after returning from his failed mission to retrieve the girls from the LRA camp in Sudan. The other parents agreed that he'd died of a broken heart. His role in the death of the girl in Kony's camp—escapees had told them what happened to her—had sealed his coffin.

The other members of the Concerned Parents Association tried to support one another emotionally (and routinely invited Florence Lacor to their meetings, to no avail); it was part of the reason they met so often. Some of the parents had mentioned to an NGO working in Lira that they needed coping mechanisms, and the organization had returned with an offer to counsel them. Angelina, having returned home, thought about Alfred and Isabella alone in Kampala, and sent them a note in the mail inviting them to this four-day special counselling session.

Now, sitting around in a room in Lira, a counsellor told the parents to stand up and clap. They clapped. "Now jump!" he said. Alfred jumped. Consy jumped. Angelina jumped. They all jumped, but their minds rebelled. They made mocking faces at one another.

The counsellor said he wanted the parents to let it go. To forget for a while. They played, acted, and shared their feelings. After four days Alfred realized that for the first time in three years he actually felt relaxed. The counsellor tried to convince them to let the emotions go, to accept that it had happened, and to know that they weren't alone. And after the counselling was done, Isabella did realize that she wasn't alone in her suffering. If she needed to talk, there were others who wanted to talk too.

IN 1998 Pope John Paul II appointed John Baptist Odama as the new Archbishop of Gulu, the diocese covering all of Northern Uganda, including Lira and Kitgum. Odama, once a Ugandan village boy born in a mud hut, had converted from animism and then been educated by the Combonis to be their leader.

Archbishop Odama and Bishop Ochola were old friends. They'd met as young priests, one Catholic, the other Protestant, who worked close by each other. One of Odama's first actions as Archbishop was to join the Acholi Religious Leaders Peace Initiative as vice-chairman. The previous Archbishop had refused to join the association, believing it made him appear too political.

In Odama's first speech as Archbishop he announced his intentions to the people of the North: "We should all unite, whether we are Catholics, Protestants, or Muslims, and see each other as images of God." He said that he would shed his blood for the people of the North. He called the rebels Uganda's prodigal sons.

Father Carlos Rodriguez, the serious-minded Spanish priest of Kitgum, became the Archbishop's fearless Catholic assistant in this new cause for peace. He stepped up his rhetoric against the abuses of the war, and resolved to expose some of the truth of the situation down in Kampala.

A colleague had arranged for Father Carlos to speak at the Makerere University Faculty of Law, and now he looked out at a class of young men and women as well as the Ugandan media he'd invited. The title of his speech was "Media Coverage of Human Rights in Conflict Situations: The Right to Information." "In a situation of conflict … the first casualty is truth," he told them. He recounted human rights abuses by the Ugandan military, the UPDF, that he had investigated. He told the students about how, a year earlier outside Kitgum, the military had targeted and then gunned down as rebels thirty recently abducted children who were still roped together. The media, he told them, had ignored the story. "If it was a businessman in Kampala, it would have been reported. But the fate of thirty children being killed in cold blood!" he said. He also told the students that, contrary to the army's claims, the rebels were in fact stealing children from the so-called protected villages.[63]

The next day *The Monitor,* Uganda's national independent newspaper, splashed the headline "UPDF KILLED 30 CHILDREN, SAYS PRIEST" across its front page.

There was no outcry. At the time, another unfolding story was fascinating Kampala's residents. That week *The Monitor* had published a photo of a screaming, naked young woman having her pubic hair shaved while being held down by a group of laughing soldiers. The caption specified that the photo had been taken inside the Gulu military barracks. The twenty-four-year-old woman later fled to Kampala, and believing she was safe, spoke to *The Monitor* about how she'd been crudely circumcised by one of the soldiers that night. The Ugandan Parliament, outraged at the newspaper's audacity in publishing such claims, had *The Monitor's* three senior editors arrested and charged with treason. The Ugandan military claimed that the photograph was of either Congolese or Sudanese forces, but definitely not Ugandan. People in Uganda were further scandalized when the woman was arrested for making a false statement and thrown in jail. *The Monitor* stood by its story.

HUMAN RIGHTS observers on the outside wondered why world powers were so silent in the face of abuses and rampant corruption inside Uganda. The American NGO Human Rights Watch, which had been trying to promote Angelina Atyam and the Aboke Girls' cases—in part by throwing prestigious awards at Angelina—concluded that the West was less interested in exposing Museveni than in maintaining a good relationship with him. He was considered a crucial leader in the Great Lakes region of Eastern and Central Africa, a power broker who, in the interest of his American ally, had helped end the Rwandan genocide (others allege he also helped start it) and had supported Zaire's rebels in their 1997 toppling of Sese Seko Mobutu. As well, by supporting John Garang's Sudanese rebels, he was useful in containing Sudan's Islamic government. Besides, he'd created stability in Uganda and had penned the slogan "African solutions to African problems," a slogan the donor countries liked to use to absolve themselves of the mess that colonialism, and later the tactical support of dictators during the Cold War, had left behind.

And yet this didn't explain why the network of hundreds of powerful NGOs working in Uganda didn't sound the international alarm themselves. Human Rights Watch came to understand that it was because Museveni played the repressive-regime game better than his neighbours. He knew what to say, and when to clamp down. First, most of the NGOs worked out of Kampala, one of Africa's safest capital cities, which is where the government wanted them. Museveni also required that all NGOs be legally registered in the country, and sometimes the government revoked registration, "in the public interest," to silence critics. NGOs were also not allowed to form group alliances, and as a result their voices were divided, the flow of information plugged. The government rationalized that because NGOs, in reality, served foreign governments, it was inappropriate for them to comment and interfere in the governing of a sovereign nation. To operate in Uganda meant that one had to be nonpolitical. For instance, NGOs were encouraged to debate prison reform, but not human rights abuses.[64] The resulting self-censorship worked effectively. In the end, the powerful voices supporting Museveni—especially the U.S. government and the World Bank and International Monetary Fund—drowned out the less-powerful voices criticizing him.

In addition, many Acholi politicians in the North saw the low-level war as part of a political strategy designed to maintain Museveni's strong-arm dictatorial leadership. With a looming all-out Northern war a continuing threat to the country, Museveni could persist in his high military spending and his outlawing of political parties other than his own National Resistance Movement.

Meanwhile, it was by now the unanimous opinion of the Comboni missionaries of South Sudan that the related larger war between South and North Sudan—which was ultimately the bigger force that trapped the Aboke girls—no longer had a moral core. It was a heartless international struggle for money and power, and religion was being distorted and misused in the process. Powerful Christian Right groups in the United States were portraying the war as a battle based on Islamic expansionism and religious persecution of their Christian brothers of South Sudan, downplaying the financial heart of the war—the battle for oil. Meanwhile, the Islamic Khartoum regime was asserting that the strict limits on freedom it had imposed in South Sudan were about Islamic shariah law, when in fact they were largely the means by which to retain power and take control of the oil wealth. Comboni missionaries also argued that international NGOs and various Western-based churches operating in South Sudan were prolonging the fighting by providing relief aid that actually supported the warring factions.

It seemed that, if the low-level war in the hidden corner of Uganda would ever find a way to end, and if the Aboke Girls would ever be able to leave Sudan and see their parents again, something was going to have to upset the international playing field.

CHAPTER 17

On August 30, 1999, men from thirty Western companies watched as the first 600,000 barrels of oil flowed from pipelines into waiting oil tankers for export. "This is a divine gift from Allah," Sudan's president Omar Al-Bashir declared. Sudan had just become an oil exporter, and by the end of 1999 the Khartoum government would receive an extra US$480 million in oil revenue, representing half of its total budget.[65]

Canada's Talisman Oil was its largest partner. The Calgary-based company had purchased Sudan's oil-concession rights from Arakis Energy the year before. Arakis had tried to hold on to its full stake, but when it proved too expensive to bring Sudan's oil to market on its own it had first partnered with state oil companies in China and Malaysia. Then, taking a large profit, it sold its remaining 30 percent share to Talisman, Canada's largest independent oil company, formerly known as BP Canada. By this time, despite having discovered oil two decades earlier, Sudan had still not sold a single barrel of oil to foreigners.

Throughout the previous decade the struggling government had lacked the military strength to defeat the Sudan People's Liberation Army and was at constant risk of losing its oil fields to Garang. Now, however, to vanquish Garang's SPLA, Sudan began investing the bulk of its oil revenue into arms. The weak army with outdated equipment now bought helicopter gunships, Antonov medium transport aircraft, mobile artillery pieces, and light assault weapons, purchasing most of it from China, Russia, and Libya. The United States government, with an embargo against Sudan and a policy of supporting the rebels, was not pleased.

The U.S. government had for years refused to engage or communicate with Sudan.[66] The Khartoum regime was now making repeated efforts to talk to Washington, but still found all doors closed. The Sudanese government wanted to enter the international community, to sell its oil to American companies, to act on the world stage as a progressive country. Clearly they needed to end their war with South Sudan, but John Garang wasn't willing to talk to them either. And so President Al-Bashir decided he would first address the secondary problem of ending the war with their southern enemy of Uganda. He sought out former U.S. president Jimmy Carter to help them negotiate peace, first with Uganda, and ultimately their larger enemy the United States.

The request for Jimmy Carter's mediation assistance came as a joint letter from Sudan and Uganda. Sudan believed that Carter, whose country had been a close ally when he was in power, was uniquely positioned to convince the Clinton administration to treat Sudan better. And because Museveni was allied with the U.S. government, Uganda also held Carter in high regard. Carter accepted their invitation to address a situation that he understood could easily lead to all-out war.

Carter's motivations were both humanitarian and political. He believed that peace in Sudan would have a trickle-down effect across Africa, and possibly into the Middle East. He had a well-known track record as a peacemaker since leaving office, and a twenty-year history in attempting to help Sudan, in large part through his health programs.[67] He also believed that the Clinton administration's foreign policy was prolonging the war in Sudan; that, but for its support of the rebels and its opposition to Khartoum, which it considered a terrorist breeding ground, peace in Sudan could have been achieved years earlier.

To Carter, the current administration was working with extremely flawed ideas that had tragic long-term consequences. He had recently written an opinion piece in *The New York Times* arguing that, instead of using time-tested negotiation to solve conflicts, the United States took what it considered a shortcut. It recruited support from the forum it could most easily influence, then propped up that group with dominant military capability, gave an ultimatum to the other parties, and took punitive action against everyone to force compliance. But in the end, Carter argued, this route further oppressed the civilian populations and caused unwarranted suffering. "Even for the world's only superpower, the ends don't always justify the means," Carter concluded.[68]

Carter invited John Garang and Joseph Kony to join the Sudanese and Ugandan government delegates at the table for peace talks. Garang, however—believing he would win the war—wasn't willing to negotiate, and Kony could not be located. The Carter Center staff decided to move ahead anyway. Preliminary talks opened in London in August 1999.[69]

The first item on Uganda's agenda was the return of the Aboke Girls, with the team insisting that the girls be returned before any other negotiations took place. In response the Sudanese delegates charged that Uganda was using the Aboke Girls to draw negative attention to Sudan. After several days negotiations broke down on the issue of the kidnapped girls.

After a few months of cooling down, the negotiations began again. In early December Museveni and Al-Bashir met in Nairobi, with Carter mediating. Al-Bashir explained to Carter that he wanted the U.S. to lift sanctions; that Sudan was misunderstood. Al-Bashir argued that Sudan was a developing country struggling with debt—it was the world's largest debtor to the World Bank, and these loans, given by Western countries, had propped up Sudan's dictatorship during the Cold War and given it the false impression that it had the strength to overpower the rebellious south. Carter responded that the present-day Sudan's relationship with Kony, and reports of slavery in Sudan, were indefensible.[70] For these actions, the world considered Sudan a pariah state. This, said Carter, needed to change.

Then he briefed the Ugandan delegation in the next room. The Ugandans told him again that the Aboke Girls had to be released before they would sign anything.

The next morning Carter and Museveni went through the main points of contention. Museveni offered up all his Sudanese prisoners of war, held since the April 1997 Ugandan offensive into South Sudan, in exchange for the Aboke Girls.

Carter went back and forth between the two presidents, each in a different room. Both agreed to exchange diplomats, both offered to stop supporting each other's rebel armies, both agreed to allow observers to monitor the pact.

Eventually, all issues were settled but one: while Uganda demanded the advance return of the Aboke Girls, Sudan argued that it did not have the power over Kony to get those girls—which was the truth. Carter pleaded with Museveni not to allow the Aboke Girls' case to ruin the chance for peace and offered to send his son, Chip, to oversee their release.

Museveni relented, and on December 8, 1999, both men signed their names to the Nairobi Agreement. Al-Bashir and Museveni then met, and with Jimmy Carter standing between them, they shook hands.

WHEN NEWS reports about the Nairobi Agreement reached the LRA camp in South Sudan, Joseph Kony flew into a rage. He hadn't received an invitation to the meeting—Khartoum hadn't delivered it. Kony would have talked, or sent some of his people to talk, but instead he'd been side-lined as if he were a mere puppet of the Sudanese government.[71] Kony felt he was being betrayed on the world stage, by his former Sudanese benefactors, and by his own Acholi people who'd been supportive of this agreement intended to marginalize and neutralize him.

Kony called his commanders together and ordered an immediate LRA assault in Gulu and Kitgum to protest the agreement. At this time Kony also accused two of his most trusted and longtime commanders of plotting to surrender with all the children. Shortly after being demoted, the men were executed.

The sleeping giant had been poked, and attacks on Uganda began days later. A one-year period of relative peace and stability in Northern Uganda had been shattered.[72]

CHAPTER 18

Fears of a Y2K worldwide computer meltdown kept most people from air travel on the first day of the year 2000. So the woman at the ticket check-in had to shout out "We're over here!" to Father John Fraser from a deserted hall at the Heathrow Airport. On the plane he stretched out on an empty row, making this his easiest flight to Uganda ever. There were more staff than passengers on board.

For the last three years Father John, now sixty-six, had lived at a Comboni Mission in Kitchener, Ontario. He'd enjoyed getting to know his various nieces and nephews, now adults. There were family parties, weddings, one-on-one lunches. Being close to family again after a lifetime away was heartwarming, but deep down Africa remained inside of him, calling him to help. Up close, not far away. When the plane landed at Entebbe Airport his spirits soared. He was home again, and filled with big plans to build a radio station.

He'd spent those last three years appealing to Catholic charities, private philanthropists, and Canadian government institutions for money to aid African bishops who had worthy projects. In some remote villages the bishops wanted bridges over waterways so that farmers could get to market or children to school. Others wanted money to build AIDS orphanages. Father John had also toured Canadian schools to talk to students about how the children of Africa, despite the wars and poverty, were just like them. He had encouraged primary-school classes to fill up shoeboxes with things that were important to them; then he'd sent the boxes to Northern Uganda or Malawi schools, whose students would return shoeboxes with their own mementoes.

The idea of the radio station had come to Father John a few months earlier, after he'd been interviewed at Toronto's CHUM radio studio about being an African missionary. As the producer explained the simplicity of the technology, the realization hit: *Why haven't I thought of this before? This would be great in Africa!* In a land of low literacy and high isolation, Father John could offer something that would connect the people and strengthen the community.

The power of radio to foster hate had become well known in the aftermath of the Rwandan genocide, but since then its power to do good—to prevent conflict and foster reconciliation, to build bridges, to dispel misinformation and rumours—had become clearer. It was an obvious tool that hadn't been used to full effect.

The United Nations and many NGOs were beginning to see the power of giving information to the people through radio—but their focus was on the higher-priority conflict areas. Africa was largely absent from their radar. It was on Father John's screen, however, and this is what brought him to his new home in Ngetta, a religious compound seven kilometres outside Lira in Northern Uganda. Scouting around, he found an abandoned brick church across the dirt road from his home and converted it into a radio station.

As he went about planning the new station, Father John happened to hear Pope John Paul II's millennium address that was being broadcast on radios around the world. "At this moment when the doors to the new millennium are opening, the Pope is convinced that humanity can finally come to conclusions about the past," the Pope said. He begged the people of the world to abhor the inhumanity of war, to respect human life and family life, to close the gap between the rich and the poor, and to realize that everyone is responsible for one another. He preached that this was what God was asking of the world, "and God never asks us anything that is beyond our strength. God also gives us the strength to accomplish whatever God asks of us." The Pope said that those who don't do everything in their power to stop war were equally as responsible as those who directly caused it.

Father John thought more about what radio could accomplish. *Will people listen? What programs would they like?* he wondered. Some in his Church wanted a devotional Catholic station, but Father John insisted on a station that appealed to everyone. He told his adversaries that if they were going to appeal to the whole community they'd have to be sufficiently even-handed to attract everyone—and to give them a voice as well.

In Northern Uganda, communication between those who weren't neighbours was almost impossible. Most people in Lira, including those with full-time government jobs, couldn't afford to buy a newspaper, and many couldn't read anyway. Nor did anyone have a telephone, and the television signals from Kampala didn't reach the North. In the midst of poverty and war, rumours and lies spread between homes with as much legitimacy as the truth. It caused distrust between them all and made fertile ground for those who aimed to manipulate the minds of an uneducated and hungry people. This was part of the reason why witch doctors could still swindle money and livestock from simple peasants, who often believed that angered spirits were causing them to suffer.[73]

The Catholic Church couldn't afford to fund the project, and no international aid agencies offered support. Father John was long broke, wearing second-hand clothes and broken eyeglasses, but he wrote to old friends in Toronto, Alberta, Scotland, and Italy, extolling the merits of launching a radio station in a war-ravaged land. Twelve responded, generously, giving him a total of forty thousand dollars for the station.

Father John found a couple of local welders willing to make him a forty-three-metre-high radio antenna out of scrap metal. That way the station could be heard everywhere within a 150-kilometre radius of Lira. He also hired five local reporters who spoke fluent English and Luo— and paid them about five dollars a day.

J.J. Kakaba, a popular radio deejay from Kampala, applied for the job as top host. Deejay Kakaba was a small man with a strong voice and a quick wit. He knew of the horrors of LRA life—his grandmother lived in a displaced persons' camp outside Gulu and a cousin had been briefly abducted by the rebels—and he wanted to return to Lira to help. Father John gladly hired him.

After consulting the community, Father John learned that people wanted a radio program to help them with farming: they wanted to know the fair price of cotton, for example, or where to get seed and fertilizer. The radio also gave instructions and advice on everything from healthy eating guidelines to safe-sex practices. And since many parents were afraid to send their children to school, and wanted to learn themselves, Father John put volunteer teachers on the radio to deliver supplementary lessons. The station also played popular music. For that, he relied on Kakaba and his young staff.

And, since Father John knew that CNN and BBC and other international media outlets were competing against each other for listeners in Africa, he picked up a free radio signal from the BBC and played it on the hour. Meanwhile, local people—police, military, teachers, politicians, aid workers—came to the studio to talk and debate. If they wanted to be on air, though, they had to follow the station's rules: ideas could be attacked, but people could not.

Thus Radio Wa, meaning "Radio for All," was born.

THE RADIO STATION succeeded beyond Father John's dreams. So desperate were the people for communication, and some entertainment, that they flocked to listen. Villagers gathered together in the evenings, gravitating to the homes that owned a radio. Within months a million people were listening, and programming was expanded from evenings only to all day long. Kakaba soon became the most famous voice of the North.

Aid agencies paid a few dollars to broadcast messages on-air. Local people with announcements also advertised. If a farmer had more grain than he needed, he offered to trade his excess harvest with someone selling goats. Or a reporter would come on-air to announce the current price of cotton. "So don't allow yourselves to be ripped off," the reporter would warn. The radio was careful not to criticize the government, though they might poke a little fun sometimes. Announcement fees and advertisements soon covered all the costs of running the station.

The radio provided fun for people. It was the simplest thing, but it just hadn't been developed before. There were skits, comical shows, serious news stories. If a goat was born somewhere in Northern Uganda with two heads, it would be the top news item for days.

The radio helped farmers find markets for their goods, it informed people of fair prices, and it taught them about health. It allowed the community to organize and coordinate together, and offered warnings and invitations to events. The poorest people realized that their voices were heard, that they had some power, and it enabled those who cared in the community to work together to find answers and help for one another. It allowed the people to come together, to debate, discuss, and find a collective viewpoint.

When people had a little money, they bought their own radios for a few dollars. And, following Father John's lead, it wasn't long before other radio stations sprang up.

CHAPTER 19

LRA CAMP, SOUTH SUDAN

Now, four years into their captivity, the Aboke Girls were reaching seventeen and eighteen, maturing into women.

None of the girls were soldiers any more. They were kept in the Sudan camps, working either as teachers for the children born inside the LRA—the "pure" ones—or as nurses in the infirmary for the soldiers.

Four Aboke Girls—Charlotte Awino, Grace Acan, Louiza Namale, and Janet Aber—were together now, as teachers, training the new generation born inside the LRA. After Judith was murdered, the girls had promised each other that they wouldn't attempt to escape without the others—it would be all or none. Charlotte prayed that she'd be the last Aboke Girl to escape; she didn't think she could bear being free while others remained captives.

Rarely could the girls speak to each other, but once every few months there were fleeting moments when two of the girls realized they were accidentally alone together: perhaps in the classroom, or fetching water, or tending a wounded soldier. When those moments came, the girls tried to reassure each other.

Mostly they prayed together, reminding each other that God was with them, protecting them. But they also reminded each other that their duty to God was to survive this experience with pure souls. Their days were spent surrounded by others who had been innocent but were now cruel. Most of the captives had passed over that invisible line, especially the boys. Cruelty directed at civilians, and at Ugandan military deemed to be part of the evil world, had been so rewarded that some now craved it, even laughed at it. Many of the boys acted as though they wanted blood, that they longed to kill, that they dreamed of violence. Some competed against each other with demonstrations of creative brutality. This was their route to graduating from being a new recruit to a commander. It meant they would no longer need to be at the front lines, no longer need to run unprotected into the path of oncoming bullets, no longer need to bash in the brains of their relatives or other frightened children. They could have their own servants, their own wives, and always enough to eat.

The Aboke Girls heard about how so many of the rebel boys cut off limbs, sliced off noses and ears, raped, stabbed, and killed with bravery, enthusiasm, and creativity. About the time the rebel boys had come across a funeral procession in Kitgum, and under threat of death made all the mourners eat the dead body. They ended up killing most of the mourners anyway, leaving a few alive to warn the others. Or about how they killed a man and then cut off the ears and lips and breasts of his wife. After gang-raping her, they made her have sex with her dead husband while they laughed at the sight.

The cruelty wasn't just from the boys. The female rebels also showed their emotional strength to kill and maim, and when they weren't out fighting, to mistreat and emotionally destroy the younger girls in the camp—in the same manner they had been destroyed when they first arrived. But the Aboke Girls told each other that their goodness was all they owned, and that it wasn't for sale.

GRACE, Charlotte, Janet, and Louiza enjoyed working at the school with the children. But today a senior commander walked into the school and ordered the four Aboke Girls into an empty classroom, looked at them severely, and announced that the Holy Spirit had reported that they were devising a group escape plan for all the Aboke Girls. He placed a tape recorder on the desk and hit the record button.

The four trembled. Janet thought she'd throw up. Charlotte broke the silence. "If you say that it is the Holy Spirit, then your holy spirit is a liar!" she said, knowing that Kony would listen to her words. "If you believe in false prophecy," she continued, "from today I will not believe what you are saying, whether it means death or something else you want to do."[74]

The commander feigned hurt and made a mocking, sad face. He took the tape to Kony, who after listening to it sentenced them all to death. The girls were collected the next morning along with another teacher, Lisa, a girl who'd been abducted from Kitgum Secondary School. They were marched out to the execution field.

One of the guards told them that if they admitted their escape plan, they'd be excused. Charlotte told the bodyguards that to die innocent was good. Janet Aber, who was married with children to Sam Kolo, a top commander, whispered to the others that they should plead guilty and be forgiven. "Would you accept lies for the sake of lies? It is good to be on the safe side of the Lord," Charlotte replied, thinking about her lessons at St. Mary's. The guards forced the girls to lie down.

Charlotte was the first to be asked. "Did you plan to escape?"

"No," she said.

Following her, Grace Acan, Consy's daughter, Louiza, Alfred's daughter, and Janet Aber, the eldest daughter of Phoebe, a Gulu teacher, also replied no. The other girl, Lisa, said yes. The men beat the Aboke Girls with one hundred strokes across their backs, buttocks, and legs while Lisa watched. But the truth was that, after the first five or so strokes, it no longer hurt much to be whipped. And the girls were well practised at going into that quiet place in their heads while being abused.

Afterward, they were ordered to stand. Blood and loose flesh dripped down their backs and buttocks. The soldier asked them again: Did you plan to escape? The four Aboke Girls still said no. They were forced to lie down, and received a hundred more lashings each, this time over mostly raw flesh, their skin having already peeled away. When the beating was over, all four were unconscious.

They were moved to the infirmary to heal. Three woke up shortly after the beating. But Louiza remained unconscious. She had lost so much blood—it looked as though an artery had been cut—that the girls thought she would die. For three days the injured girls prayed over

Louiza's body while they themselves healed. On the third day Louiza woke.

When they were well enough to move, Kony called for them. As they stood before him, he declared them innocent and released them back to their husbands. But first he sent them to the firing squad. There they watched as Lisa, the only one to plead guilty, was made to stand in front of a tree. The soldiers shot her dead.

Afterward, the girls told each other that God had kept them alive.

CHAPTER 20

CARTER CENTER, ATLANTA, GEORGIA, SPRING 2000

Ben Hoffman, from the small town of Eganville, Ontario, considered the slogan inside the sprawling Carter Center headquarters—WAGING PEACE, FIGHTING DISEASE, BUILDING HOPE—and wondered just what Jimmy Carter expected from him. It was his first day on the job as the former president's right-hand man.

He sent a note to Carter, asking semi-rhetorically, "Do we really wage peace at the Carter Center?" As a professional mediator he knew that the basic tenet of mediation was not to take sides but rather to step back from the conflict and create an opening, a path, that peace could follow. Mediators didn't wage peace, they facilitated dialogue. It was an academic question, but Hoffman, at forty-nine, was a philosophical man with a recently acquired doctorate in peace studies, and he was intrigued by the possibilities. He also asked for further clarification of Carter's interest in Sudan.

Two days later Carter arrived at a meeting with the board of directors of his organization. He threw his agenda aside and looked at Hoffman. "Ben, when I say we wage peace, and when I say we wage peace in Sudan, I mean it. And you're in charge." Carter had just made Hoffman responsible for implementing the failing Nairobi Agreement.

A few days later Hoffman headed to Washington to ask Secretary of State Madeleine Albright to look differently at Sudan. Carter had already briefed him on the U.S. policy to support the rebels attempting to take over the nation's oil-rich territory. A week later he got on a plane and, for the first time in his life, headed to East Africa.

Hoffman had already come a long way: from a long-haired hippie driving a dump truck to a short-haired prison guard in Ontario's tough northern jails and eventually an international mediator navigating some of the world's most complicated wars. In the early 1980s he'd been at the centre of a movement in the Canadian criminal justice system to switch from "retributive" to "restorative" justice with its stronger focus on healing, reconciliation, and victims' rights. In 1992 he cofounded the Canadian International Institute of Applied Negotiation, which trains Canadian peacekeepers working abroad. He'd also obtained a string of graduate degrees from Tufts, Harvard, and more recently, York in England.

Hoffman's call to the world mediation stage came in 1994 after he'd spoken at a UNESCO seminar about the emergence of inter-ethnic disputes in the Balkans and elsewhere following the collapse of communism in Eastern Europe. Most of those present agreed with the explanation, advanced by writers and academics, that these conflicts were related to feelings of deep-rooted ethnic identity. Hoffman, however, argued that they were only disguised as ethnic conflict and were in reality a struggle for power and resources. He impressed the delegates, and soon found himself travelling to places such as the Ukraine and Romania—assessing, mediating, and attempting to prevent violence from breaking out.

In late 1999 a headhunter working for Jimmy Carter called. The former president had a well-known track record as a peacemaker: he'd helped bring the Korean peninsula back from the brink of war, prevented a U.S.-led invasion of Haiti, mediated in Liberia, Ethiopia, and Eritrea, and created an opening for the peace process in Bosnia. Carter wanted the entrepreneurial Hoffman to direct the conflict resolution section of the Carter Center.

Now, as an impartial observer, Hoffman was about to take a crash course in African politics, talking to everyone from warlords to government officials and taking no one at his word as he filled in the gaps and worked out the puzzle of why peace couldn't be attained. He didn't know much about Sudan or Uganda, but he knew, since everyone said they wanted peace, that someone was lying.

His first problem was that SPLA rebel leader John Garang wouldn't talk. Nor did Hoffman have authority from either the Sudanese government or the southern rebels to broker a peace deal. But he did have a place to start: the recently signed Nairobi Agreement between the presidents of Uganda and Sudan. Hoffman looked through the agreement and could see that it was deeply flawed. Neither the SPLA nor the LRA—key stakeholders—had participated in the talks, and not surprisingly, the agreement had fallen apart before the ink was dry.

By using his mandate to revive the Nairobi Agreement, Hoffman intended to get close to the warlords and presidents who were collectively killing off a generation. It would be his back-door entry into solving Sudan's intractable war. He'd do it, covertly, while working overtly on the Sudan–Uganda issue.

Backgrounding himself on news stories, he saw how icy the relations between Sudan and Uganda remained. Since Museveni kept making bold statements in the press antagonizing Sudan, one place to start was to encourage the players to use more gentle language. Hoffman wanted to establish himself as the new guy, and to show Sudan and Uganda that with him around they were going to do things differently.

A DRIVER PICKED UP Hoffman at the Entebbe airport forty-five minutes east of Kampala. Cars and minibuses sped along the highway, overtaking one another at breakneck speeds. Impoverished Ugandans lined the road with small shops and crowded the highway sides with foot traffic. He noticed how well dressed everyone was, in ironed shirts and smart dresses, wearing their poverty with dignity. It smelled of dust and grass.

Museveni, ensconced under a shade tree on his manicured lawns, greeted Hoffman warmly. When the Americans came calling, he responded. Museveni acted as their ally in Africa by helping them promote their interests across the continent, and in turn America and Britain were Uganda's primary benefactors—they'd given billions to the nation over the years, and now 50 percent of its annual budget came from foreign donors.

Museveni explained to Hoffman the crest of the problem: Sudan had had the opportunity to be a bridge between Northern Africa's Arab peoples and the black Southerners, but instead its government had designs on Islamizing all of Africa. The tension between the north and south spread farther than Sudan's borders, and threatened Uganda. As a result Museveni refused to stop supporting the SPLA, saying that he would always back his persecuted brothers in southern Sudan. And yet if Sudan stopped supporting Joseph Kony in accordance with the Nairobi Agreement, Museveni would end his military support for Garang. This was what Hoffman wanted to hear.

After the meeting, Hoffman went to dinner in downtown Kampala with Uganda's minister of foreign affairs and its minister of the interior. The ministers grilled him: Did he understand Africa? Did he know who the Aboke Girls were? Did he understand the Islamizing agenda Khartoum had? Hoffman was ready. "I'm going to learn, I'm going to be balanced and fair, and I'm going to Khartoum tomorrow—and we're not going to do business as we used to do it," he replied. "You people say you want results. You want the LRA children home, the Aboke Girls back, you want Khartoum to give up support of the LRA. They want things equally as well." Hoffman added that in order to get the Nairobi Agreement back on track he wanted the Ugandan delegation to return to Atlanta for a meeting with their Sudanese counterparts.

The Ugandans nodded. "We can always have a meeting," one of the ministers said. "We'll meet. But we want you to go and see Joseph Kony. Make the Sudanese make him available to you."

A few days later, after Hoffman met with Sudan's president, Omar Al-Bashir, and told him he wanted to meet Joseph Kony, Sudanese authorities set up an appointment for him to meet with Dr. Yahai Babiquer, Sudan's deputy director of internal security. Hoffman's assistants had informed him that Babiquer was in charge of militia armies—the cloak-and-dagger operations of Sudan.

Hoffman was taken to a gated compound inside a residential neighbourhood. Babiquer greeted him in his plush office with a dozen television monitors. He was in his late-forties, Arab, hospitable. He told Hoffman that he'd done his Ph.D. in the United States. Hoffman and Babiquer hit it off. He could talk to this man.

Hoffman told Babiquer about his meeting with the Ugandans, and how they'd requested that he meet with Kony. He wanted to know if Babiquer would help him get together with Kony.

"Certainly, when do you want to go?" he asked.

TWO WEEKS LATER Hoffman was fumbling nervously over what to wear for the meeting inside Kony's compound. He settled on dress pants and a pressed shirt with no tie. Before dawn he and his assistant were heading to the Khartoum airport. Just in case, he called his wife Ann to tell her that he loved her, then caught a flight to Juba. There he was greeted by two Sudanese officers. Before leaving town, the group stopped at a corner store to purchase a crate of Coca-Cola, then bumped along the dirt road into the countryside. As they drove they passed Dinka villages, fields, broken-down military equipment. Hoffman saw soldiers walking home, civilians pushing bicycles, huts with children running outside in the countryside, women waiting around for their military husbands to return. Forty-five minutes later they drove up to the LRA compound in the middle of the bush.

LRA commander Sam Kolo, who looked to be in his mid-thirties, greeted the visitors and led them in. Several large, thatched-roof buildings surrounded an inner courtyard. When the group walked into the largest building on their right they saw thirty uniformed men sitting in an assembly. On the left was an open bearpit, where Joseph Kony and his senior commanders stood. Hoffman noticed curious young faces peering at them through the compound windows, but he was careful not to look back. They all followed Kolo down into the pit.

Sam Kolo introduced Joseph Kony as a great man of God. Kony wore a lace shirt with an open collar and blue jeans. His hair was short, not the dreadlocks he'd been photographed in. Kony invited the visitors to sit down. The Sudanese nervously began cracking open the pop and handing it around to everyone. In the silent observation gallery above, no one dared so much as cough.

Then Kony began theatrically waving around a red book that Hoffman presumed was the New Testament. Kony ranted and raved, in English, spewing insults. Hoffman already knew he wouldn't be defensive, that he'd absorb the accusations without rebutting. "If you're really serious about democracy," Kony finally said, "why doesn't President Carter hold a national reconciliation political conference in Uganda?" This supposed psychopath appeared to make sense, and Hoffman's mind raced with the implications. Had Kony been portrayed as insane as a tactic to delegitimize him?

Kony went on to say that they weren't just criminals living in the bush. "We have a political objective. The people in the North have been neglected." Kony wanted a genuine democracy, and was upset that he hadn't been included in the talks that had produced the Nairobi Agreement. And then he looked at Hoffman. "I don't know why you, UNICEF, are abducting our children." He spouted an angry message for him to give to Museveni.

Hoffman took a deep breath. He didn't want to look nervous, or like a spy assessing his surroundings, so his eyes remained either on Kony or the commanders sitting next to him. "I am here to request that you meet with representatives of the government of Uganda and have talks with them," he said. He talked about measured steps. Gestures of trust.

The conversation, while tense, grew increasingly civil. But Hoffman felt he had to show Kony some of the trust of which he spoke so that it could be reciprocated. Wanting to emphasize that he was an agent of neither the Sudanese nor the Ugandan government, he turned to his Sudanese handlers and asked them to leave the room. The men were taken aback, but complied.

Kony shifted in his seat and looked to his adviser, Sam Kolo, for advice, but Kolo remained silent. When the Sudanese were gone, Hoffman began. He said that he was a servant of peace, that he was working under the auspices of the Nairobi Agreement, and that the government of Uganda had asked him to ask Kony to enter talks. But as he spoke he could see that Kony was growing more agitated and confused. Hoffman worried that if Kony's stress grew, he could turn violent. He sensed that Kony needed some time to himself. So he stopped talking and announced, "Now I too am going to leave the room."

He got up and Vincent Otti followed. Outside, Hoffman glanced through a window and saw that Kony was lying down with someone massaging his head. He wondered if one of Kony's spirits had arrived, or if he merely had a bad headache. Trying to lighten the mood, Hoffman made small talk with Otti. They discussed the grass roofs of the buildings, but when Hoffman met Otti's eyes, he saw the fierce gaze of a warrior. Although Hoffman was nervous, he knew he couldn't show it.

Once Hoffman sensed that Kony had calmed down, the entire group went back in. Hoffman took his seat across from Kony, who was again seated at the table. Kony now looked at Hoffman, made a gun out of his finger and thumb, and pointed it at Hoffman's face. Everyone was silent. Kony stared wide-eyed at him, as if attempting to penetrate his thoughts. Hoffman returned the gaze, and as he locked eyes with this man accused of such barbarism, who claimed spirit possession, who was trying to read his mind, his imagination took over. When Kony pressed his finger down, triggering the imaginary gun, Hoffman felt the bullet go through the back of his head.

"You are not my enemy," Kony said at last. "My enemy is Museveni." Kony now turned his other hand into a gun and pitted the gun barrels together. He told Hoffman that Museveni came to power by the gun and only the gun. That Museveni understood only the gun. Kony then set his hands on the table, laying down his imaginary weapons. "We agree to talks. But we need time," he said.

As Hoffman felt relief sweep through him he saw the tension give way in everyone else in the room. The conversation shifted to planning. Kony wanted to meet with Acholi elders so that they could voice their demands through him; the group of elders must not include any government spies.

Delegates exchanged small jokes as the prospect of peace lifted everyone's spirits. Kony wanted the meeting to be here, in Nisitu camp, expressing concern that if he left his compound a trick could have him hauled off to a war crimes tribunal somewhere, just as Chile had tricked Pinochet.

At the end of the meeting the men all shook hands warmly.

On the way back to the truck, Hoffman and Sam Kolo talked. Kolo told him about coming into the bush when he was eighteen, and that this was a cause he believed in. Hoffman was impressed with Kolo, and before leaving said he hoped to see him again outside of the bush one day soon.

That night Hoffman's Sudanese handlers treated him to goat stew in a home in Juba. "That was the best meeting we've had with Kony in a long time," one of the intelligence officers said, telling Hoffman how difficult Kony's group had become. Hope was high that night that peace was on its way.

WEEKS LATER Hoffman was back in his office in Atlanta, wondering what had happened in South Sudan. It seemed as though the LRA wanted talks, and yet something always stalled the process. So who was doing the stalling? Was Kony not serious after all? Was he really just a fickle psychopath as Uganda described him, or given half a chance, would he come through? Hoffman wondered if Sudan, despite having facilitated the meeting with Kony, could be the ones secretly upsetting all the plans at the last minute. Or perhaps it was Museveni, or his senior commanders siphoning off their military budgets and wanting to continue living off the avails of war. Hoffman knew that the southern and western Ugandans controlling the country had an enmity toward the Acholi people that went back to British colonial times, when the Acholi were put in charge of the military and did England's bidding in keeping Ugandans down. Some now thought that the Acholi were an intrinsically violent people finally getting their due.

Nor did Hoffman feel that either Sudan's Islamic President Al-Bashir or the SPLA's General John Garang were particularly interested in peace. They both said they were, but neither wanted to negotiate.

Al-Bashir was a military man, a general who'd led Sudan's military operations against the SPLA in the 1980s. He'd come to power ten years earlier in a joint coup with the fundamentalist Islamic group spiritually led by Hassan Al-Tourabi. Al-Tourabi was fiercely anti-American and the man behind giving Osama bin Laden and other terrorists haven in Sudan in the 1990s. But now Al-Bashir's and Al-Tourabi's union was unravelling. Al-Bashir felt that Al-Tourabi was too extreme, and Al-Tourabi—whose niece was married to bin Laden—felt that Al-Bashir was too weak. Al-Bashir had recently placed Al-Tourabi under house arrest, but if he moved too far away from the established party line the fundamentalist core supporting him could cut him loose. Hoffman's sense was that Al-Bashir might personally be a little more secular, but that if he compromised the political desires of the Islamic agenda he'd be overthrown and the fundamentalists behind Al-Tourabi would be in charge. In that scenario, the situation could get worse.

Then there was Al-Bashir's man in charge of internal security, Yahai Babiquer. Hoffman found him one of the most amenable, gracious, and sophisticated people he'd ever met, and they'd gotten to know one another reasonably well, even meeting with their wives for a pleasant dinner in London one night. That was always part of the complexities of international mediation in war zones: meeting fascinating people, often intellectuals, who had the blood of innocents on their hands.

Or was it John Garang, who, although technically a rebel leader, travelled the world with an entourage and was treated in many Western countries, especially the United States, as a head of state?

The answer to who was doing the stalling evaded Hoffman. If he had the answer he could strategize, manipulate, appease, encourage, and apply pressure. He could drag that party kicking and screaming to the negotiating table. It had worked many times before.

CHAPTER 21

WINNIPEG, SEPTEMBER 12, 2000

Lloyd Axworthy, in his fourth year as Canada's foreign affairs minister, was opening the first international UN conference on children affected by war. Hallways buzzed with organizers setting up tables and chairs as newly arrived delegates filled the hotel bars of downtown Winnipeg. Axworthy, who had just arrived from New York, was handed a request from one of his staff members to meet some children from the Northern Uganda war. Pressed for time, he sighed unenthusiastically, but his staff member persisted and he agreed to slot in time the next morning.

His room at the Fort Garry Hotel had deep, oversized chairs. The two Ugandan girls were swallowed up inside them. Accompanying them were Angelina Atyam and Geoffrey Oyat, an Acholi employee of an NGO called Canadian Physicians for Aid and Relief (CPAR).

One of the tiny girls told her story of abduction and rape. She'd been forced into military service at age nine and now, at thirteen, she already had a child from a rebel commander and lived in one of the squalid, disease-filled displaced persons' camps in constant fear of re-abduction and a torturous death for her betrayal.

Axworthy was shocked. The heartbreak of the girl cracked his shield. He had a granddaughter her age. As the group was leaving, Axworthy promised her he'd visit Uganda someday to see what could be done. For a while he sat there, wondering in a way he hadn't before about how far one's responsibility for others went. Where was the line drawn? Did Canada's collective conscience take the country as far as the camps of

Northern Uganda? And given that most Canadians remained indifferent, was he expected to be as well?

The next morning protesters gathered outside the Pantages Theatre in Winnipeg as the conference delegates poured in. "Ismail is a killer," a Sudanese man with a bullhorn shouted in outrage at the imminent arrival of Sudanese foreign minister Mustafa Ismail as one of the conference delegates. Others carried placards that called for Talisman Energy's expulsion from Sudan. A recent government-funded study had estimated that 80 percent of the money the Canadian oil company gave to the Sudanese government was redirected into battling South Sudan through the purchase of weapons and other military support. Yet Canada's politicians continued to allow Talisman to conduct business with Sudan, turning a wilful blind eye, clouded by economics, to the massive horror in which they were complicit.

Axworthy had earlier promised Canadians that he would intervene if it was found that Talisman's oil business with Sudan was involved in prolonging the war or otherwise linked to human rights abuses. But when the report came out, and Axworthy attempted to bring forward new laws on Canadian companies working in conflict zones, he found that he didn't have the backing of Cabinet, many of whose members had been heavily influenced by the Cadillac of Ottawa lobbying firms, Hill & Knowlton, which worked in support of Talisman.[75] The power of economics had trumped Axworthy's power as minister of Foreign Affairs.

Now, with 130 leaders from around the world gathered here in Winnipeg, Axworthy saw an opportunity to help end part of the war, to bring Sudan and Uganda together. He also thought he could work out a deal to release the estimated six thousand LRA child soldiers. Without dialogue, deals were impossible, he told reporters questioning his decision to invite Ismail. And with the world watching, Axworthy knew that the conference would be an excellent forum in which to exert political muscle.

When Mustafa Ismail arrived the next day, the fact that a Sudanese villain was on Canadian soil made front-page news across the country. Ismail met with a *Globe and Mail* reporter to complain that the UNICEF conference was being hijacked by organizers, protesters, and

Joseph Kony, leader of the LRA, in July 2006.

Credit: Acholinet.com/Mike Odongkara

Junior LRA commanders during one of their first meetings with the Acholi religious leaders in 2001.

Credit: Father Carlos Rodriguez

An LRA child soldier poses for the camera.

Credit: Acholinet.com/Mike Odongkara

Father Carlos Rodriguez speaks with an LRA rebel during one of the LRA meetings with the Acholi religious leaders in 2001.

Credit: Father Carlos Rodriguez

Sudanese President Omar Al-Bashir (left) shakes hands with Ugandan President Yoweri Museveni upon the signing of the Nairobi Peace Agreement on December 8, 1999. Jimmy Carter looks on with Kenyan former president Daniel Arap Moi.

Credit: The Carter Center

A 2001 interfaith peace march led by the Acholi religious leaders.

Credit: Father Carlos Rodriguez

Activist Angelina Atyam, whose Aboke schoolgirl daughter Charlotte Awino was kidnapped by the LRA, speaks at the United Nations in New York in 2004. Former UN undersecretary for humanitarian affairs Jan Egeland watches as Angelina shares her testimony.

Credit: UN Photo/Evan Schneider

Ugandan president Yoweri Museveni addresses the meeting on Financing for Development at the World Summit 2005 in New York.

Credit: UN Photo/Paulo Filgueiras

Father John Fraser looks out over the scene of the massacre in Barlonyo in June 2005, with the Ugandan military standing behind him.

Credit: Mike Blanchfield

A counsellor at the Rachele Rehabilitation Centre in Lira interviews a group of girls who escaped from the LRA during a battle with the Ugandan military that same morning. One Aboke Girl was among this group.

Credit: Kathy Cook

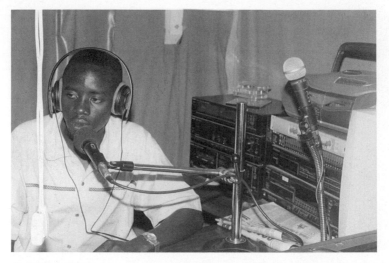

A deejay news reporter during his show in the Radio Wa studio, 2004.

Credit: Radio Wa

A group of night-commuter boys have a little fun for the camera before settling in to sleep for the night at St. Mary's Lacor Hospital, June 2005.

Credit: Kathy Cook

Escaped Aboke schoolgirl Grace Grall Akallo with the child of Jessica, another Aboke Girl. Jessica was killed in February 2004 in a Ugandan military attack on the LRA. This child was found alive, still strapped to her back. The boy's father is Raska Lukwiya, who was indicted for crimes against humanity by the International Criminal Court in June 2005. Jessica's parents are now raising the child.

Credit: Mike Blanchfield

Sylvia Alaba with her baby, Joseph Kony's child, stands with her former teacher, John Bosco Ocean, at St. Mary's school on June 3, 2005. Sylvia escaped from the rebels that morning.

Credit: Kathy Cook

Rebecca, daughter of Joseph Kony and Aboke schoolgirl Jackie Wagesa, safe now with her great-grandmother, June 2005.

Credit: Kathy Cook

A group of escaped Aboke Girls now back at high school together, June 2005.

Credit: Kathy Cook

delegates. "To come and wage a campaign against the government of Sudan, and that becomes the whole scenario of the conference, that's unfair," Ismail said. "There is no acknowledgment about what we are doing."[76]

But to most at the conference, Sudan was at fault. Stephen Lewis, the former Canadian ambassador to the United Nations and now deputy director of the United Nations Children's Fund, had accused Sudanese officials of lying and manipulating Western governments into believing they were trying to win the freedom of the LRA captives. "[The LRA] would not survive without the government of Sudan," Lewis said. "They have chosen together, consciously, to pursue their aims using children as sacrificial fodder."[77]

Lewis also said that Calgary-based Talisman Energy's continued partnership with the Sudanese government was "a terrible cross of dishonour for Canada." Canada's reputation as a world advocate for peace and the protection of children was being revealed as a sham, he said, given that the country was allowing its financial interests to come before the lives of children in Sudan.

Delegates at the conference made speech after speech calling on governments to put children ahead of oil and to do more than express moral outrage. The case of the LRA children was repeatedly held up as the worst scenario in the world.

For Ben Hoffman, though, it all spoke to the hypocritical nature of politics. For months he'd been knocking on UN doors, trying to get someone to commit their government to helping in even just a small way. All had refused. In his opinion, leading up to this conference not one person working inside the United Nations cared about these abducted children. Perhaps they cared personally, but Northern Uganda simply did not rank on any country's political radar.

Hoffman did not attend the conference. There were always so many conferences.

MEANWHILE, in the village of Kabedo-Opong, seven kilometres north of Gulu, Esther Owete, thirty-six, knew nothing about the high-level discussions going on in Winnipeg—although she would soon drastically affect their outcome.

Her fever had worsened. She was shivering cold in the hot tropical heat. Before long the mother of five felt pains in the muscles in her legs, and her throat was sore. That night, her chest hurt, and diarrhea struck unrelentingly.

Her family and neighbours thought Esther had malaria. Her mother brought her on a bicycle to St. Mary's Lacor Hospital the next morning, where she was given an injection of chloroquine and sent home to rest. Lying in bed in her tiny mud hut, she spent the night wracked in pain. Early the next morning she began vomiting, and by daybreak she was dead.

With broken hearts, Esther's mother and two daughters bathed her body, as was the custom, and sat inside the hut with her for two days to say goodbye. A neighbour walking by overheard Esther's distraught mother cry out for her grandson, one-year-old Sam: "Suck your mother's last milk so you too can die. There is no one here to look after you now."

Sam, it seems, did as he was told.

A few days later everyone who'd lived inside the hut was dead. And a farmer who went to Esther's funeral, Albino Ciero, was soon admitted with a fever and diarrhea into the general ward at St. Mary's Lacor Hospital.

The deaths frightened the community. It didn't make sense how an entire family could die so quickly. They called the thing "gemo," which in Luo means a type of ghost or evil spirit: no one knows about it, but it comes and takes you in the night. Someone inside that family must have done something wrong, very wrong.

At Lacor Hospital a young student nurse perched herself at Albino's bedside and fed him by hand. She didn't use gloves. She was used to treating HIV patients, and considered it rude to treat them with gloves on. It seemed likely to her that Albino was suffering from a complication from AIDS.

A few days later she fell ill with a fever and was admitted into the hospital herself. It only took her two days to die. Stool and blood samples failed to reveal the cause of death, but the hospital suspected a virulent strain of malaria. Her parents took her body home to their hut in Gulu to prepare her for burial. No one yet suspected that the most feared virus known to humankind, identified only in 1976 next to the Ebola River in Congo, had just resurfaced, appearing for the first time in a densely populated area.

THE COLD CHILL of fall descended over the prairies as Lloyd Axworthy announced on September 20, the final day of the conference, that a deal to release the children inside the LRA had been reached. He explained that intense meetings had taken place, international pressure had been put on Sudan, and Canada had seen to it that the captive children would soon be rescued. The "Winnipeg Communiqué—Joint Communiqué on Immediate Action on Abducted Children" was signed by government representatives of Sudan, Uganda, Canada, and Egypt.

The communiqué stated that the case of the LRA children was "one of the most condemnable examples of the suffering of children in war and that the release of these children was an urgent and unconditional humanitarian priority."

A series of statements condemning universally deplored things, including land mines and trafficking arms, was included. The most important were these two sentences:

> The Government of Sudan, for its part, will take all measures to ensure the release and safe return of these abducted children.

> The Government of Uganda, for its part, will take all measures to engage in dialogue with the LRA which will allow for the amnesty, reconciliation and rehabilitation, including return and resettlement of members of the LRA and abducted children.

It was also agreed that the governments of Canada, Egypt, and Libya would meet regularly in Khartoum and Kampala in the following three months to ensure that all was going according to plan. By January, the children should be free.

The exciting news was announced in front of reporters. "As we said all along, it was important to have the ministers here, to meet face-to-face," said Axworthy. Canada, he added, would cover the cost of returning the children to their families.

Mustafa Ismail stepped up to the microphone. As he spoke, a handful of the Sudanese-Canadian demonstrators beat drums outside in continued protest. "Sudan is committed to put all efforts in order to relocate and rehabilitate these children. We have been trying several times," he declared. Ismail went on to say that he was glad Canada had been added to the peace process already underway, in part because it may help refute the incorrect notion that Sudan was the problem.

Olara Otunnu, the UN undersecretary for Children in Conflict who had earlier in the conference met with Angelina Atyam, watched from the sidelines. He was glad that Axworthy had taken up the cause, but he didn't believe anything would come of this latest effort. In his opinion, that wouldn't happen until the world turned on Museveni. Otunnu, who'd been shortlisted as secretary-general of the United Nations only to have his nomination actively undermined by Museveni speaking out against him, was increasingly convinced that Museveni was one of the most diabolical leaders in the world today.

The day after the conference ended, a front-page headline of *The Globe and Mail* announced: "CHILDREN OF WAR RESCUED BY CANADA."

CHAPTER 22

ATLANTA, GEORGIA, LATE SEPTEMBER 2000

"President Carter, I think we're being jerked around." Hoffman stood in his boss's office at the Carter Center. "Blocks are being put up at every step in the way."

Hoffman had prepared a meeting between Kony and the Acholi elders, as requested, to be held in Juba, but the plan fell apart at the last minute when Museveni refused to allow Kony's parents to be part of the delegation. It didn't make sense, and seemed to point in one direction: that it was Museveni who didn't actually want peace talks. After that mix-up, Kony had ignored Hoffman's subsequent requests to meet.

"Perhaps we should withdraw until all the parties are serious," Carter said.

Hoffman wasn't yet prepared for that; he wanted to keep working through the hurdles. Next item on the agenda: Hoffman told Carter about the meetings in Winnipeg, the resulting announcement, and that another meeting among the foreign affairs ministers of Uganda, Sudan, Egypt, and Libya had been scheduled in Kampala for early October to discuss the agreement.

Hoffman told Carter that he smelled a dangerous political game brewing. Suddenly politically motivated, wanting to help end the kidnapping of children because it would give Canada, and Axworthy, some good PR in the world, Canada was coming on board. Hoffman didn't mind the help, but he worried that Axworthy might be inadvertently undermining the Carter Center's own attempts to broker a deal.

"It's like a rerun of the Nairobi Agreement," he told Carter. He went on to say that he'd send a representative to monitor the October meeting.

AFTER THAT MEETING took place, an intern at the Carter Center handed Hoffman an Associated Press news story whose headline read: "KONY TO BE RELOCATED 1000 KILOMETRES NORTH OF THE UGANDAN BORDER." The location proposed was Darfur, a desert land in western Sudan. Hoffman nearly fell off his chair. It was preposterous. Kony hadn't surrendered, and since his ultimate aim was either to topple Kampala or to take control of all of Northern Uganda, relocation even farther from Uganda was nonsensical. Kony would never agree to such a thing. Hoffman called his assistant, who told them that this plan had been discussed at the meeting. Someone in attendance must have leaked the story.

Hoffman felt sick. From what he knew, this was the kind of statement that would incite Kony into yet another brutal rampage. Hoffman tried to talk with the political players involved, but everyone was quite serious about this new plan. Hoffman felt that an insane chaos had just set in.

Nonetheless, the plans moved ahead. Further meetings established that the Egyptians would pay for the tents, the Libyans were offering money for other supplies, Canada would help with the costs for the children, and there'd be lots of work for UNICEF when they began relocating the children back to Uganda. The top priority was the Aboke Girls. The more complicated parts of the peace process—namely, that war still raged—were being ignored.

LIFE HAD BEEN QUIET in Northern Uganda for many months. There had been no abductions and the LRA had stayed away, holing up in Sudan, and so the people had relaxed a bit. They'd taken to driving down the roads again, believing themselves safe from ambush.

But now Joseph Kony, learning of Sudan's plans to relocate him, without permission, to Darfur, was indeed furious. Believing that Sudan was betraying him, Kony ordered his soldiers to abandon camp in Nisitu, where they would have been vulnerable to a Sudanese government attack.

Kony's group, Command Altar, moved into the no man's land of the hills along the Uganda–Sudan border. He sent a squadron of his soldiers into Northern Uganda to abduct children and therefore punish the Acholi for their perceived role in assisting Museveni.

That night the LRA went to Alokolum village, next to St. Mary's Lacor Hospital, where they abducted twenty children and killed nine adults. The following night thousands of frightened and vulnerable villagers descended on the hospital grounds to sleep within the protection of its surrounding wall. None of them knew that the world's most deadly disease awaited them there.

ATTEMPTING TO REGAIN control over negotiations, Hoffman set up a meeting in Khartoum in early October for everyone involved, which now included Canada, Libya, Egypt, Sudan, Uganda, Save the Children, the UN's International Organization for Migration, and UNICEF representatives. But the Ugandans missed the first round of meetings, and Hoffman could tell that the newcomers to the table were suddenly wondering if the Carter Center was the best candidate to be leading these peace talks. He could hear the innuendos: *Maybe the Egyptians should take over.…*

Hoffman knew what was happening. The conflict-mediation community had a term for it: "duelling mediators," or "table hopping." It was a tactic designed to undermine negotiations—if you don't like what's happening at one table, try another one. It was also a stall tactic.

So Hoffman called a meeting with all the newcomers. He began by addressing the innuendos, and everyone assured him they were comfortable with the Carter Center leading the way. With that item settled, he went on to assert that although Uganda had narrowed the meetings' agenda to two imperatives—relocating the LRA and getting the Aboke Girls back—there was a lot more that needed to be discussed, such as an exchange of diplomats between the two countries, talking with the LRA to secure their approval, and getting the rest of the children released. "Does anyone here disagree?" No one did.

When the Ugandan delegation finally showed up at midnight, Hoffman sat down with their leader, Busho Ndinyenka, and told him they were planning to have full talks the next day. Ndinyenka's nostrils flared in rage as he stared at Hoffman. To Ndinyenka, the only thing open for discussion was relocating the LRA and getting the Aboke Girls returned.

"It's just not on," Hoffman said, adding that they needed to talk about bringing Kony to the negotiating table. Ndinyenka fumed and asked him why he didn't get it. Hoffman felt that Ndinyenka wanted him to buckle under the pressure of Ugandan power. "What?" Hoffman asked.

"We have been telling you in so many ways! No, we don't want a dialogue with Joseph Kony."

The words hit hard. "I guess I've been stupid. And I'm sorry if I've insulted you," Hoffman replied. He thought out his next words carefully. "But I was under the impression that your government had asked me to meet with Joseph Kony, which I did at great personal risk, and they wished to talk to him, which I got him to agree to. And everyone would prefer a peaceful resolution ultimately. Am I wrong?"

Ndinyenka said he'd see him in the morning.

Hoffman couldn't make sense of why the next day's meetings focused on the logistics of the new LRA camp in Northern Sudan and of returning the Aboke Girls while flagrantly ignoring the reality of the continuing war. He listened with perplexity as the politicians in the room even expanded the plan to include disarming the LRA before they were relocated.

It was all quite earnest and serious. But in the corridors during breaks, those who weren't politicians playing a game mumbled disapprovingly among themselves. *How is Kony going to react to this? Are we not aggravating the LRA?* Without a massive military offensive to essentially destroy his forces, Joseph Kony and his army would not be getting on a plane to relocate a thousand miles away from Uganda.

But as the day passed, the meetings went surprisingly well. The Sudanese revealed more intelligence on the LRA than ever before: where they were, how many were sick, what arms they had, how many were old, how many were young.

A plan was sketched out: the government of Sudan would establish the location of the new LRA camp, likely in Darfur. Next, everyone would help identify resources required for the new camp. Funding issues for the camp would be referred for immediate attention to a finance working group. Both Egypt and Libya were offering money. The job of relocating and disarming the LRA went to the government of Sudan. And finally, the LRA would ultimately be disbanded. "It was noted that disbanding the LRA contained many complex elements. The Carter Center will convene the relevant parties at the earliest opportunity to hold such discussions," read the minutes with understatement.

Meanwhile, Ndinyenka was allowing Hoffman to insert into the discussion items that Sudan wanted. A second committee worked on the details for creating an SPLA observation team that would guarantee to the government of Sudan that Uganda was not secretly supplying the SPLA.

Finally, every organization and country wanted to be a part of the team involved in the release and return of the Aboke Girls.

Sudan agreed to obtain the early release of the girls—within the week—and the remaining abductees would follow. Their identities would then be verified by Sister Rachele and Angelina Atyam, who were sitting in on the meeting as observers. Libya would provide the air transport for the Aboke Girls and the others. The mood in the room was becoming jovial.

Suddenly, Yahai Babiquer, the Sudanese deputy minister for internal security, stood up and announced that he would personally meet with Kony and ask for the Aboke Girls. At this news, Angelina and Sister Rachele jumped up from their seats and shouted their approval. In three days it would be the fourth anniversary since Angelina lost her daughter to the LRA.

Babiquer said he couldn't guarantee anything, but that he'd make his best efforts.

"You can do it!" the women shouted. And Hoffman knew that, indeed, if anyone could do it, Babiquer could.

When the meeting adjourned a group of Sudanese officials, mysteriously in tandem with the Libyans, whisked off to the airport to head to Juba to meet Joseph Kony at an undisclosed location in the bush.

Aha! thought Hoffman. The veil was lifting. These meetings had been a smokescreen between the Libyans and Sudanese, with the rest blindly following along. Pawns in the game of war. Now, Hoffman figured, Colonel Muammar Gaddafi, Libya's president, was about to secure the release of the Aboke Girls by offering Joseph Kony a ransom payment.

PART 4

GEMO, THE EVIL SPIRIT, VISITS

CHAPTER 23

UGANDA, OCTOBER 9, 2000

St. Mary's Lacor Hospital was now seeing an upsurge in communicable disease. Malaria was also thriving, especially in the children. The children, without fat reserves, were also the first to suffer the effects of insufficient food in the family. Children under six, and women, made up 80 percent of all admissions. Meanwhile, AIDS was also, once again, on the increase.

Uganda had been ground zero for the spread of AIDS across the globe. International scientists would eventually track the world spread of AIDS to the villages along the shores of Lake Victoria in Southern Uganda—villages that had been built atop the remains of the Buganda kingdom's royal court where the martyred Christian pageboys had lived. By 1990 Uganda had the highest AIDS rate in the world, with 30 percent of its adults infected. Since then, aggressive prevention and education campaigns had reversed the epidemic, and now less than 8 percent were HIV positive, although infection rates in the displaced persons' camps of Northern Uganda were climbing again.

The Lacor Hospital staff had tried to conduct outreach programs, offering AIDS education and explaining the need for behaviour changes, but the war was taking such a toll on everyone's psyche. People were crowded in camps, and teenage girls often stayed together with military men who offered food, money, and drink in exchange for sex. The children saw the immoral activities of their neighbours, and parents found it hard to stop them from following suit. And with the roads lined with land mines, and ambushes a nightly occurrence, the staff could offer outreach education only on a haphazard basis. They'd go into a community, teach the people, and for two months the people's behaviour would improve. Then the depressed, hopeless people, knowing death was coming anyway, returned to high-risk behaviours.

Matthew Lukwiya, Lacor Hospital's head doctor, pulled away from his textbook and answered the telephone at his temporary home in Kampala. He was completing a master's degree in health administration at Makarere University as part of Dr. Piero Corti's plan to soon retire and leave the hospital in his hands. Lukwiya was a brilliant doctor, an Acholi from Kitgum who through a string of scholarships had gone from a child born in a mud hut to graduating as the top student of tropical pediatrics at the school of tropical medicine in Liverpool. His name was known across Northern Uganda as the brightest Acholi still living in the North. He was an inspiration to all the younger Ugandan doctors and nurses at the hospital.

The vast majority of newly qualified Ugandan doctors left their impoverished country for the relative wealth of South Africa or farther abroad. But Dr. Matthew's home was with his suffering people, and his home was the Comboni missionary hospital, St. Mary's Lacor, outside Gulu. It didn't matter to him that he was devoutly Protestant and about to head up a Catholic facility.[78]

"There seems to be a strange disease killing our student nurses," Dr. Opira now said on the phone to Dr. Matthew. "It is very strange, I don't know what to do." Neither stool cultures nor blood samples gave answers. He explained that the last student nurse began bleeding from the mouth just as she died. Dr. Corti was away visiting family in Italy, and Dr. Opira needed help now. Dr. Matthew flew to Gulu that day.

THAT NIGHT, a small group of rebels crossed into Gulu district. Unaware that the LRA were close by, a few hundred young people in Gulu had decided they deserved a little fun. The next day was Uganda's Independence Day. It was a night to celebrate, so a crowd descended into the Opit Travellers Inn, whose hall had been converted into a dance club.

At 11 P.M. the rebels walked into the village at Customs Corner and killed four people as they continued their march toward Gulu. At midnight, three rebels cut through a fence and skulked around the outside of the inn as African rock music boomed out from the hall.

The rebels hurled two grenades into the crowded dance floor as another rebel standing at the hall entrance shot a volley of bullets from his AK-47 into the crowd, killing four on the dance floor and effectively preventing the others from fleeing the building before the bombs exploded into the screaming crowd.

Gulu Radio announced that the rebels had left leaflets saying they would kill two hundred people a month in Gulu as punishment for the Acholi people's failure to support the LRA.

The next evening, more than nine thousand frightened children and parents from the surrounding villages crammed inside the walled grounds of Lacor Hospital. At 9 P.M. the gates to the compound were closed and locked shut.

WHILE DOCTORS continued removing shrapnel and stitched wounds, in another wing of the hospital Dr. Matthew frowned while looking at blood samples in a research lab. The disease was odd, spreading quickly, and highly lethal. By his count, at least eighteen patients in his hospital were suffering from it and twelve had already died. He took to the internet, which he accessed with a satellite connection, and began reading medical diagnoses for Ebola. He'd hoped it was just viral fever, but it was killing too quickly.

Dr. Matthew called the Ugandan Ministry of Health in Kampala and reported his beliefs. The world had been free of Ebola for over four years, since the last outbreak in Congo in 1995. If he was right, that it was Ebola, it would be the first time the virus had hit a densely populated area. The world's most feared disease—quickly fatal, highly contagious, and without a cure—had never struck Uganda before.

Outside the hospital, the war-frightened villagers slept on the ground, crammed in head to toe. The nearby camps were packed with people and water was communal. And given the local custom of cleaning the dead before burial, the entire population of Northern Uganda could be wiped out within weeks. The disease could easily creep into Kenya, through Sudan, and it would take just one infected person to get on a plane to spread the disease around the world.

Dr. Matthew spent the night reading a manual he'd downloaded from the internet: "Infection Control for Viral Hemorrhagic Fevers in the African Health Care Setting."

At 7 A.M. the crowd outside was dispersing, returning to their homes for the day. At 7:30 the day staff of nurses had all arrived on duty. Over the PA system Dr. Matthew called an immediate emergency meeting. The nursing staff, orderlies, and doctors all gathered together.

Dr. Matthew headed to the front of the crowd. There was no fear in his voice when he told the group that Ebola was in their hospital. He now had no doubt. "Some of you are almost certainly already infected," he said. He told the hospital staff that they must not leave the compound. "If you leave you'll take the virus with you into the community."

He laid out to the frightened audience the plan adopted by the World Health Organization after the virus had struck in Congo. They needed to enact a rigid system of barrier nursing, preventing any contact between suspected cases and hospital workers. During the previous outbreak in a remote, sparsely populated area of Congo, sixty-three health-care workers had died, almost two-thirds of all the victims.

Dr. Opira was sick with fear. "I think, doctor, we're going to die on duty," he whispered later to Dr. Matthew.

"We won't die," Dr. Matthew said. "We just need to be careful. We can't make mistakes."

After the meeting, he and his staff started setting up a barrier-nursing environment using whatever resources were on hand. They built hands-free boot removers from scrap wood and constructed an incinerator out of a 55-gallon oil drum. They fashioned aprons from duct tape and plastic sheeting and converted a hospital pavilion into an isolation ward. Then, from behind these crude protective layers, they began nursing Ebola patients.

The doors and windows of Lacor Hospital were quickly wrapped in white plastic sheeting. At the door, a hand-painted sign warned: NO

ENTRANCE WITHOUT PERMISSION. The sign was illustrated by a stick man with an X drawn over it.

That night, the hospital caretakers closed the gates before the night commuters arrived. From now on, the people would need to find other places for safe sleeping.

The night-commuting refugees moved on. For most it meant another ten-kilometre nightly walk into Gulu. Others quietly moved into the bushes, bringing nothing with them that might alert rebels to their hiding places. But now they also feared one another. Word of the deadly disease spread through the community, but was not yet international news. They understood that a plague-like disease transmitted by a simple touch, or a shared airborne particle, had now also invaded them.

Shortly after sunset, the Red Cross CB radio crackled in Gulu: "There's gunfire on the road near the Lacor Hospital." North of Gulu, a Ugandan military soldier in an armoured truck had broken out in a fever and was vomiting red inside the vehicle. The other soldiers had run away. "Can you send an isolation ambulance?" the commander pleaded to the Red Cross.[79]

KENNETH BANYA was amazed when he heard the news about Ebola: he remembered listening to Kony's "spirit" telling them years earlier that another disease, not just AIDS, would come to Acholiland. Kony's spirit had called the disease "don't touch me," and explained that it would cause people to explode in blood and die within hours.

Banya truly believed that Kony was in touch with the spirit world; Kony's prophecies had come true so many times. However much Banya questioned some of their more horrific and bizarre acts, he knew that Kony understood more than he ever could. In fact, just weeks earlier Kony had forced Banya to return to the Libyans the $5 million ransom they'd offered for the release of the Aboke Girls. Kony's spirits had revealed that the money was laced with poison.

Banya became careful not to touch anyone in the camp, especially the soldiers who'd recently returned from Uganda. He warned all his wives to do the same. He was particularly concerned about his Aboke Girl wife, Grace Acan. She had just given birth to their first son together, and Banya loved the little boy.

Kony's own attention was soon transfixed by the news of Ebola he was hearing on Gulu radio. He called a doctor he knew in Juba for instructions, then contacted his field commanders stationed outside Gulu and ordered that all new recruits taken from Gulu and surrounding area be let go and left unharmed. Everyone else was ordered to return immediately to Sudan and forbidden from touching one another in case the disease had penetrated them.

For the next weeks the rebels holed up inside the LRA camps in Sudan, waiting. They kept themselves busy with gardening and harvesting in the fields around their camps. No one in South Sudan was fighting.

In fact, while Ebola raged in Northern Uganda, life in the LRA camps was rather peaceful. Some of the Aboke Girls were allowed to watch old cowboy movies from a television run off a generator in the camp.

St. Mary's Lacor Hospital, November 20, 2000

Inside the Ebola ward a hulking male nurse, Simon, started to hemorrhage from his lungs. His eyes flooded red and blood drained out his nose and gums. Struggling to breathe, he sat up in bed and pulled off his oxygen mask. He coughed violently and bright-red blood and mucus sprayed on the opposite wall.

Disoriented, he mumbled angrily to himself as he ripped off his catheter, climbed out of bed, and lumbered from his private room into the hallway, his intravenous dragging along behind him. The terrified nursing staff and other patients ran from him.

Another male nurse on night duty pleaded with Simon to return to his room, but he stood in the hallway, blood dripping down his gown onto the floor and growling in frustration. "Please, Simon!" the nurse shouted again as everyone ran farther back, but Simon ignored them.

Not knowing what to do, the nurse ran to Dr. Matthew's quarters at 5 A.M. on that November 20th morning and woke him. "Blood is pouring from Simon's eyes and nose like tap water. He is confused, fighting death. He seems violent," he said. Dr. Matthew jumped out of bed, ran up the dirt path then down the corridors of the hospital, and entered the isolation unit. Within five minutes he'd stepped into his protective boots and gown, pulled on his apron, gloves, mask, and head cap, and run into the Ebola ward, forgetting his eye goggles. Simon had stumbled back onto his bed and was heaving for air. As a small consolation for having put his life on the line, Simon, like the other nurses who'd contracted Ebola, had been given a private room.

Dr. Matthew lifted Simon into a sitting position to open his airway. Then he cleaned him up, removing his blood-soiled gown and changing his soaked bed linen. As Dr. Matthew mopped the floor around him with bleach, Simon died.

A few minutes later Dr. Matthew removed his gear, washed his hands with bleach, and walked back to his home for breakfast before returning to start another fourteen-hour day.

The nurses were terrified for their lives, but still they worked, and still more died. Dr. Matthew couldn't understand why. They were doing everything right. And yet, between November 23 and 24 seven people died, including three nurses. Two of the dead nurses had never even worked on the Ebola ward.

A FEW DAYS LATER, on Dr. Matthew's birthday, his wife and children called from Kampala and sang "Happy Birthday" to him. Feeling exhausted, he told them he couldn't talk. He fell into a deep sleep and woke in the morning with a sore throat. The next day he tested positive for Ebola.

The most senior hospital staff teamed up with World Health Organization Ebola specialists to save Dr. Matthew's life. The death rate among Ebola patients was 50 percent, but they'd gotten to him early and had kept his body hydrated, a factor affecting Ebola survival. Still, despite the attentive care, his high fever remained and his breathing was increasingly laborious. Fearing the damage Ebola was causing to his organs, the staff opted for an aggressive, experimental therapy, and artificially ventilated him.

His fever diminished and a chest X-ray showed improvement. The hospital announced to the media that Dr. Matthew's condition had improved.

But then, on December 5, his lungs began to bleed. He was put on an oxygen supply machine, but it was not to be. On that final night, when it was clear that Dr. Matthew was beginning to hemorrhage, marking the last stage of Ebola, the entire staff on duty gathered in prayer. An Italian Comboni Brother who worked at the hospital kept saying "We are all orphans." Then Dr. Matthew's lungs exploded, blooded poured out his mouth, and at 1:20 A.M. he died. His infectious body was doused in bleach and wrapped in plastic.

The next morning he was laid in a casket. Gravediggers in full protective gear lowered him with ropes into a grave within the hospital compound, while another man in protective gear sprayed bleach on the casket to keep the infection from spreading. Four metres from the grave a line was drawn over which no one was allowed to pass. Although burials were strictly curtailed, hundreds had gathered. Bishop Ochola, leading the service, compared Dr. Matthew to Gandhi.

With morale low, the grieving health-care workers returned to their posts. Some thought the hospital would soon close and that they'd all run for their lives as the plague took over to kill off everyone. Others simply assumed that their own deaths were imminent. Some called it the Apocalypse.

Instead, the health workers already suffering from Ebola began recovering, and the rate of new cases diminished. Dr. Matthew was the last health-care worker to die.

But as the disease lingered, it would take another six months before the international community would again risk their health by entering Northern Uganda. By that time the peace deliberations and ongoing negotiations resulting from the Winnipeg conference had lost their momentum. And when January came and went, and still the children hadn't been brought home by the Winnipeg-imposed deadline, no one in Canada seemed to notice. The world's press told only the story of Ebola in Northern Uganda, and nothing of the stolen children. The local community was on their own.

THREE WEEKS AFTER Dr. Matthew's death, the Acholi religious leaders delivered a New Year's message to the people of Northern Uganda. In small and large churches across the North, in makeshift services within the displaced persons' camps, in the Gulu Cathedral, in the mosques— almost everyone gathered for prayer and worship. Those who still had decent clothing wore their best, and the children had been washed. In the crowded camps most were barefoot. Mothers held babies, children held babies, and all gathered to listen to a single interfaith message written by Bishop Ochola, Sheikh Musa Khalil of Gulu, and Archbishop Odama and sent down through their networks.

"Dear people of God, our brothers and sisters. Praise be to our merciful God, who is always with us in our trials. We greet all of you, who have just celebrated the religious feasts of Christmas and Idd El-Fitr."[80] The religious leaders spoke about the difficult situation and told the people not to fear, that God was with them. They offered words of hope, and then turned political.

They began by denouncing those profiting from the war, calling on them to repent their grave sins. They said the guilty knew who they were, and proclaimed that forgiveness was the only way out of the war. The people had suffered too much in the displaced persons' camps and should be helped to return to their homes. They appealed for the LRA to release the children, for the international community to intervene, for children to be rehabilitated and not recruited into local defence units. They wanted Uganda to withdraw all its troops from the Democratic Republic of Congo and to end the distribution of guns to civilians in dispute with neighbours. They encouraged religious leaders to be united among themselves.

Then they asked the LRA to cooperate with the Acholi people in finding peace: "Trust the goodwill of the local population, who are ready to forgive the evil of the past and accept you back." In the end, the Acholi leaders greeted their populace in the name of God and assured them of their solidarity with them all.

One day later it was New Year's Eve. John Bosco celebrated with his mother in her tiny home. Grace Grall was at her father's home in Lira, cooking food for her younger half-brothers. Grace Acan and the rest of the Aboke Girls sat beside hearth fires in their prison camps inside the LRA, cuddling their newborn children. Angelina Atyam and Consy Ogwal and the other parents at the Concerned Parents Association spent the night praying to Jesus inside the Lira Cathedral.

CHAPTER 24

Years of trying to find the LRA had proved a dead end. The Acholi religious leaders' original plan was for Sudan to put them in touch with Kony and for the United Nations to encourage the Ugandan government to enter talks. The hope was that before long everyone would be at the table negotiating peace. But instead the religious leaders found themselves detoured and deceived at every turn. The Sudanese government offered encouraging words and no action. The group claiming to be the political spokespeople for the LRA, based in Nairobi and London, proved to be con men unaffiliated with the LRA. The LRA itself remained a shadow mystery group.

Finally, their inquiries led them to an old Italian priest working north of Kitgum. Father Tarcisio Pazzagli, barrel-chested with a full beard and grey hair, looked more like a tough old fisherman than a priest. Like Father John, he had lived in Northern Uganda for forty years, in the same area where the LRA had first surfaced. In fact, Father Tarcisio had baptized many of the LRA boys at birth. They'd grown up attending his masses every Sunday, and he'd watched their young faces turn to glee when he offered sweets. Later, he consoled their parents when they were abducted. And on a few occasions he had spoken to the boys when they returned to the community to attack it as rebels.

Although he risked being imprisoned as a rebel collaborator if the government found out—since Museveni had made it illegal to communicate or meet with rebels—Father Tarcisio had quietly talked to families that had lost boys to the LRA. He believed that some of these families, perhaps rebel sympathizers, must have ongoing contact with those within its ranks. Finally, in the small village of Pajule, about seventy kilometres south of the Sudan border, he'd found a brave young man, Dominique, who was willing to admit to the priest that he was in contact with the LRA. (For Dominique's safety his particulars remain a secret, but it appeared that he had brothers inside the LRA's higher ranks.)

Father Tarcisio wrote letters to his former parish boys who were now LRA commanders and Dominique quietly delivered them. Before long these letters prompted a response, and in April 2001 Father Tarcisio stepped into the dreaded bush of LRA territory and met with a top commander who'd brought along some of his junior commanders. The old priest encouraged them to take the amnesty offer that Museveni had put on the table the year before and that now included commanders. The commander responded that he was tired of war but didn't trust that the Ugandan military wouldn't simply kill them all as they attempted to surrender. He asked for a demilitarized safe zone so that he could gather his men, who were spread out across the bushland, and surrender together, with witnesses.

Father Tarcisio and other Acholi elders later met with the Ugandan military to inform them that the LRA platoon was willing to surrender in a ceasefire zone. The military commander was skeptical of their motives, however, and refused: the rebels had to either come out or face attack.

Joseph Oywak, the area's district chairman and one of its few remaining respected cultural leaders, offered to enter the bush to assure the rebels that the amnesty offer was real. The military approved, its commander giving his word that those at the meeting wouldn't be attacked: "You're free to go and try to convince them to come," he said.

Father Tarcisio and Joseph Oywak ventured into the bush for the second time to meet the rebels. But as they approached the designated location bombs and gunfire erupted from the bushes: they had been ambushed by the Ugandan military. Joseph Oywak was shot in the leg and Father Tarcisio narrowly escaped with his life.[81] None of the rebels were caught, and the LRA's and military's mutual distrust grew.

For several months after this incident there was no further contact with the rebels, but one day in the late summer of 2001 Father Carlos Rodriguez, who was now working closely with Father Tarcisio to locate the LRA, received a hand-delivered message that a group of rebels under a top LRA leader wanted to talk to the priests.

When Father Carlos arrived at the remote homestead he found a group of ten children, including two girls. They were posturing, acting tough, carrying guns, and claiming that their friends were in the bush watching. But Father Carlos sensed their fear and understood that they'd escaped from their commander the day earlier. He told them about the amnesty offer, and then asked how he could help.

"We want to meet our parents, to be sure we'll be accepted," a boy said.

After five hours of reassurances the children gave Father Carlos their guns. He drove them to the Pajule Mission, gave them food and beds, then went looking for their parents. He even brought in the local media to highlight the successful reunion. The parents were overjoyed. They hugged their children, crying and laughing and then crying again. Dozens from the community gathered around and watched with curiosity and a little fear.

Those first contacts encouraged the religious leaders, and, more significantly, broke the myth that one couldn't talk to the LRA.

BUT THEN ON September 11, 2001, everything changed forever. By December 2001, as the war on terror was underway, the U.S. State Department published a list of the world's terrorist organizations. The Lord's Resistance Army was on it, effectively putting an end to negotiations with Joseph Kony. As George W. Bush had said, you were either on the side of the terrorist or you were on the side of freedom. Museveni said the same of the LRA, adding that, like the U.S., he would not negotiate with terrorists. The fact that almost all the rebels were abducted children was overlooked. Plans to eradicate the LRA began in earnest.

The world political climate had rapidly changed in the months after the September 11 attacks. Suddenly, Sudan feared that it might be invaded by the United States. Acting quickly to prove their alliance with

Bush in his war on terror, the Sudanese government ended all residual support for the LRA and joined Uganda in devising plans to attack the LRA terror machine.

Old enemies Uganda and Sudan now strategized together. Their military planners considered surgical strikes to capture Kony but rejected them as unworkable. By early 2002 they came up with Operation Iron Fist, giving the Ugandan military unprecedented legal authority to cross into South Sudan up to the so-called red line, the Juba-Torit highway a hundred kilometres into the country.

The Sudanese government would not participate in the operation, however; nor would they allow a military collaboration between the Ugandan military and the South Sudan rebels, fearing that Uganda might use the collaboration to resupply and otherwise assist John Garang's SPLA rebels. By now, with Sudan having received hundreds of millions of dollars in oil revenue to strengthen its military, Khartoum had reached a stalemate with the SPLA, with each holding their own territory but neither making advances.

THE ACHOLI religious leaders wrote about the state of the world after the terrorist attacks of 9/11. "One of the lessons we have learnt from those tragic events, and also from our own tragic experience in Northern Uganda, is that our future does not lie on the quality of our weapons, but on the quality of our relationships with others," they said in a quote read out at churches and mosques on New Year's Eve 2001, also a World Day of Peace.[82] Days after September 11 the religious leaders had also written to Uganda's American ambassador urging him to show "restraint and wisdom at this hour in which the future of the whole world is at stake."[83]

The religious leaders nonetheless felt that peace would soon arrive in their country, given that, with the LRA remaining in Sudan, the year had thus far been relatively nonviolent. Only a hundred children had been reported abducted from all of Northern Uganda. The people of Acholiland had returned to farming and to scavenging in the bush for firewood, and the numbers in the displaced persons' camps had declined to under 500,000. The people even talked about when the camps would be disbanded.

But that relative peace was not to last. It was a few weeks into the New Year when the Acholi religious leaders noticed a huge military buildup in the Northern Ugandan countryside. It was clear that a military offensive was in the making.

CHAPTER 25

KONY'S CAMP, FEBRUARY 2002

Joseph Kony called his commanders together and told them that the spirit was warning of an imminent attack. He ordered everyone to pack up. The Aboke Girls working in the sick bay quickly bundled up the medical supplies while others gathered their clothes, cooking supplies, and food.

One month later, ten thousand Ugandan soldiers stormed into Kony's camp. They found it abandoned. They moved to the next LRA camp, finding that it too was empty. The Ugandans followed the LRA's trail east into the barren, rock-faced Imatong Mountains bordering Uganda. These were Sudan's highest mountains, with steep peaks rising more than ten thousand feet in the air.

The Aboke Girls walked along quickly, watched always by guards, as together they marched toward eastern LRA hideouts along the South Sudan–Kitgum border. The rebel boys moved ahead, obediently burning down villages, looting for food, and raping and killing South Sudanese villagers along the way. As the LRA militia advanced the Dinka civilians ran for their lives. Some ran ahead to warn their kinfolk, delivering messages from the LRA demanding that everyone be gone before their arrival. After that the LRA marched onward to find villages abandoned, which had been the plan all along. It meant that no spies would remain to report LRA positions.

But as the LRA marched, Ugandan helicopter gunships followed, blasting away. The rebels scattered through the mountains. Kony periodically called Kenneth Banya on his satellite phone to ask for advice, but before they could figure out a plan they'd be shelled from the skies again. So they kept running, little pockets of rebels moving through the mountains, carrying their wounded and their dwindling supplies of ammunition, food, and medicine.

Now desperate and confused, the LRA made no distinctions as they attacked, raiding villages aligned to Khartoum and to Garang's South Sudan rebels alike. They stole weapons, ammunition, and food, and killed everyone who got in their way.

Following along with the rebels, the Aboke Girls, along with two thousand other young mothers and children, climbed up into the remote Imatong Mountains. Behind them the rearguard kept an eye out for the Ugandan gunships and the SPLA.

Grace Acan had a babysitter assigned to help her carry her two children—General Banya's children. Palma had two children by General Tolbert, who was now the overall army commander. Jackie was heavily pregnant with Kony's child and was surrounded by guards.

Agatha Longoria, the Aboke Girl from the Karamojong tribe who had been raped on that first day, was carrying her two children, the one-year-old girl on her back, the infant boy in her arms, and was further loaded down with luggage and saucepans both on her back and head. She was now on her third husband, a particularly brutal man. He was an African Muslim from Darfur who'd told her that he had willingly joined the LRA rebels because they provided him with a livelihood and wives. He told her he liked to kill and pillage. He was miles ahead now, leading the way with Vincent Otti.

Back in 1996, Agatha's initial luck in being given to a kind man who never touched her had run out quickly. He died in battle in the first weeks of their marriage. General Tolbert then assigned her to a new husband, a lower-ranking man, but a month later he was sent away to fight, whereupon he too died. Her third husband was never kind to her. He was the father of both her children.

Alfred Olum's daughter, Louiza, and Florence Lacor's daughter, Angela, both carried the children of other mothers. Louiza and Angela had been co-wives to a top commander who had died of AIDS in 1999, as had several of his other wives. They never had children with him. But because he died of AIDS, these two Aboke Girls were no longer considered marriageable. They served as slaves to other commanders and wives, leading, in many ways, harder lives than the girls who had husbands.

Agatha and the others now climbed the steep, rocky hills of the land that bordered Uganda, keeping up a fast pace to ensure they stayed ahead of the advancing Ugandan army. They followed treacherous routes, knowing this would slow their pursuers. Sometimes rebels lost their balance and slipped, falling hundreds of metres to their deaths. They were all nervous, climbing and descending in silence, carefully placing their callus-hardened bare feet along the rock ledges while loaded down with supplies.

As Agatha climbed, she could tell that her one-year-old girl had too much pressure against her from the saucepans also strapped to her back. She wrestled with the pots and pans, trying to keep their weight off her little girl, but they kept falling back against the child.

Finally, they stopped for lunch. Agatha untied her little girl and saw that her child's arms and legs were swollen from lack of circulation. The baby girl was quiet and unresponsive. Agatha cooked some porridge for her, and the girl did eat, but minutes later her little body heaved its last breath.

Agatha buried her daughter under a tree and offered a swift prayer. Then she strapped her luggage back on, picked up the boy, and moved on. Her heart ached, but the commander was motioning for the group to head onward, and she had no choice.

EVENTUALLY, the LRA was able to lose the Ugandan military that trailed them. Not only did the LRA know the terrain, but also the underpaid Ugandan soldiers were suffering from low morale. Many had come directly from deployment in the dubious war inside the neighbouring Democratic Republic of Congo—a war that was in reality a scramble for wealth. President Museveni's family and top generals were using their own military to help them steal the vast natural resources—diamonds, gold, mahogany—of the essentially failed state.

For two months the LRA continued moving through the mountains. They sent contingents in opposite directions, they set decoys for the Ugandan military to track, and finally the men, women, and children of the LRA, led by Commander Vincent Otti, secretly crossed back into Uganda.

Announcing their arrival, the rebels first blew up a Kitgum nightclub filled with dancers. Two days later they reached Gulu. With the Ugandan military still inside Sudan, the town was unprotected and unprepared.

The people panicked. By nightfall, thirty thousand men, women, and children arrived at the gates of St. Mary's Lacor Hospital seeking entrance for the night.

The Ugandan army said it knew what Kony was doing: Vincent Otti was trying to confuse them, to lure them back into Northern Uganda while Kony escaped. But the military declared they would not let up. "Otti and Kony must know we shall get them," said the military spokesman.[84] Whether Kony was actually in Uganda or Sudan remained unknown.

Nonetheless, a few days later the ten thousand–strong Ugandan military returned to Northern Uganda. To evade them, the LRA commanders and their troops spread out into small cells. Each night they raided and abducted children from the defenceless villages and displaced persons' camps. By daytime they'd be gone, back to the secrecy of the bush. The LRA commanders organized their own collaborators, finding civilians—often relatives of abductees or simply those who feared to say no—who gave food, information, and airtime for cellphones. Kony's whereabouts remained a mystery.

As the weeks went by, the hunted LRA realized that it was becoming difficult to move quickly with the pregnant and breastfeeding mothers and children. Kony ordered them all released, and nearly two thousand mothers and children suddenly found themselves free again. But in his orders Kony had cautioned that none of the Aboke Girls, who continued to offer him bargaining power—and he may have still believed his earlier prophecies that they were the future of the human race—be released.

Instead, the Aboke Girls who were now travelling through Uganda (some remained in Sudan with Banya) were brought together to a hidden cave in the Kilak Hills, fifty kilometres outside of Gulu. Here the girls holed up, waiting, cooking, tending their children, and periodically offering a secret nursing base for injured LRA soldiers.

The vulnerable civilians ran for their lives to the safety of the displaced persons' camps. But the LRA didn't want them in the camps; they wanted them to hold their ground in their villages and support the rebellion. So they attacked. After one attack, a local camp councillor found a letter left for him by LRA commander Matata, who had just led a massacre: "Don't stay in the camp. Museveni has put you in the camps to finish you and take over the land in Acholi. We will kill everybody in the camp. There will be nobody left to bury the dead.... We want peace talks. Traditional leaders, religious leaders of local council V, and other elders should be present."[85]

AT ST. MARY'S SCHOOL in Aboke, Sister Alba was worried. Every day she called the Ugandan military intelligence to find out whether there had been any sightings of the LRA within fifty kilometres. She had also secured more guards around the school.

On June 22, 2002, she heard that the LRA were coming for the school. The school administration told the girls to wait for instructions, but instead they ran in panic, dispersing into the fields and behind houses and jumping onto passing trucks to make it to safety. The rebels didn't come, though, and after a few days the school reopened. A month later another warning came. This time Sister Alba hired a truck, and all the girls were driven to Radio Wa in the centre of Lira town. It too turned out to be a false rumour.

Before long, all schools in Gulu and Kitgum closed down. Over the next months thousands of children were captured and indoctrinated into the Lord's Resistance Army.

AS THE WAR continued, and with the death toll climbing into the thousands, Commander Tolbert sent word to his guards to move the Aboke

Girls and children from Kilak Hills. The girls and their captors began walking southward to Murchison Falls National Park. Occupying both sides of the Nile River, the park's vast forest and grasslands, far from human settlement, contained dense populations of lions, elephants, hippos, giraffes, and monkeys.

The girls and their children made camp in the park. They lit huge fires at night to keep the predatory animals at bay, and waited to be collected. Days turned to weeks turned to months.

The Aboke Girls, their children, and their ever-present guards survived by eating fruit and boiling the leaves of wild plants. But those who had been newly abducted, who were without allies, ranking, weapons for hunting, or husbands to give them food, suffered from constant hunger. Unable to help, the Aboke Girls watched while the young ones around them weakened, wasted away, and died.

BACK IN GULU, Lacor Hospital tried hard to cope with the thousands of overnight visitors. Although most people built themselves mud homes inside the displaced persons' camps cropping up around the North, those who lived within ten kilometres of Lacor Hospital chose to walk there each night, confident that it was safer than both the camps and their former homes. Inside the hospital compound, just two years after fighting off Ebola, the number had swelled to thirty thousand people who slept, crammed in together, arms and legs draped over one another as they struggled for ground space. Every morning the hospital staff bleached the ground and its walls, killing the germs left behind from disease and human excrement.

Godfrey Acaye, the hospital's kind-hearted security chief, struggled to keep these masses of people in order. The hospital hired twenty police officers who strolled around the grounds inside, trying to keep the desperate from stealing from the hospital or one another. But Acaye's biggest problem was keeping the children, who would be children, controlled. He assigned the under-sixteens to the back corner of the hospital, within tents provided courtesy of Doctors Without Borders. The youngest slept in the middle. He kept the teenage boys and girls at opposite ends to prevent sexual and rowdy behaviour. Adult men stayed in the hospital's admitting centre, where police watched over them. Mothers and their youngest children, under seven, slept together in the day clinic and chapel. Young women slept under the verandas, where they had greater protection.

But with so many thousands, it was hard to keep everyone safe. Girls were raped, or exchanged their bodies for loaves of bread. Teenage boys were always sneaking over and preying upon the young women. When the boys were caught, the security chief took them aside to counsel them. "This is not why you're here. You're spreading AIDS." If they kept it up he found the boys' parents and shamed them. But in the end, no matter how unruly, no one was ever forbidden from taking shelter at the hospital.

CHAPTER 26

Two kilometres from Lacor Hospital, Catholic Archbishop Jean Baptist Odama hosted Anglican Bishop Macleord Ochola in his home. Odama was sick with worry. He had just visited nearby camps, where he'd seen people fleeing the camps in fear and others running toward the camps in fear. His people didn't know where to go, and the suffering and death was unbearably high.

"We must not keep quiet. We must talk to the president," the Archbishop told Bishop Ochola.

Some Acholi members of Parliament had recently received a secret note from some of the rebels asking for peace talks. Since it would have been unlawful to communicate with the rebels themselves, they'd passed the contact to the Acholi religious leaders.

It was decided. The two good friends, the Catholic Archbishop and the Anglican Bishop, headed off together, driving down to Kampala to Museveni's office.

The religious leaders were desperate to end the assault. Thousands of children were being abducted. Massacres were occurring every night. The entire population of Acholiland was now living in displaced persons' camps. In a matter of months, since Operation Iron Fist had been launched to wipe out Kony, the number of displaced people had climbed from 400,000 to 1.7 million.

The Archbishop told the president that they wanted to make contact with the rebels. "We must talk to you about this, because it's causing a lot of suffering to our people," the Archbishop said. He told Museveni that they had a secret contact. Museveni gave the religious leaders permission to talk to the rebels.

The first meeting, on July 14, brought Archbishop Odama and Bishop Ochola together with three LRA generals—Sam Kolo, Vincent Otti, and Nyeko Tolbert—in the hills outside Gulu. The group sat under a tree and talked. "We're not here to preach at you," the Archbishop said. He wore a long white and red robe with a large cross around his neck. "We just want to listen. Tell us your points and we'll take them to the government."

For seven hours the rebels and religious men talked. The rebel commanders were extremely concerned about their own security, asking if they'd be arrested if they gave themselves up. Although the amnesty offer was on the table for all commanders as well, they didn't believe it. Finally Sam Kolo said, "Go and tell the president: if he's ready to talk with us, we shall talk. If he wants to continue to fight, we shall fight."

The Archbishop and Bishop relayed Kolo's words to Museveni. The president agreed, and gave them twenty-one days to attempt to mediate peace with Kony.

Three days later, Archbishop Odama, Bishop Ochola, and Father Carlos again met with Vincent Otti, Sam Kolo, and Charles Tabuley, who together constituted the LRA's highest command. Kony's whereabouts remained unknown.

Odama began with a prayer, and then he spoke, likening the rebels and the government to two elephants fighting, crushing the grass beneath their feet; the Acholi people were the grass. He appealed to the LRA to reconsider their position: "If the issue is so important and serious, why don't you sit down and talk about it, instead of crushing us?"

A few days later the LRA team gave the religious leaders a letter to be delivered to Museveni, who responded with a long letter denouncing their violent actions but agreeing to engage in talks. He proposed three venues in South Sudan. Two days later Bishop Ochola and Archbishop Odama returned to the bush and delivered the letter. Sam Kolo and Nyeko Tolbert warned that it would take a bit of time to respond, since Kony would need to see it.

Toward the end of the meeting, after the formal discussions were over, Father Carlos said to Commander Tabuley, who sat next to him: "Hey, if you want people to take you seriously, you have to release captives."

Tabuley didn't respond, but a week later he sent a note to Dominique, the religious leaders' secret contact, saying that he and General Raska Lukwiya had released thirty girls and young children. Father Carlos went to the location he named, and sure enough he found the frightened children.

Over the next three weeks the LRA released two hundred more abductees. But for all the goodwill that suggested, Father Carlos had reports that other LRA cells were killing and abducting more civilians. In Mucwini, Kitgum, they massacred sixty-two people, and in Acolipii displaced persons' camp they killed dozens of Sudanese refugees, sending twenty thousand running for their lives.

Finally, after a month of silence, the rebels called the Archbishop's cellphone and said they had a reply. Because the twenty-one days had passed, Archbishop Odama and Bishop Ochola went to the president to ask for permission to collect it; they found him inside the army barracks in Gulu leading his troops in the ongoing Operation Iron Fist offensive. A few hours after Museveni gave his permission they returned with the letter. He read it and scribbled another reply. Five times Bishop Ochola and Archbishop Odama, and now also the Muslim Khadi sheik, went back and forth, delivering the confidential communications between the president and the rebels.

Two days later Museveni went on air at radio Mega FM, a former Ugandan military station that was now sponsored by the British government and whose signal could be heard inside Sudan. Museveni announced that he was ready for a ceasefire and named his negotiating team.

WITH NEGOTIATIONS about to begin, Father Carlos, in a bid to encourage the public mood for peace talks, sent off an article he'd written for *The Monitor* entitled "Army's Victory Against Kony Not in the Gun." In it, he criticized Operation Iron Fist and extolled the virtues of peace talks.

The next day the religious leaders met with General James Kazini— the Northern Ugandan army chief and Museveni's nephew—and other army brass to discuss the proposed peace talks. The army stressed that if talks were to succeed the LRA abductions and ambushes, which were still occurring on a daily basis, had to stop. The problem was that although the Bishop and Archbishop were meeting regularly with the top commanders outside of Gulu, who supported ending the violence, the lower-ranked rebels in the Kitgum and Pader areas, cut off from communication with their higher ranks, continued to abduct and ambush every night.

Meanwhile, Father Tarcisio in Kitgum called Father Carlos and told him that he'd received a letter from one Major Topaco, who headed up this wayward group of ambushing rebels, asking for a dose of syphilis injections. The old Italian priest saw this as a good excuse to meet these rebels and appeal to them to end the attacks, at least temporarily. He'd already asked permission from the military in Kitgum, who'd readily approved the meeting. Father Tarcisio now asked Father Carlos to come with him to the bush, and suggested they bring Father Giulio Albanese, the editor of the Rome-based Missionary News Agency, who happened to be visiting. It was rare to have such a visitor.

Father Carlos and Father Giulio readily agreed. Before the priests left for Kitgum, its regional district commissioner gave them a letter to deliver to the rebels. Joseph Oywak, the Acholi cultural leader, also gave them a letter from the Acholi diaspora in London, written to LRA commander Charles Tabuley and encouraging an end to all acts of violence. Meanwhile, in Kitgum, Father Tarcisio also picked up a letter from the local government official and then briefed two senior military intelligence officers on the details of the rendezvous.

In the rush to get going, none had read that morning's *Monitor*. In it was an angry opinion piece written by Museveni in response to Father Carlos's article. Museveni called him a misleading and erroneous pacifist who was part of the problem, a man who condoned crime, a man without solutions. "What I am trying to put to Fr. Carlos is that … only a capable, legal and legitimate state apparatus can, eventually, bring discipline in a country; not unprincipled appeasement peddled by people like him."[86] Museveni went on to claim it was a lie that his government had failed to defeat Kony. "In fact we have defeated Kony repeatedly! Every time he was defeated, he would flee to the Sudan....

"If we do not strengthen our security and defence capacity what guarantee do we have that a new Kony will not emerge even if we grovel in the dust begging this Kony who has 'only' killed 20,000 people to 'please' not kill more?" the president wrote. "That is not how we should build a country or future. Investments cannot flow to such a country...." He talked about his days fighting in the bush to free Uganda from Idi Amin's butchery; that he had accepted the sacrifice and struggled for justice. It was through such painful but principled actions, he continued, that Uganda, indeed the whole of Africa, was where it was today.

UNAWARE THAT the president had so publicly railed against him, Father Carlos and the other two priests now drove the orange dirt road into the countryside. Museveni was a man who could be gracious and enlightened, yet he could turn instantly into a fierce dictator and commander. He did not allow true threats to his authority.

In the middle of the bush the priests were surprised to find a military roadblock. Three soldiers approached their truck. "Where are you going?" a soldier asked.

"A meeting with the rebels," Father Carlos replied.

"Where are you going? What are you going to do?" the soldier asked again.

"I already told you, we're going to the meeting with the rebels. We have all the permissions."

"What are you carrying?"

Father Carlos showed them everything: batteries for the rebels' radios so that they could hear peace messages, some newspapers for them to read, a little medicine for the commander, the letters of approval. It was strange to be questioned so repeatedly, but eventually they were allowed to continue on. After a few kilometres, they stopped and grabbed the supplies—only then realizing that the soldier had taken the medicine. They decided to walk ahead anyway.

Father Carlos was nervous, as he was each time he entered the bush. As they walked along a footpath a passing farmer whispered to them,

"The rebels are in the village, under a tree." They walked on, eventually reaching two armed young boys in military fatigues who ordered the priests to sit before them. "Are you coming with soldiers?" one of the boys asked.

"No, we just want to talk with your bosses," Father Carlos said, guessing the child to be about eight. He felt anxious around the boy, knowing that the youngest ones were often the most dangerous.

The boy motioned with his gun for them to rise, and now they walked together to their lay preacher's homestead. They found it surrounded by young boys with guns and a group of women with small children. Six older rebel boys greeted the priests and offered them chairs under a tree.

The rebels explained that although Major Topaco wasn't with them, they were happy to talk. Father Carlos glanced at the group and was shocked to see among them the frightened eyes of his young religious teaching assistant, Matthew Obote. Matthew stuttered that he'd been abducted hours earlier and was now a captive. Father Carlos told the rebels that this was his personal catechist, and to show him goodwill they released the young man.

Father Tarcisio opened the meeting with a prayer, and then the priests introduced themselves. Father Carlos asked if they'd heard the president's ceasefire message broadcast on Gulu Mega FM the week before. The boys said they'd heard that he spoke, but hadn't known what he'd said.

Father Carlos explained that they were in a critical moment of the war, and that violent acts must stop in order to allow a real ceasefire that would in turn allow peace talks to begin. The boy in charge conceded that Kony had ordered them to stop abductions and ambushes.

Suddenly a branch cracked in the bushes. One of the rebel boys stood up and grabbed his gun, his face etched with fear. Then a barrage of gunfire and explosions surrounded them. Father Carlos dove flat to the ground as the other two priests ducked behind a tree. Finally, after half an hour of gunfire, there was silence.

Father Carlos saw Ugandan military soldiers walking toward him and raised his hand in the air to signal he was alive. They walked up to him and kicked him. The soldiers motioned for him to join the other two priests. Father Carlos staggered over.

A soldier, gun drawn, demanded to know what they were doing. The priests explained the peace mission, but the soldier angrily yelled at them to lie flat on the ground. Another called them arms dealers for Al Qaeda. A third cocked his gun and pointed as if to fire. "Please. No," Father Carlos said.

"No what?!" the soldier yelled. He kicked Father Giulio and jumped on Father Carlos's back. A wounded woman lying next to Father Giulio was picked up and thrown a few metres away, left to die.[87] The priests believed their end had come. The two remaining catechists were tied together and beaten. Two other boys who were abducted just that morning, and who had thought they were being rescued, were also tied up. The signaller called on his radio: "We have captured four enemies!"

When war comes the first casualty is truth, Father Carlos thought. Other soldiers continued to taunt them, calling them terrorists.

Forty minutes later they were told to stand and march. "If you try to escape, we will shoot you and kill you," a soldier said. The three priests walked twenty kilometres with the hot sun bearing down on them, without a drop of water or food. Father Giulio's weakened kidneys hurt, and within hours dehydration left him screaming in pain. Father Tarcisio, at sixty-eight, had already had two heart bypass operations and his spleen removed. He was now staggering.

Six hours later they stumbled into Pajimu barracks. There Father Carlos watched as the soldiers beat their lay preacher while questioning him. Father Carlos yelled out that the UPDF was better than that. The soldiers responded by arresting the priests, stripping them to their underwear, and throwing them in a back shed.

"What is the charge?" Father Carlos asked.

"Talking to the wrong people," a soldier replied.

"We had permission from you!" But the priests' cries went unanswered as they were thrown into a cell. The parched men pleaded for water, but were refused. Father Giulio cried in pain. Father Carlos begged for water in every language he could: English, Acholi, Kiswahili,

Luganda. He offered one soldier money for water. The soldier apologized, quietly explaining that he was under orders.

The priests now stood together, their eyes communicating what each knew: their deaths could be imminent.

Father Carlos turned to the other priest. "May the Almighty God have mercy on you, and forgiving your sins, bring you to life everlasting...." He raised his right hand toward Father Tarcisio and Father Giulio. "May the Almighty and Merciful God grant you pardon, absolution, and remission of your sins...."

Father Tarcisio recited the absolution back to him. He made the sign of the cross over Father Carlos. Then, after being absolved of his sins and spiritually prepared for death, Father Tarcisio found a corner of the cell and relieved himself. He was suffering diarrhea, and access to the latrines had been forbidden.

It was a long night, lying near-naked on the bare concrete, hoping that sleep would stop the pain, praying that sleep would not bring death. That morning the state-owned *New Vision* paper splashed "UPDF ARRESTS THREE WHITE PRIESTS IN NORTH" across its front page.

... Fr. Rodriguez was reportedly arrested on Wednesday in the company of three Kony fighters who were armed with a gun each. They reportedly had a grenade and were travelling in the same vehicle. Military sources said the team carried "an amazingly" large quantity of drugs.

The independent *Monitor* interpreted events differently, writing that Father Carlos was arrested for the article he'd just written criticizing the military.[88] But the army spokesperson corrected that notion. "In fact they are captives. They are not the ones authorized by government to talk to rebels. We did not know their mission and they did not inform any authority," he said. The Ugandan minister of defence publicly questioned whether these men really were priests at all.[89]

At 9 A.M. a soldier brought in a jerry can of water. A few hours later the priests were brought forward to give their statements, after which they boarded a military helicopter and were taken to headquarters in Gulu. They were given food and sodas, and questioned again.

"This is outrageous, we had permission from you," Father Carlos told his military questioners.

"From whom?"

Father Carlos gave the names.

"We don't know those people," the questioner said.

"But we have a letter from the district commissioner," Father Carlos said.

"Where is the letter?"

"In the bag." But when they looked inside the bag, the letter was gone.

Father Carlos changed tactics. He apologized, explaining that he'd made the mistake of assuming that one army division would communicate with the other, and that in the future he'd be more careful to get full permissions. And he explained that they held no grudges against the UPDF. "It's important to move beyond this unfortunate incident and to keep the peace process on track," he said.

Meanwhile, the Italian embassy was demanding answers from Museveni, and the international press was closely following the story of three arrested white priests.

That evening the priests were taken to see General Kazini inside his Gulu barracks office. He welcomed the men, but told them they'd made a mistake in not giving a report to the 4th Division Headquarters before meeting the rebels. He handed them a statement to sign that said they did not inform the military. Father Carlos answered that Father Tarcisio had informed them in Kitgum, but Kazini countered that the Kitgum office had denied it.

The priests complained that they didn't like the wording of the statement, but signed it nonetheless. Kazini told them they were free to leave.

The next day Father Carlos, hoping to keep the peace talks alive, greeted the commander of the Ugandan military in Kitgum. "My friend, where we have made a mistake we say sorry, and where you have made a mistake, we say: we forgive."

"We haven't made a mistake," Brigade Commander Kazoora said, unwilling to show any weakness in the power and ultimate authority of the military way. Father Carlos was then taken to the hospital.

A few days later Archbishop Odama released a statement exonerating Father Carlos and the other two priests, saying that they'd had permission and were working for peace. He also pledged no ill will toward the officers who arrested and detained the priests. But the Ugandan military spokesman rebutted the explanation: "They are lying. Having been embarrassed they are trying to cover up."

Father Carlos believed that the military's attack against him was actually directed at the Archbishop, and that he'd merely been the scapegoat. It was a warning to back off. But the military understood that the internationally respected Archbishop Odama was Northern Uganda's equivalent of a Gandhi or Nelson Mandela, and that to publicly attack him would only backfire. For Father Carlos it was a tough role to play, but he had long before decided he was willing to die for the Acholi people.

When Father Carlos was released from hospital he called *New Vision* demanding a retraction; during the call he answered the journalist's questions. The next day's paper didn't carry the retraction, but Father Carlos was quoted in an article titled "Priest to Continue Peace Talks": "I have returned to the bishop's house ready to resume work.... We are ready to talk peace to anybody for the sake of peace to return to Acholiland."[90]

A few days later, the Ugandan defence minister wrote a letter to the *Monitor* telling it to stop telling lies. He called the paper a "forum for psychological terrorism on the public."[91] The *Monitor* defended its integrity and continued reporting events. But when a journalist wrote that a Ugandan military gunship helicopter had crashed in the hills of Northern Uganda, possibly shot down by LRA rebels, the government had had enough. They called the allegation a lie. Fifty soldiers stormed the station and began searching through reporters' computers and notes. The reporter was arrested and the newspaper closed, an act the Ugandan government justified by citing its new anti-terrorism law that restricted civil liberties and that had been inspired by the U.S. law passed in response to the September 11 terrorist attacks.

NGOs and media groups around the world cried out for the *Monitor*'s restitution and donor countries spoke to Ugandan officials about the importance of a free press in democracies. Eventually the paper was reopened, the journalist freed, and the brave and idealistic reporters returned to their jobs, albeit with treason charges hanging over them.

MEANWHILE, the Acholi Religious Leaders Peace Initiative tried to move forward in their peace efforts, but the next time Archbishop Odama and Bishop Ochola entered the bush for a meeting, the rebels didn't show up. Trust was broken. For months the religious leaders sent letters through their contact, hoping to talk, but they received no reply.

Operation Iron Fist carried on under a president who was unwilling to throw off his guerrilla warrior background, set his authoritarian ego aside, or accept even the slightest dissent in an effort to mediate a peaceful end to the war. Others, like Father Carlos and his colleagues, had risked their lives for peace, but the terror of the LRA against the Acholis continued.

CHAPTER 27

It had taken four years for news of Judith Enang's 1997 murder to reach St. Mary's. Now, a relatively new escapee—an Aboke Girl who asked not to be identified—sat before Sister Rachele and Alba to tell Judith's story.

The girl had escaped Kony's camp in 1999. She'd found a Sudanese Dinka civilian who said he'd help her, but instead of delivering her to authorities he gave her to an Arab Sudanese relative, a charcoal maker in Juba who kept her as a sex slave. She was trapped there for months, and was pregnant by the time she met an escaped LRA boy on the streets of Juba who agreed to help her. The two followed a treacherous path across the Imatong Mountains and months later made it to safety. Along the way she had miscarried the charcoal maker's baby. When she returned to St. Mary's she was a silent teenager. But two years had since passed and now, at last, she had resolved to share the story of Judith's savage murder.

Those who now heard the story—Sisters Alba and Rachele along with a group of parents that included Angelina Atyam and Consy Ogwal—prayed together.

It was time to share the truth about Judith. Angelina called Judith's uncle, Dr. Otim, at his office in Kampala, and told his secretary that they wanted to see him in Lira. Otim had been taking care of Judith's mother and children since her father had died some years before. Some referred to him as Judith's father; in African tradition, brothers took responsibility for the wives of their dead siblings. He came without asking why.

The Concerned Parents Association brought him to St. Mary's to pray, then invited him into Sister Alba and Sister Rachele's home. Sitting at the kitchen table, Angelina took out a tape recorder and began playing the tape of the girl who'd witnessed Judith's execution. Dr. Otim listened for a few minutes, then got angry.

"This is nonsense, Angelina! Nonsense. Don't tell me nonsense."

She turned off the tape. At least they'd communicated it to him, she reasoned. Leaving the school, she and the other parents decided to visit Otim's village home, which was on their way back to Lira—and over these years they had all become like extended kin to one another. Before getting out of the car, Otim turned to Angelina. "Don't tell my mother. If she hears about it, she will die. And don't tell the mother of Judith, because they'll all die."

And so when they arrived they made small talk with Judith's relatives. Judith's mother, Mary, was critically ill; the emotional pain of finding out the truth could indeed have killed her.

Mary was Consy Ogwal's best friend. Consy's daughter, Grace Acan, and Judith had been friends all their lives. Now, though, because Consy knew the truth about Judith, she felt a distance between them. Consy wondered if she was sinning by not speaking the truth, but she told herself that since her friend had other children who needed their mother's love, her concealment would be forgiven.

Still, lying to Mary wasn't easy. So when she visited her one day, Consy led her to the living room, grabbed her hand to pray together, and resolved that this would be the moment to speak the truth. "One day the children will come back, but if they don't come back, we have to praise God for that, because we never know God's plan," Consy began, trying not to cry. Mary nodded and Consy found the strength to continue. She told Mary that anything could happen to their daughters and they needed to be prepared for that. Consy looked at her friend squeezed her frail hand. They both understood that the word *anything* meant their daughters could die. Mary nodded her agreement. "So if it happens to me, let me thank God for it. If it happens to you, you thank God for it," Consy said, hoping Mary might also agree.

But Mary sat silent, holding Consy's hand, pain etched across her face. Consy continued her prayers, and after a while knew she couldn't tell Mary the truth. She went home with a heavy heart.

Within weeks Mary passed away. Consy took some solace in knowing she was now with her daughter.

A SHORT TIME LATER, on October 10, 2002, the Aboke Girls' parents travelled by lorry together to the sixth-anniversary memorial of their daughters' abductions. Thousands of parents, students, religious leaders, and the greater community gathered. They carried posters, placards, and banners, whose messages included PEACE, FORGIVENESS AND RECONCILIATION, DON'T DRAW CHILDREN INTO POLITICAL CONFLICT, and WE WANT OUR CHILDREN BACK.

Members of the Concerned Parents Association, including Alfred and Isabella from Kampala and Father John and his staff at the radio station, all gathered and prayed at the school. It would be the last time most of them would see Sister Rachele and Sister Alba again. Not long after this, both sisters were reassigned. The head office of the Comboni sisters in Rome had decided that the strain on the two nuns had reached its limit. Father John agreed that it was time to close that sad chapter and open another. Besides, the new generation of girls at St. Mary's deserved to be led by nuns who did not have this deep loss burrowing down on them and inadvertently affecting the happiness and tranquility of the younger ones.

Before the sisters left, the government—whose posts were increasingly filled by graduates of St. Mary's—insisted on throwing the nuns a party in Kampala. Graduates who now lived in the city gathered together for the goodbye party at the infamous Nile Hotel in downtown Kampala—the hotel that in the 1970s had been converted into Idi Amin's interrogation and torture chamber.

After the dinner, Sister Rachele stood up and gave a speech to the crowd of women before her. "If you remain in unity and keep each other in your hearts, that's when the girls will come back. Never give up praying. It is only prayer that will bring the girls back," she said. "One day I will come back to Uganda, when all the girls are found." All the women clapped.

And with that, Sister Rachele was on her way to Rome, reassigned as the general secretary of the international Comboni sisters. And Sister Alba, now seventy, would soon make her way up to a Comboni House in the outskirts of London for retirement.

Jinja, Uganda, October 2002

While the war continued to rage in her homeland, Grace Grall, now a first-year college student at Uganda Christian University, walked into its midday prayer meeting hall where most of the students gathered. Stephen Noll, an American theologian and the school's president, welcomed the assembled freshmen. The Jinja campus, located on the grounds of an old seminary built in 1913, was just a few hundred kilometres from the war, yet seemed so far removed. The hall was open on all sides, allowing for a cooling breeze.

Grace, who'd been free from the rebels for five years now, stood with her classmates and recited the school's oath, promising to "promote Christian moral spiritual principles in the spirit of the university motto: God, the beginning and the end."[92] Dr. Noll, wearing a saffron gown and clerical collar, told the students to study hard and to stay on the straight path. That they should not go to the disco on Friday nights, but instead gather in the meeting hall to watch movies he'd chosen for them. The first movie, that Friday night, would be *Lord of the Flies;* it elaborated on the theme of sin, he said.

Recording the meeting was Henk Rossouw, a freelance journalist from South Africa who was writing a story about African women triumphing over the odds and making their way into university. He'd read a brief online *Monitor* article mentioning that five former child-soldier women of the LRA were now in university in Kampala, and had convinced his Washington newspaper to fund his trip to Uganda for a month so that he could find and write about these unnamed women.

Grace Grall had stayed at St. Mary's school in Aboke for two years after her abduction. But in 1999, when the rebels came close to the school, Grace fled in fear to her father's home in Lira. She transferred to St. Catherine's School there, where she thought she might get a fresh start, but the story of her past had made it into the school halls. Grace was taunted as "Kony's wife" and rejected by her peers. Upset, frightened, and lonely, her grades suffered. But when she graduated she learned that a Belgian philanthropist who'd read about the Aboke Girls' plight had offered to pay the tuition of any of the escaped girls once they were admitted to university. Grace was accepted at the Uganda Christian University, a private university-college founded in 1997 in Jinja, near Kampala, by the Anglican Church in America, and so received her scholarship.

Grace was Catholic, but it didn't matter. She now studied journalism. She felt it was good work, that it could make a difference. Her father didn't understand or support her aspirations, but too much had happened to Grace for her to want to lead a "normal" life. She had no desire to settle into the married life of hard labour and repeated pregnancies known to most women of Northern Uganda. Because Grace had survived her ordeal, she felt it was her moral obligation to try to help her suffering people.

It didn't take Henk Rossouw long to find Grace, and she readily agreed that he could follow her around campus and get a sense of her life. Grace liked journalists; she'd been reassured and encouraged years ago by the few journalists who visited her at St. Mary's. She asked Henk only that he not tell her schoolmates about her past. He assured her that her story, for a remote education magazine in Washington, D.C., would not be published in Uganda.

After Dr. Noll's speech ended, groups of students mingled and flirted around the canteen. Grace, having no interest in potential romances, instead headed back to her small room in town, in a boarding house whose walls were concrete and whose makeshift roof was a corrugated sheet of iron.

She loved movies, and so on Friday night, because Henk had offered to take her—she wouldn't risk walking alone after dark—they returned to the school to see *Lord of the Flies*. She watched as well-behaved young cadets became shipwrecked and slowly turned to mysticism, then savagery, in a continued descent into evil. The crowd of students gasped when the shipwrecked children, faces streaked with ceremonial blood, whacked a crying boy to death at their feet. Grace turned away and grimaced at the blood, but later told Henk that the scene wasn't realistic—she knew the boy should have taken longer to die.

The next day Grace decided to throw a dinner party in her small room. She liked having friends around, and was quick to make new ones. On Saturday morning she hopped on a minibus that brought her to the bustling market in downtown Kampala. The prices were outrageous compared with Lira's, but she picked up some bean leaves and okra to make boyoyo, a rich, buttery sauce. She already had the millet, cassava, and yams, kept stored under her bed, that she'd cook and spread the sauce over.

Later in the afternoon, on the paraffin stove in her room, she added sesame-seed paste, eggplant, fried plantain, and peppers. She cut up a melon and pineapple for dessert. Her female classmates living nearby, and Henk Rossouw, who she said was writing about African girls in university, joined her in her room. The evening passed with good food, laughter, and new friendships. She told no one of her past.

Her new best friend at the school, Doreen, missed the dinner party because she was on a college-sponsored outing to Lake Victoria. But at the end of the evening Doreen burst into Grace's room, excited to tell them all about the day's adventure. On the outing the school chaplain had asked everyone to sign a statement promising to wait until marriage before having sex. She showed Grace the yellow card she'd signed. "True Love Waits" was the slogan—adopted for Uganda's AIDS policy from an American church campaign emphasizing abstinence. Grace handed the card back and said how nice it was.

Back in class on Monday, the professor asked a moral question: should a working woman be promoted if her husband was already successful? A male student raised his hand. He suggested that the word *woman* was derived from "worker for man." Grace's hand shot up angrily. She argued that a woman's merit should not be assessed based on her husband. The husband's job was irrelevant. Her early self-esteem lessons from the nuns at St. Mary's, who told them all that they could be anything they wanted to be, combined with her experiences as a soldier, had made Grace—uncharacteristic of most young women from the North—a staunch believer in women's equality.

At lunch, Grace and a new friend were joined by a young man from their broadcasting class. He turned the conversation to an essay they were all writing about Joseph Kony, and asked Grace if he could read her version. Grace made excuses, saying she didn't know anything about Kony. The young man expanded into bravado. He told the women that he could be a famous war journalist if he went north. He could be the first one to photograph Joseph Kony. The world would know of him then. Grace hoped the conversation would soon change, afraid that something might give up her secret.

As the weeks and months went by, Grace began to excel at school. She felt safe, proud, and free, and no one here called her "Kony's wife." Life was as she'd dreamed it as a child, but sometimes the memories flooded back unexpectedly. In one communications class, the students viewed a documentary film about Martin Luther King Jr. When Grace watched a scene where two captured black girls escaped from the Alabama policemen who were bundling them into the back of a van, tears welled. She covered her eyes and no one noticed her crying as she struggled to stop thinking about her friends still trapped inside the LRA.[93] Not a day went by that she didn't think of her fellow Aboke Girls.

CHAPTER 28

EGANVILLE, ONTARIO, DECEMBER 2002

Ben Hoffman's phone was ringing off the hook with calls from LRA commanders deep inside the bush of Northern Uganda and South Sudan. Operation Iron Fist had been raging for nine months and killing thousands of LRA rebels.

"We want talks. We're telling you we want talks!" the rebels shouted. Their phone, which Hoffman had sent Kony months earlier, had been rigged by U.S. intelligence agents so that it dialed only three specific telephone numbers that only Hoffman answered.

While Hoffman took the calls, and tried to figure out what more he could do, his boss, former U.S. president Jimmy Carter, was in Norway accepting the Nobel Peace Prize. Carter used the occasion to talk about what he called the world's greatest threat today: the increasing gap between the world's wealthiest and poorest people. Neither terrorism nor religious divisions were the root cause of the world's problems, he declared, but rather the growing financial inequity between the West and the impoverished Third World. Carter blamed Western greed.

When the rebels called Hoffman he often heard gunfire in the background, at which point the rebels would quickly get off the phone. Days might go by before a commander would call back to announce, "Okay, we're safe now. We can talk."

Joseph Kony never called, but Hoffman did hear from Vincent Otti and other junior commanders fighting in the bush. Hoffman would listen, but he increasingly understood that he had no power to launch a fresh round of peace talks. Although convinced that the top commanders around Kony wanted to negotiate, and that Kony himself needed only to be coaxed to the discussion table, Hoffman was beginning to believe that it was indeed President Museveni who was secretly blocking progress. Every time they got close to talks it seemed to be the Ugandan government that upset the process, either by delays, by "accidental" uncoordinated ambushes on the LRA during ceasefire talks, by blocking Kony's parents from visiting him (although it was clear that Kony longed to see them and that it could be key to his stopping the fighting), or by encouraging competing peace efforts that would end up working against one another. Hoffman seriously wondered whether Museveni was simply using him and the Carter Center to make it look as if he was interested in a peaceful settlement.

Still, since Hoffman increasingly understood that Northern Uganda's peace prospects were affected by the dynamics of the war in Sudan, he shifted his primary focus back to that conflict. For the last two years he'd already been trying to get the SPLA and Al-Bashir government to talk to each other, but each time a breakthrough seemed to be at hand something went wrong and the door to peace talks kept slamming shut. The main parties simply would not get together. The United Nations was no help, having become preoccupied first with Afghanistan and then with Iraq, and the U.S. government simply would not support efforts to negotiate peace with Khartoum.

Hoffman had by now reckoned that the biggest roadblock to peace was not the people of Sudan—they all wanted the carnage to end— but rather special interests in the United States, specifically the long and influential arm of the Christian Right, which had placed itself in opposition to the "evil" Khartoum regime and in the process had also financially strengthened the rebels.

After September 11, when it looked as though Sudan could be a target of future U.S. attacks, Hoffman and Carter had redoubled their efforts to push Washington toward a peace process. Hoffman met with diplomats and think-tank executives across the world. He also set up meetings with influential members of the Christian Right, such as Franklin Graham, to explain the importance of trying to negotiate with Sudan's Islamic rulers in Khartoum. He asked these men to use their power to convince George Bush to back negotiations, and he emphasized that Khartoum's leaders would still be held accountable for the crimes against humanity that they were accused of.

Slowly, it seemed that Washington was listening. In October 2002 Bush approved the Sudan Peace Act that called on North and South Sudan to enter good-faith negotiations. The new initiative combined the carrot of more aid with the threat of reprisal. And the Sudanese government, which had seen the U.S. topple the Taliban in Afghanistan in December 2001, proved receptive.

MEANWHILE, the LRA themselves continued to push for peace talks. On December 28, 2002, Vincent Otti called in during a program on Gulu Mega FM that was airing live interviews with Ugandan military spokesmen. Shockingly, Otti told the program that Joseph Kony wished to speak to the people. Then Kony took to the airwaves, allowing the people of Northern Uganda to hear the voice of their oppressor for the first time.[94]

"On matters of peace talks and dialogue, I want to assure you that I am one of those who are seeking peace. That is why I am in the bush fighting. There is nothing I am struggling for, apart from peace," Kony said in Luo.[95]

"I am interested in peace but it is the government of Museveni, or Museveni himself, who is against peace.

"I want to inform you Acholis, listen carefully that Joseph Kony says he is interested in peace. There are indicators to that effect. I am the one who initiated peace with government. I have done it two times already. The problem lies with the government.

"In the past, Carter Center took some of you to meet me in Juba. When all arrangements were made, Museveni destroyed the program. He even confiscated the passports of some delegates, claiming that they would defect to me.

"The government's method will never bring peace. The other day I prepared my delegation led by Brig. Otti Vincent. He met with Archbishop Odama. I would not have allowed that meeting if I was against peace.

"We are all clever and alert. We know things; if we knew nothing, would we dare fight a government like Museveni's? We are all capable of moving things. None of us is stupid. How are we able to sustain a war with a superpower like Uganda?...

"I want to repeat that the LRA is not against peace. A few minutes back you were talking to Brig. Otti Vincent. That is a typical soldier who may not be able to make a political statement. He may be sad at events taking place but it is I who is the mother and father of the LRA, I know that I want peace. My only quarrel is the way government treats me. That is not a peaceful way. It leads to a bloodbath...."

The army spokesperson for the North responded that the government also wanted peace talks, but that first the LRA must stop abducting and ambushing.

"My friend.... You are setting for me conditions that I should not abduct, not ambush, and all other nonsense. The most logical thing would be the preliminary negotiations before such conditions are set. If we are genuine, this can lead to ceasefire. Once that is achieved then real negotiations can begin. It can't be in the way you want it done....

"Let me say this to my brothers in Gulu, Kitgum, and Pader; there is a war going on between Museveni and Kony. You should know by now how you can preserve yourselves wherever the war gets you. The Acholi are not made out of trees or from the soil of Palabek or Odek. Acholi are God's creation whom He loves very much. What is happening in Acholiland is a plan from God. Remember Acholi proverb, which says; the first may become the last. This is the first time you are experiencing a guerrilla warfare. You who support government must deal humanely with the people under you. Don't despise them. If you think you can manipulate Acholi, then you are wrong....

"God should bless you and protect you. We shall meet some other time."

Kony hung up.

Shortly afterward the Ugandan government declared it illegal for the Ugandan media to publicize any statements by the LRA or to allow rebels to talk on air.

Joseph Kony was not heard from again.

CHAPTER 29

MURCHISON NATIONAL PARK, UGANDA, JANUARY 2003

Still hiding in Murchison National Park, a half-dozen of the Aboke Girls along with their children and their guards celebrated Christmas and New Year's 2003 with hymns and prayer and song. It was a desperate time, with death hovering ever closer.

Occasionally the girls considered escaping, but none knew where exactly they were, and all feared the wild animals. Kony had told them now that he would never let the Aboke Girls go. That Museveni wanted them back so badly had, paradoxically, sealed their fate. Kony also told each girl separately that their parents had died from Ebola. The reality was that none of them knew whether their families were alive or dead.

Sometimes Kony spoke of his bad reputation in the world. He had told them that he was the messiah, the prophet, and that the whole world would one day know about him. Now he said that those who called him the devil would die because he was, in fact, God.

Suddenly, in early January, they received word from Commander Tolbert—Palma's husband—to join him outside of Gulu, in Pader district, whose inhabitants were almost all now displaced. Together they walked each night through the still villages of Lira and Apache, farther south than the rebels normally travelled.

At each village the rebels looted and killed, reminding the people not to give them away to the government and that the government did not protect them. They criss-crossed back and forth, and finally headed north to join Tolbert and his group.

While the rebels hid in the bush outside Gulu, news went around the North that Obol Aluji, Joseph Kony's father, had died of natural causes. He was given a proud burial in Gulu, presided over by Archbishop Odama, who preached that in death there must be no enmity. Aluji had worked as a religious teacher for the Catholic Church for many years, and despite the sins of his son, was respected in the North. He had also served as a soldier in the Second World War for the British colonial army known as the King's African Rifles.

Showing respect to Kony, hundreds attended the funeral, which Museveni had paid for. Kony's mother, Nora Anek Oting, told those gathered around the gravesite: "I am grateful that Museveni has buried Aluji with dignity. I want Kony to come back home. Many of my children have died. I want this message to reach Museveni and all the people of Uganda that I want peace."

Although Kony's family village had, like so many others, been abandoned years earlier for displaced persons' camps, Museveni had brought Kony's parents to Kampala, where they lived in comfortable anonymity. Museveni's condolence message expressing sorrow and love for Obol Aluji was read at the burial.

SHORTLY AFTER the funeral Archbishop Odama's mind turned again to somehow reaching Kony. There had been no communication for months, but perhaps after the funeral there could be again, so he asked Father Carlos to deliver a letter to Nyeko Tolbert via their secret LRA contact person.

After Father Carlos dropped off the letter near the Comboni mission house in Pajule, Kitgum, he decided to spend a few nights visiting the quiet pastoral land, taking testimony, and sharing knowledge. But at 6:30 P.M., while Father Carlos sat outside the Comboni mission house with an Acholi priest, the serenity was shattered as a volley of gunshots pierced the air. Children who'd been playing ran for cover as the two priests fled into the house followed by two young brothers, aged five and twelve.

Father Carlos grabbed the children's hands and they all snuck into a room, locked the door, and hid under a bed. Moments later the rebels stormed into the house and opened fire. They walked down the hallway, opening doors. When they reached the locked door where the four hid, they stopped and shouted. "If you don't open we're going to throw in a bomb."

For the first time in his life Father Carlos was paralyzed with fear, but the Acholi priest climbed out from under the bed and let the rebels in. The rebels, four boys who looked to be about twelve years old, said they wanted the radio communication system and solar panels.

Father Carlos and the boys remained hidden, but the rebels prodded under the bed with their guns, fishing them out. Now standing before the young soldiers, Father Carlos held the boys close to him. He softly told the soldiers to take anything, trying to show them he wasn't a threat.

The rebels pointed a gun at the older boy, Jimmy, and told him to come with them. Father Carlos held tight to Jimmy's arm. They grabbed Jimmy's other arm and pulled him, but Father Carlos wouldn't let go. The boy wrestled free from Father Carlos. "Do not die for me Father," he said. "Don't worry. God will protect me. Please take care of my brother," Jimmy added as rebels left with both him and the Acholi priest.[96]

Father Carlos and the five-year-old boy again crawled under the bed. The child nuzzled up to him and soon fell asleep, leaving Father Carlos alone, bathed in a cold sweat, fighting off curious rats who chewed on his hair and aching with guilt for allowing the abduction of the older child. Loud explosions and heavy machine-gun fire periodically filled the otherwise quiet air.

The next morning, when Father Carlos heard the Ugandan military moving about, he crawled out from under the bed, got in his truck, and headed back to Gulu.[97]

As he drove the priest played with his radio dial looking for news reports, but there was nothing on any of the stations about the attacks. He wasn't surprised. There were now dozens of small local radio stations in Northern Uganda, but they mostly limited themselves to music and devotional themes. They feared reprisals if they spoke about the war, whether from the government or the rebel perspective. The Ugandan government was so sensitive about allowing information to flow, and so adamant that the rebels not be given a voice, that the Northern Ugandans knew they could be arrested for treason if they allowed anti-government messages on the air. Conversely, they also knew that if they broadcast the government line they'd make themselves a target for the rebels. On unrelated matters the country was benefiting from a relatively free press, but the topic of the Northern war was a different matter altogether.

Radio Wa, Lira

Father John Fraser's Radio Wa had paid heavily for reporting on the war. When the rebels moved into the area the station had given early warnings of their whereabouts. Civilians with cellphones would call in to report where the rebels were and in what direction they were headed, giving people a chance to run for their lives.

But a few months earlier, around dawn on September 27, 2002, the station had been attacked. Father John had feared it would happen; he'd seen rebels that week outside of town, and the day before had called the Ugandan army major a dozen times for reinforcements to protect his station. But the promised men never showed up. He'd considered temporarily closing the station down, but that meant depriving the local people of their early warning system.

Early that morning he was lying under his mosquito net listening to machine gunfire and rocket-propelled grenades exploding, looking out at the still-black sky and hoping it wasn't the radio station. But at 6 A.M. the morning deejay from Radio Wa called him. "There's smoke coming from the station!"

Father John jumped in his truck and drove to the radio station he'd built just two years earlier. He found the roof blown off, and everything—the walls, the soundproofing, the floor—still on fire. It was all destroyed. Twelve soldiers had been guarding the station at the time, but all had fled when the rebels came. Father John soon learned that the rebels had also abducted a group of children and killed two neighbours.

He shuffled through the wreckage, looking to salvage working spare parts. But everything was burned, and looking around at the CDs, radios, recorders, batteries, and other expensive equipment, he noticed that the only thing missing was the Coca-Cola he kept stored in his office refrigerator.

When she heard the news, Angelina Atyam flagged down a bicycle driver and paid him three hundred shillings to take her the seven kilometres to Ngetta. There she saw Father John, his eyes red and traumatized. "God help support these people," she prayed, looking around at the anxiety and pain on everyone's face.

Radio Wa had been the best thing to happen here in years. Angelina felt that the region's people had so little to be thankful for, and yet Radio Wa had united them, restoring a sense of neighbourhood, of normalcy, of protection. By 8 A.M. thousands of people from Lira had joined Father John in mourning. It was everyone's radio station.

MONTHS WENT BY in radio silence around Lira. At first Father John thought that perhaps launching the station had been a mistake. It was expensive, and had lasted only two years before being destroyed. It could even have become a destination for the rebels, meaning that all those missing kids around the station might have been living normal lives today if he hadn't created it in the first place.

But one day, a few weeks after the station was destroyed, Father John was shopping in the Lira food market when two village women approached him. They each gave him five hundred shillings—a day's wages from trading in the market—toward the cost of rebuilding "their radio station." That was enough convincing for him, so he went home and wrote letters to his mostly Canadian friends, asking for more money and explaining that this time they'd build inside the safe confines of Lira town where the rebels couldn't reach them. To those who questioned the rebuilding, he explained that the attack had been proof of their success. Of the fifty radio stations in Northern Uganda, only Radio Wa had been destroyed. Clearly they had been annoying the rebels. "We were giving information, talking to them. They didn't like us," he said.

Radio Wa management wrote a letter directly to President Museveni explaining what had happened. When the army sent an investigator, Father John gave him the documentation of the major's repeated promises to send more troops and heavy equipment. The major was court-martialled and sentenced to two years in prison for neglect of duty.

Father John's friends came through for him again, with another thirty thousand dollars. As well, a quarterly Comboni Missionary newsletter published out of Cincinnati reported on the attack and asked readers for donations. Hundreds of new CDs, mostly gospel and country music, arrived from the people of Cincinnati.

CHAPTER 30

CHICAGO, ILLINOIS, MARCH 2003

Angelina Atyam's world travels continued. Determined to voice the pain of the thousands of mothers who suffered as she did, her life purpose now was to speak out about the war. Sometimes she would cite an Acholi saying: "One blade of grass can cut the heart enough to cause a leak for others to see."

It was when Angelina was in the United States attending a conference on Human Trafficking that the Women's Commission, a New York–based division of the International Rescue Committee and another attendee at the conference, was able to arrange for her appearance on *The Oprah Winfrey Show.*

And now she was sitting next to Oprah Winfrey in her Chicago studio, cameras on. Angelina wore a beige headwrap and a pink shawl over a long traditional Ugandan dress. Oprah spoke to the camera: "For seven years, one Ugandan mother has been struggling to free her daughter and her daughter's classmates from rebel soldiers."

Angelina cried. "Inside me, we failed, we didn't do enough," she sobbed to millions around the world.

"Every day she dreams of her daughter's homecoming," Oprah said to the audience.

"I cannot give up hope, I long for that day," Angelina replied.

After the interview, Oprah's charity, the Oprah's Angel Network, gave the Concerned Parents Association a large, four-wheel-drive truck. Oprah explained that it would help the parents keep in touch with each other in the North.

Angelina was grateful. She hadn't known of Oprah before, but now she understood that her story was being broadcast to tens of millions of homes in the powerful United States. She hoped to reach them emotionally so that they might rally the American government to help. The vehicle was a welcome gift, equivalent to a lifetime's salary for most Ugandans. It meant that the parents could travel into such treacherous locations as Kitgum and Pader, collect information, and leave without spending the night in danger of rebel attack.

ATLANTA, GEORGIA, JUNE 2003

Although the war in Northern Uganda raged on, by early 2003 peace talks between South and North Sudan had finally ramped up and a ceasefire was being honoured. Around this time Canada's Talisman Oil sold its operations in Sudan, largely as a result of external lobbying and mounting pressure over the ethics and legality of their involvement. A consortium of companies from China, Malaysia, and India took over the oil operations.

A surprise route to the talks had opened up when the Sudanese government offered to allow South Sudan to hold a referendum on self-determination six years after peace was established. Ben Hoffman had been thrilled. For three and a half years he and his team of eleven at the Carter Center had been working day and night to bring the two sides together. Hoffman had provided negotiation training workshops for most of the SPLA's top commanders (other than John Garang, who refused to participate), for the government's negotiating team, and for some Acholi religious leaders. He'd coached the official mediators on how to lead the talks, and had even drafted the first peace agreement for the two sides to discuss and negotiate over. When the talks began, Hoffman and the Center had received accolades from the diplomatic community around the world.

But the Carter Center had recently been pushed out of the way by the newly arriving U.S., British, and Norwegian teams now backing the process. And as the weeks and months passed, Hoffman had grown increasingly uneasy about a gaping hole he saw in the peace process. He well understood the power of elites to carry the community along—a top-down process that was much more efficient than grassroots efforts in swaying leaders—but these talks were ignoring the community altogether. The American diplomats were excluding all groups other than the SPLA and the Sudanese government. Those from the west and east, from the disgruntled region of Darfur, women's groups, religious voices, other interested parties—all were being cut out of the process.

It was a mistake, an obvious mistake, and Hoffman begged Carter to remain involved in order to address it. Sudan had a long history of ignoring not only outlying areas but anyone not of the elite Arab class. Hoffman thought the Carter Center could wire the community voices into the talks. That way, the people might not actually be in the room, but they could be heard.

Hoffman asked President Carter for US$2 million a year to attain this inclusion, explaining that the process might take a few years. But Carter had one firm rule: the Center didn't duplicate efforts. Now that the United States was leading the peace talks, it was time to move away. Hoffman countered that the United States' agenda was too narrow. The people of Darfur, for instance, who wanted to be at the talks, should be heard.

The Darfur region in western Sudan, population six million, had a long history of skirmishes between nomadic Arab Muslim herdsmen and black Muslim landowning farmers over limited water and grazing lands. And by early 2003 it was beginning to overheat with tension. Two new rebel groups had emerged with grievances against the Sudanese government for neglecting Darfur, and when the peace talks became imminent these Darfur rebels saw an opportunity for these grievances to be heard. Their voices weren't being represented by Garang.[98] But the American mediators behind the talks wanted a simple process, not a complicated one. They wanted a tight negotiating table limited solely to John Garang and either Omar Al-Bashir or his top spokesman. Once the details were hammered out, they said, they'd bring everyone along behind.

Hoffman didn't like it when diplomats became mediators. They often didn't know what they were doing and were too arrogant to take advice from those who did. And sometimes diplomats got things wrong, badly wrong, especially when state politics played a secret hand.

Years of building had brought them to the moment of a classic fatal error. Rule number one of mediation: bring all the interested parties to the table. That way, the secret forces that might sabotage the talks could be assessed and hopefully manipulated. There would be no broadsiding. It could be done with ongoing parallel tables. It didn't have to upset the talks.

Carter, however, still refused to give him the go-ahead to address the problem. "I guess we don't understand each other," Hoffman said, bitterly disappointed.

Now, in June 2003, his work in Sudan was done. Frustrated, hurting, and sensing the needless deaths he felt could only be the result—and which he believed he could have prevented—Hoffman retreated to the woods of Ontario, needing a break. He would not return to the Carter Center.

CHAPTER 31

KITGUM, NORTHERN UGANDA

Each evening the night-commuting village children arrived in Kitgum town. The Comboni Mission House was now cramming in five hundred each night, sent by worried parents who feared at every twilight that this could be the night the LRA arrived at their doorstep demanding to take their children.

Father Carlos, who continued to document the war, also slept there. His notes revealed the sad details of the rural Kitgum people's terror. And despite parents' efforts to save their children—either by sending them in to sleep each night or by moving to displaced persons' camps—by Father Carlos's count, every single day an average of thirty children were abducted. It was also clear to him that famine was growing. The World Food Programme would travel only with a military escort, and only to registered camps. But hundreds of thousands were sleeping in the bush and thousands more in remote, unregistered camps.

Now back at his home at the Bishop's House in Lacor, just outside Gulu, Father Carlos sat down to write another article for *The Monitor* about the atrocities and the pointlessness of the military path to peace. He also sent his report to the Catholic news service in Rome.

"For the last two weeks the Lord's Resistance Army (LRA) rebels have been very active," he began. He detailed fresh abductions and even more massive displacements. He asked readers why thousands of reporters would explain the minutest detail of the war in Iraq and yet ignore every massacre in Uganda. "But who can understand this long boring war where everything is so illogical?"

Father Carlos wrote that although Sudan claimed it was no longer supporting the LRA, he knew they were again. Many recent escapees had reported as much to him. The children had told him that just months before they'd fought alongside the Sudanese government forces to recapture Torit, a Sudanese town very close to the international oil drills. The SPLA rebels had won Torit in battle shortly before that, and that win seemed to precipitate the renewed LRA–Khartoum alliance.[99] Although Khartoum had denied the allegation, the regime could not be trusted, especially over the issue of oil wealth.

THEN, one early May morning, days after writing his report, Father Carlos's phone beeped. A priest at the Catholic seminary school in Lacor had sent him a text message: *The LRA is abducting the boys.*

Father Carlos called the priest, who answered in a whisper from his hiding spot inside the seminary. The priest said he wanted to follow the rebels, just as Sister Rachele had eight years earlier.

Father Carlos said he'd go with him. At dawn he stopped in at the Archbishop's room and told him of their plan. By now they knew that forty-three boys between ages twelve and seventeen, all studying for the priesthood, had been taken.

The Archbishop gave them his blessings, just as Sister Alba had given hers to Sister Rachele all those years ago. But before the two men left to follow the trail, Archbishop Odama called the army division commander, who forbade them from going, arguing that he wouldn't be able to protect the priests in the crossfire. The priests agreed to allow the military to do their jobs.

But when the military followed the trail, all they found were the remains of four of the weakest boys from the seminary school. The boys had been hacked to death.

Sacred Heart Seminary School was closed. Another nightmare began for yet another set of parents. Father Carlos felt massive sadness. It seemed that the horror was beyond any of their capacities for endurance.

The terror across the North was out of hand. The rebels were on an offensive, expanding their territory toward the Kenyan border and farther south into Soroti and Lira. Nowhere was it safe. Vehicles on the road were ambushed in daytime. Villages were attacked at night. Displaced persons' camps were targeted for murderous attacks and abductions. Ninety percent of the people in Acholiland had now moved to the camps. But people felt like exposed targets there, and so tens of thousands hid in the bushes, camping out without cover or supplies, hoping to evade the rebels. And even there the rebels found them, sending their child soldiers up trees as scouts, identifying sleeping bodies hiding below in the grass.

And now the Catholic Church seemed another target. The desperate priests wondered what had happened. Had they done something to anger Kony?

The answer came a few days later when an LRA message was intercepted. On June 17, 2003, Kony's voice was recorded issuing this order over CB radios to his operations in Northern Uganda: "Destroy Catholic missions, kill priests and missionaries in cold blood and beat nuns black and blue." Kony declared that the Catholic Church had defied him and become a pawn of the Ugandan government.

The message filled the Catholic diocese with fear. They could all retreat, but they had promised to stand by the people unto death. So the priests stood their ground and prayed to God to protect them. Across the North, as the sun went down and night descended, the frightened priests of Acholiland settled in for a night of terror.

That night the rebels attacked the Comboni mission in Amir Omina, looted it, then burned it down. The parish priest, from Costa Rica, hid himself and wasn't discovered. The rebel boys then moved on to Anaka parish a few kilometres away, where they bombed all three vehicles, broke down locked doors, beat up a ninety-year-old Italian priest, and forced another Italian priest to come with them carrying their stolen goods, although they ultimately released him without harm a few hours later. The next night rebels attacked the people in two displaced persons' camps and murdered a Catholic priest. The following night the target was a Comboni orphanage, where they abducted more than a dozen young girls. That same night the rebels raped four nuns in Gulu.

WHAT WERE they to do? The Acholi religious leaders talked with one another. No one was safe, including them. The threats made them feel the same terror the locals had felt for years. Like the Northern Ugandan people around them, they were unprotected and targeted.

Father Carlos began changing his sleeping place every few days, rotating between St. Mary's Tailoring School in downtown Gulu, Lacor Hospital, and the parish in Gulu town.

Although desperate with fear, the religious leaders realized that this was, in fact, an opportunity: the attacks on the Church might attract international attention to the people. They would have to somehow publicize their plight. But how? they wondered. The members of the Acholi interfaith religious leaders now gathered regularly, sharing ideas. On Sunday, June 22, after mass, they met at St. Mary's Tailoring School in Gulu town. Father Carlos suggested that they publish a press release. But a Muslim leader said that people were tired of documents and words.

Then someone remarked how intolerable it was to have their children sleeping on the streets night after night. It had been going on for almost a year now. "Why don't we go and sleep with them?" a voice asked. Immediately there erupted a chorus of excited approval. The leaders decided that for four straight nights they would sleep amidst the thousands of frightened and homeless night commuters.

They would start that evening. Father Carlos was glad for the quick action. The military, he figured, might prevent it if they heard advance word.

The religious leaders resolved to march in a way that was as close as possible to what the children were experiencing. They'd leave their homes in the early evening, with just a blanket and a piece of plastic sheeting, march on foot, without supper, then walk the five kilometres to the bus park and sleep under the night sky with the children.

That night, Anglican Bishop Ochola and Catholic Archbishop Odama wore their clergy gowns. Around them hundreds of children marched down the same road, some laughing, some singing or playing with sticks, but most in silence. The children looked at the religious leaders but stayed back a respectful distance, assuming that the men were simply out for a walk. But as darkness filled the sky they arrived at the Gulu bus park and Archbishop Odama spoke.

"Today we want to sleep with you. Because you must be thinking: 'Why are we abandoned here? Nobody seems to care about us.' So we shall sleep with you, and show solidarity with you, and we hope that doing this will open the eyes of the others to your plight."

The children looked in stunned silence at these powerful men before them. *What? Coming to sleep with us, out in the open?* They were taken by awe. None spoke to the priests, but they stared wide-eyed as the men lay out their plastic sheets and sat on the ground. *Is this true, or are we dreaming?* their eyes said. Military and government authorities in the town rushed to the bus park, intending to stop the spectacle. The police told the Archbishop that what they were doing was illegal.

"If it's illegal, then what the children are doing is also illegal," Archbishop Odama said.

"But you're VIPs," the police said.

"We are not VIPs, because children have a special status at the UN and religious leaders do not. So they are more important than us."

"But you need protection."

"Are you telling me the children are not protected?"

Neither the Archbishop nor the other religious leaders slept that night. The best the Archbishop could do was close his eyes. Heavy shooting just two kilometres away rocked the town at midnight. The children looked at each other, not daring to say a word as they pricked their ears to the varying echoes of gunfire, distinguishing the machine guns from the big booms of mortar fire, listening closely for sounds that the echoes were drawing nearer.

After forty minutes the gunfire stopped, but the silence soon gave way to a night filled with coughing children. And then a child screamed. Father Carlos got up and climbed over the bodies sleeping around him to find a child in the midst of a nightmare. He reassured the child before returning to his plastic sheet. Minutes later another child cried out, then another.

The next morning Archbishop Odama, Father Carlos, and Bishop Ochola walked home together without many words. Father Carlos's back and head ached from the hard night. His mind turned again, as it did so often, to the mystery of why they had been abandoned by the world. Other wars had gained the world's attention, Bosnia and Kosovo, but those were different: they were in Europe. Even in Africa, though, the world was helping to end other wars, in Sierra Leone, Angola, Congo, Sudan. All those countries had help. But in Sierra Leone there were diamonds. Sudan and Angola had oil. Congo had gold, diamonds, coltan. *In Northern Uganda there are just the children,* he thought sadly. It was always a struggle to reconcile oneself to the world's indifference. They all knew that indifference was a sin—a massive sin that pervaded the West. And God was asking them to find the way to overcome it.

That morning Archbishop Odama sat down at his computer and sent out emails to the people in the world who had expressed care. Back in Canada, Lloyd Axworthy opened his email to find this message from the Archbishop of Gulu: "Quick! Help! Come do something. We need international intervention quick."[100]

The next night the men again headed out without dinner. This time the children ran up to them, walked alongside and behind them. Archbishop Odama, already tired and sore, greeted the children. "My colleagues. My fellow night commuters," he said as the children walked beside him.

When he settled in to sleep, the children nuzzled up tight, as close as they could. Eventually the children worked it out: they slept surrounding the priests and the Khadi Sheik, their heads all bent toward them. And then it rained. Everyone got up and ran under ledges for shelter.

The next night, when the priests set off again for town, the children were waiting for them outside the Bishop's House. The children laughed when the men stepped out to join them and called them "colleagues." And so the children were encouraged. It was very important to these suffering little souls.

When the men reached the bus park the international media had already arrived. It had been the visuals—religious men in cloth sleeping outside with thousands of desperate children, praying they'd see morning—that had brought them forth.

Father Carlos saw a UNICEF vehicle and recognized some of its Kampala staff. "Did you come here to have your picture taken?" he said, his lack of sleep forcing open his true feelings. He couldn't understand why, when children in no other part of the world suffered such serious, continual abuse, the world's organization for the protection of children hadn't come. The hypocrisy hurt. He knew he had to welcome them, though. Their presence was what they all needed.

On the fourth night the religious leaders called a press conference at the bus park. Bishop Ochola asked, "Why is the international community turning a blind eye on us? We have no homesteads in Acholi now, we are all displaced. Why is the world keeping quiet?" He appealed to the government to stop its arrogance and ask for help. The Sheik told the press that the Acholi were all victims.

Closing the press conference at 10:15 P.M., as the children settled in for bed, Archbishop John Baptist Odama asked: "Why has the UN Security Council not addressed our problem? I would like our government to answer this crucial question. African Union, where are you? East African Community, where are you? Are we not part of you? ... United Nations, are we not a part of you?"

And while they slept, a hundred kilometres away, in an area of northeastern Uganda normally safe, eighty-eight teenage girls were stolen from their beds at Lwala Catholic Girls Secondary School by Lord's Resistance Army rebels.

CHAPTER 32

GULU, NORTHERN UGANDA, NOVEMBER 2003

Jan Egeland, the UN undersecretary general for Humanitarian Affairs, decided during a tour of Africa that it was time to visit Northern Uganda. Months earlier the Acholi religious leaders had travelled to New York to meet with the United Nations, and now Egeland felt he should see for himself. He visited for two days. He arrived in Gulu on November 11, visiting the World Vision Child Rehabilitation Centre where Florence Lacor continued to work. After Egeland met with former child soldiers, Archbishop Odama took him on a tour of the displaced persons' camps.

Then Archbishop Odama brought him back to his home for a Coca-Cola and talked to him about the depth of his people's suffering. He handed Egeland a letter that the Acholi religious leaders had written months earlier to Francis Deng, the UN secretary-general special representative for Internally Displaced Persons, asking for assistance. He had received no response. Egeland read the letter:

> ... We must be very frank and tell you that our people in Northern Uganda feel abandoned and betrayed by the international community. Particularly, the UN is not doing enough to end the war. The good thing done is that some relief aid has been delivered, for which we are very grateful.
>
> We are aware that this is a war that has remained for long in the dark, and which fits in the category of the world's forgotten

conflicts, most of whom seem to take place in Africa. A number of reasons may account for this, particularly that our region does not have any significant commercial or economic interests. We are also aware that these days the world's attention and resources are being directed towards places like Iraq and the Middle East, as some years ago they were towards Eastern Europe. Moreover, we have a feeling that too many times this tragedy has been put on the label of internal affairs, closing the door to any outside international intervention that may help bring this war to a speedy end. We firmly believe that people's interests must come first, so that when levels of human suffering become unbearable there is no situation which becomes just "internal," since we are all part of the same humanity...

Dear Sir, we are very happy that you took the time to come and take interest in our situation. What you have heard and seen here, go and tell the whole world so that something is done without delay. May the Lord of peace bless your endeavours and grant you wisdom to perform your very important task.

In their letter the religious leaders went on to detail what was required: that the UN immediately discuss the Northern Uganda war, whose eighteen-year duration had yet to draw its attention; that food distribution in the camps be adequately protected; that the UN issue a clear statement of the temporary nature of the displaced persons' camps; that the fighting sides commit themselves to peace talks; that the international community send peace observers to the conflict areas; that UNICEF fulfill its pledge to open an office in Gulu; and finally, that the UN help educate the war-affected children of Northern Uganda.

Troubled and with a deep sense of purpose, Egeland flew out from the North and told international media that the tragedy of Northern Uganda was "the worst and most forgotten humanitarian crisis in the world." He called it a moral outrage that the world had ignored the suffering of these people, especially the children. Egeland then launched a $130 million campaign for an emergency supply of non-food items to

Northern Uganda. He issued a press release saying that he'd been shocked to his very bones, that the humanitarian situation was worse than anywhere on the planet. "I cannot find any other part of the world that is having an emergency on the scale of Uganda, that is getting such little international attention," Egeland told the BBC. He called it one of the world's last dark spots.

In the rush of media attention that followed Egeland spoke repeatedly to major news outlets around the world about Northern Uganda and the war against its civilians. He announced that the United Nations would fund peace talks between the LRA and the Ugandan government to their conclusion, and urged the government to find a peaceful solution.

It would take some time, but Egeland's visit would ultimately be seen as a turning point for the war.

A short time later the Ugandan Parliament unanimously resolved that the government declare Northern Uganda a "disaster area" so that humanitarian assistance could be given directly to vulnerable people in the dispaced persons' camps. Museveni refused, however, insisting that the war was nearly over.

As an immediate result of Egeland's visit, the United Nations opened new offices in Gulu, Kitgum, and Soroti, managed by international staff. It also increased its humanitarian aid, although not by enough to keep the people from dying. In the squalid, fetid, disease-ridden camps, the wretched and forgotten people, most of them now children with distended bellies from long malnutrition, waited for peace, and as they waited continued to suffer and die.

PART 5

"YOU SHOULD PRAISE GOD THAT I'M BACK ALIVE"

CHAPTER 33

RADIO WA, LIRA, JANUARY 2004

Deejay Kakaba, the most famous voice of Northern Uganda, entered the morning meeting at Radio Wa wanting to talk about the government's amnesty offer to any rebel who stopped fighting.

It wasn't the government's first offer. Years earlier the religious leaders had pushed Museveni to provide amnesty, and in late 1999 he'd finally agreed. Back then, however, the amnesty didn't include the top commanders, the men who held all the lower-ranking ones captive. In 2000 Museveni changed his mind and offered amnesty to them all, but the rebels didn't trust the offer, and only the surrounded or injured gave themselves up. That amnesty had since expired, and now, once again, Museveni was offering a complete pardon to all. But, as before, hardly any rebels were surrendering. To make sure they knew about the offer, the government had even air-dropped pamphlets on rebel locations explaining it. Even the Aboke Girls had read the notes.

Deejay Kakaba knew that the LRA leaders had always considered the amnesty a trap, believing that if they gave themselves up they'd be imprisoned, tortured, even killed. The deejay, whose own cousin had been abducted years earlier, told Father John Fraser and his staff that they needed to work harder to get the message out to the rebels that the amnesty offer was real and that the community wanted them back.

Deejay Kakaba proposed putting former child soldiers on air. Only two kilometres away the Belgian government had built a new child-soldier rehabilitation centre—named the Rachele Rehabilitation Centre in honour of Sister Rachele—and this would give them a steady supply of kids who'd successfully escaped and who might be willing to talk.

Kakaba's proposal was greeted enthusiastically, and before long the *Welcome Home* program, known as *Karibu* in Luo, was broadcasting three nights a week.

"This is *Welcome Home* of Radio Wa, greeting you rebels in the bush. It is a rainy night, we hope you have cover tonight," Kakaba began. "Tonight I bring to you two of your own, who recently escaped from your ranks. Please, tell your colleagues who you are."

A shy sixteen-year-old boy sat in the studio and leaned into the microphone. His name was Okello Moses, and he had been under the command of Vincent Otti. He'd escaped just one week earlier after three years with the rebels.

Kakaba asked him to tell the listeners how he'd escaped.

The boy explained that he'd remained at the back of the line while they walked, and that one day, realizing there was no one behind him, he ran away. Before long he found two women who were carrying firewood. He stopped them and pleaded for their help, explaining that he'd been abducted and wanted to find a way back home. The women told him that he was safe now, and together they led him to the military barracks, where they handed him off to the military.

Deejay Kakaba asked the boy what time it was, knowing that the rebels would think this was a taped message that had been forced from Moses before the Ugandan military killed him. Moses relayed the current time. Then he sent a message to his friends. He called on others in Otti's group—Matthew, Simon, and Sam—to come back, to give themselves up. "You see, now I am back. They don't hurt you. They lied to us when they told us that whenever we go back they kill us," the boy said into the microphone.

Gulu Mega FM, the newly British-sponsored station, followed suit. They too began interviewing former child soldiers and speaking directly to the rebels, but their stronger signal meant that the message was heard hundreds of kilometres away in the hills of Sudan where the rebels hid.

The voices of the children were clearly communicating the truth. And some of the rebel commanders listened, fantasizing about a life back with the families and friends they'd left behind years before.

THE ABOKE GIRLS knew nothing of these radio broadcasts. Trapped in the Imatong Mountains of South Sudan, the group of the Aboke Girls who stayed close to Kony and his Command Altar battalion were feeling the growing stress of LRA life. They were now hungry all the time.

Although they had now spent many more years inside the LRA than they had at St. Mary's, none had forgotten the idyllic school life they'd once known. When they had a chance to talk, each revealed that they dreamed of the gardens of St. Mary's, of the classrooms and teachers, and of their own homes and families.

For the past six years Louiza Namale, Alfred Olum's daughter, had been living as a slave to Kony. After the commander husband she shared with Angela Atim had died of AIDS in 1999 she had toiled from morning to night inside Kony's camp. In the daytime she was a teacher in the school, but she also served Kony's wives and his guards. She cut grass, cleaned, carried supplies, and cared for his children. In the last year, however, her health had been deteriorating. She secretly had frequent cramps in her stomach that slowed her down.

But in late January 2004, she felt well enough one day to volunteer herself when Nyeko Tolbert, Palma's husband and now the overall army commander, came around looking for a team to head off to Uganda.

The thought of being in Uganda gave Louiza hope of escape, and she swore to Tolbert that she was strong enough to go. Although an Aboke Girl, she was without a husband, childless, and thought to be suffering with AIDS, so she wasn't as desired as the others. He nodded. Louiza was filled with excitement. She said her goodbyes to Angela, but not before confiding her deepest thoughts to her friend. Then she marched off with the other soldiers, dreams of escape and of seeing her parents filling her head. It would be her first time back in Uganda since her abduction.

Days later, using heat-sensing equipment, the UPDF detected the LRA troops in the bush and aerial-bombed their location. One of the bombs hit Louiza Namale and ripped her apart. Nyeko Tolbert, their chief army commander, also died in the attack.

Louiza's body was never recovered. It would take a year before Alfred and Isabella would know that their daughter was dead.

RASKA LUKWIYA, who now had twenty other wives besides his two Aboke Girls, Charlotte and Jessica, swiftly assumed control from Tolbert. Lukwiya was a hard man who took mercy on no one. In order to evade detection he ordered the junior commanders to fan out across the North with small groups of rebels. It was around this time that Palma and her guards and two children finally reached Tolbert's intended destination and learned that the father of her two children was dead.

The rebels continued raiding, pillaging, abducting, raping, and terrorizing. But each night, under the dense forest canopy and away from headquarters' control, the rebels settled in to sleep while listening to the radio. Although Joseph Kony had forbidden it, the commanders and their trusted sergeants tended to listen most evenings. And now, instead of the usual popular music and sports, they heard the voices of former rebels and of family members calling out to them to come home.

The radio program began to shatter Kony's myth that the rebels could not escape. Every night another voice told their story over the radio, and soon many in the LRA ranks understood that they could go home again. The children, in their innocence, were so convincing.

After a few months hundreds of rebel soldiers, having found the courage to escape their commanders, began reporting to army barracks. Some commanders led their entire units out to surrender. And almost every child soldier who returned asked to appear on Kakaba's *Welcome Home* program so that they too could tell their former colleagues in the bush that they'd made it to freedom.

Between the ongoing UPDF military assaults and the rebels' surrender, LRA ranks began thinning. It didn't take long before the government began claiming that the rebels had been defeated.

KONY, always sensitive to statements being made against him, ordered his soldiers to prove their strength, sending out three hundred fighters to target the so-called protected camps. In their first act, Kony's fighters overwhelmed the Ugandan army guards and opened fire randomly on the Abia camp outside Lira, killing forty-five, wounding seventy, and abducting yet more children.

Then they moved on to Barlonyo camp. On February 21, 2004, on Saturday night at 5 P.M., the LRA walked single file through the bush toward the camp that was home to five thousand displaced people. Just before entering the camp they stopped. Their leader blew a whistle and the rebels fanned out, surrounding the camp in a horseshoe formation. Dogs started barking, and just as the people looked to see what the disturbance was the rebels opened fire, first on the local defence unit barracks and then on the rest of the camp.

Some ran out from their huts, others ran into them. The LRA strode through the camp setting huts ablaze and shooting at anyone who dared run from their burning home. Others were caught while running, ordered into huts, then the grass roofs were set on fire. Dozens more were hacked to death with machetes and clubs. Before the rebels left, more than two hundred people were dead and the camp was destroyed. It was the largest single massacre on Northern Ugandan civilians in seven years.

Father John arrived at the camp at daybreak the next morning as corpses still smouldered. He loaded injured survivors onto his truck and brought the first load to the Lira Hospital.

The army wanted to keep the attack quiet, and so it went unreported in the news. But the religious leaders insisted on the truth; one even systematically counted all the bodies that morning before the military could bury them. The priests called international media outlets and reported that hundreds were dead and hundreds more injured. At first the army denied this casualty count, but then conceded its truth.

Thousands of frightened people in Lira took to the streets to protest against the government for not protecting them. Some held banners that read THE UNITED NATIONS MUST INTERVENE. Lira shopkeepers locked up their businesses as the crowd passed through. Motivated by their collective fear the people had rallied together, demanding protection from the murderous rebels.

But then small groups of angry male Lango teenagers, carrying clubs, broke away from the main protesters and formed a lynch mob. They burned and looted about fifty Acholi grass-and-mud homes, as if these Acholi were somehow to blame. The Acholi and Lango were kin, closely related and aligned, but now the angry Lango youth clubbed to death two Acholi women and two men suspected to be LRA sympathizers.

The Ugandan police walked into the crowd and opened fire. An Associated Press reporter covering the event witnessed the police killing two protesters and wounding five.[101]

World bodies and NGOs responded—as they had many times before—by condemning the atrocity and demanding that the LRA stop attacking civilians. UN Secretary-General Kofi Annan begged anyone who had the power to protect civilians in Northern Uganda.

At the Lira Hospital three days later, Museveni, flanked by soldiers and wearing military fatigues, spoke to reporters before driving off to the massacre site. In a major policy shift, he apologized to the people for not protecting them. "We have got a big struggle, but we shall win. We have won previous battles," he said.[102] He seemed upset, and blamed the local military commander for not doing his job.

In a renewed offensive—named Operation Iron Fist, Part 2—Museveni's army followed the rebels through the bush, and within days of the attack killed half of the three hundred rebels. The remaining rebels retreated to Sudan. Uganda received permission from the Sudanese government to chase the rebels across the border, and soon thousands of Ugandan soldiers were fanning out across Northern Uganda and South Sudan. Kony's Command Altar group was forced to run from their Imatong Mountain base in South Sudan.

CHAPTER 34

NORTHERN UGANDA, MARCH 2004

In response to the government offensive, the Aboke Girls were now spread out in units across Northern Uganda and South Sudan. Agatha Longoria, the Karamojong teenager who had buried her baby girl in the Imatong Mountains two years earlier, had been sent to a Northern Ugandan hideout in the mountainous forest to wait for her husband. And now, amidst the hail of gunfire and exploding bombs, she was fleeing from the ruthless Amoka soldiers, a private youth army hired by the UPDF and known for not taking prisoners. Finally she stopped, hiding behind some trees with six others. She was the only one among them with a child.

As soon as the group stopped running, the soldiers directed a bomb over their hiding spot. The bombs fell from above and the Amokas searched on the ground, but they did not reach the hiding rebels.

Still, in the darkness and through the forest, Agatha ran. She could tell from the gunfire echoes that the Amokas had moved to the western side of the mountain, so she headed east. She held her hand over her two-year-old son's mouth to keep him quiet.

In the morning she started moving again. Knowing that her fellow rebels were looking for her, she was able to find a group and sit with them. She had no food for her child, not even a cup of poshe to keep him from crying. But soon the UPDF, following their sounds, were after them again.

Agatha again ran with her child. But as she fled she met a girl who'd been abducted close to Aboke. She felt some kinship toward her and, desperate to save her son's life, she found the courage to ask the girl if she wanted to escape with her.

The girl agreed. Agatha whispered that when they escaped they should not carry extra supplies lest the others suspect. A woman saw them talking, and inferring their plan, said she wanted to join them too. Now they were three.

They decided to make a run for freedom when their group crossed a main road, which Agatha knew was coming up in a few hours. They'd have to make sure they weren't spotted by anyone, that all rebel eyes would be on the road. Agatha whispered that they should separate themselves, so the three moved apart within the line of rebels. At 6 P.M. they started to inch their way closer to one another, and an hour later, as they reached the main road, they were together.

The commander instructed everyone to spread out to prepare to cross the road as one. Agatha and the other two girls were the last people in line on the far western side. Agatha thought to herself, *God is with us, because the commanders have forgotten to assign someone to watch us.*

The sign to cross the road was given, and Agatha and her two co-conspirators ran for their lives. Behind them two girls, one with a baby of her own, ran after them, not knowing why they were running but quickly realizing that they had just inadvertently escaped as well.

The five escapees headed west then doubled back to the eastern side. They decided to run back to Pader, a village they had passed some hours ago. They ran along the road for just seconds, then dove into the next bush. They looked around, saw it was clear, and ran again before diving into the next bush for cover. Before long they were within sight of a village, and no rebels were upon them. They dove into another bush, and decided to stop for a meeting.

Conferring under the bush, their spirits suddenly soared at the realization that they were free. They found a fresh garden just metres from the road and dug for vegetables. But Agatha stopped them after a few minutes. There were too many of them, she said; they could be spotted. Ugandan soldiers were everywhere and might bomb their location during the night. "Let us just move under a bush and sleep for the night," she said. "Tomorrow we'll call out to the main road."

They found a bush large enough that they could lay out under its branches, and as darkness covered the land they settled down to sleep. Agatha gave her son a breast to suckle, but she had no milk for him. It had been almost two days since he'd eaten.

The group awoke at dawn to the sound of people talking. Agatha listened closely. They were UPDF soldiers, not the Amoka boys. The girls looked at each other, not sure what to do. But they lay low, knowing that their being layered in dirt would give them away as rebels. The voices passed. Quietly, the girls moved away from the road and came upon a tilled garden. One found a cup that had been left behind. The soil was wet, so the girls dug two feet into the ground and pulled up about three cups of water. They shared the water among the five of them, rubbing themselves clean. One of the girls also found an oil nut, so they smeared oil on their faces, legs, and arms, hoping the shine would make them look even cleaner.

Deciding this was the best they could do, they straightened their dresses and stepped out onto the road. Five girls, two babies. The moment they walked out the UPDF patrol saw them and understood instantly that these were escaped girls. A soldier greeted them. He kept his gun down and walked over. "Where are you from?" he asked.

"We just escaped," Agatha replied. They all bent their heads in a gesture of submission.

"We'll go to the barracks," the soldier said, and led the girls away. Inside the barracks, Agatha didn't say she was a Karamojong tribal woman. She said she was from Aboke.

A few days later a soldier from the Ugandan military called Sister Anna Maria Spiga, who was now the headmistress at St. Mary's. A girl had returned from the bush, he said, and they were bringing her to the school. Upon hanging up, the nun told the new deputy headmistress that she didn't know what to expect.

They prepared a room for this child, who would be a woman now, wondering who she might be and in what condition she would return. Would she even still be mentally sane? Eight years had passed. Neither

Sister Alba nor Sister Rachele, nor any of the students from 1996, remained at the school. The woman would be returning to strangers.

A truck pulled into the school. Two soldiers stepped out, and then a skinny woman holding a baby climbed out from the back seat. A matron who had been at the school for twenty-five years shouted, "It's Longoria!"

The children in the school ran to Agatha. None of the girls knew her, but still they felt a strong bond with her. During every single morning prayer the girls asked God to ensure the safety of the abducted Aboke Girls who remained in the bush. It was a tradition that had begun in 1996 and had continued to that day.

And so now, without even saying hello or thinking she might be frightened of them, two hundred girls surrounded Agatha and lifted her up into the air. Others took her baby from her arms and lifted him up as well. They danced and sang around the two while the soldiers looked on, astounded.

It was March 22, 2004, and Agatha was back.

All the mediation efforts, the high-level meetings, the clerics' bravery, the ceasefire in Sudan, the engaging of some of the most powerful people in the world—none of it had successfully brought back the girls. Ending the fighting in Sudan had deprived Kony of his sanctuary and brought the girls into Uganda. But really, it was something else. It was the girls themselves. After eight years in captivity, the Aboke Girls had adjusted, learned, coped, grown up. And now these formerly obedient girls had begun to find the inner strength to risk it all. They were still young women. Eight-and-a-half years had been long enough. It was time to make their own way home.

A few days later another military truck drove through Lira and turned into the Rachele Rehabilitation Centre.

During the same battle, in the confusion after her husband died, Palma Achieng had been left unguarded and had also managed to escape.

News spread swiftly. Angelina Atyam and Consy Ogwal and others in the Concerned Parents Association, along with Father John and hundreds of well-wishers from town, came to greet Palma. Agatha also came. The two girls told the parents news of their missing ones. Hope had suddenly arrived, cracking through the darkness that had smothered them for so long.

WHILE THE WAR continued in Northern Uganda, an American woman working at the American Institute of Indian Studies at the University of Chicago sat back in her chair, picked up *The Chronicle of Higher Education* newspaper, and read the cover story about an Aboke Girl who had escaped from a terrorist army and was now attending university in Uganda. Grace Grall, the story said, had escaped from the LRA back in 1997.

For twenty years Elise Auerbach had volunteered with Amnesty International. Each month she and twenty others got together in the basement of a local church. They wrote letters to governments calling for the release of political prisoners, prepared greeting cards for sale, set up information tables at public events—anything they could do to help the disadvantaged of the world.

Elise had never been to Africa—her own special interest was working on cases in the Middle East—but the fact that Grace could overcome so much, and now be excelling at university, humbled her. At the next Amnesty meeting Elise told her group about Grace Grall and suggested they bring her to the United States to talk to some schools.

Everyone agreed. They had enough money in their budget for Grace's plane ticket. Elise emailed Grace a letter making the offer.

Grace Grall, now with long braided hair, a style popular among university students, sat in front of a computer at her campus lab in Jinja, Uganda. The wind blew strong outside, and then the sky cracked open and the rain poured down. Rainy season was just getting started. Grace had recently found herself thinking even more about her old school-mates she'd left behind. Although not a day went by that she didn't think of them all, she had put them in a place in her mind with a wall around it. It was a tough shell, and encompassed a belief, somehow beyond her understanding, that this was God's plan. But now that Agatha and Palma were back, she had found herself dreaming more vividly of them all coming home.

She logged onto her email account and trembled as she read the letter from Amnesty International. Visiting the United States was a dream she'd held onto since her early youth.

A few short weeks later, on April 9, 2004, Grace Grall left Uganda to fly halfway around the world. At New York's John F. Kennedy airport Elise hugged her. Then she brought her to the five-star Marriott Hotel near the Brooklyn Bridge in Manhattan.

When the door to her room closed behind her, Grace looked at the king-size bed with big pillows and feather duvet and thought that tonight she'd be sleeping like a president.

The next day she stood in front of a crowd of a thousand people at Amnesty International's annual meeting. Everyone clapped. She looked side to side, saw everyone staring at her, and realized with a sinking fear that the clapping was for her. Her body went numb, but she looked down at her speech and began talking.

People cried. Afterward, women hugged her. They asked questions. Others whispered to Elise that Grace seemed like a pro. And when it was done, Grace felt she'd conquered more than she had dreamed possible.

That evening a producer from *The Oprah Winfrey Show* called Elise to ask Grace to appear on the show. The Amnesty International communications staff had managed to use a back channel to contact the *Oprah* staff, and Oprah had said yes, she was interested in Grace's story.

Two days later Elise and Grace flew from New York to Chicago courtesy of the show. A limousine waited to take them to the studio. Grace—following whatever path was laid before her, and not really knowing who Oprah was—crawled into the back with Elise and the limousine pulled into traffic.

And now Grace sat in the front row of the *Oprah* show, waiting. Suddenly the audience around her began shouting. "What is happening?" she whispered to Elise sitting next to her.

Everyone stood up and clapped. Someone in the audience yelled out, "Oprah is coming!" Grace forgot to clap, mesmerized by the beautiful woman walking on stage, her presence filling the room. She hadn't known what Oprah looked like.

Oprah interviewed a girl trafficked from Africa to America, then spoke to a filmmaker who had documented male teenage prostitution in Romania. Finally she turned to Grace in the audience, asking her to share her story. Suddenly feeling shy, Grace spoke quietly, narrating her story to audiences across the world: three failed suicide attempts, live burial, rape, the killing of others, escape, and now, college.

When Grace was done speaking, Oprah called out, "Get up, the world wants to see you! You are a great woman!" Feeling shy, and uncomfortable with all the attention, Grace didn't want to stand up, but she did.

Over the next two weeks Grace spoke at campuses across the northern states, in Chicago, New York, Boston. After her talks, people often asked if she would return to Uganda, and what she had learned from her life as a child soldier. Grace always explained that she was in America to shed light on her country and that she must return there.

On May 6 Grace was taken to Capitol Hill in Washington. Until now, the United States—as the world's only superpower and Museveni's best ally, the single country that could make a difference—had ignored the suffering in Uganda. Amnesty International had arranged for Grace to speak to Congressman Tom Lantos and Senators Russ Feingold, Joseph Biden, and Sam Brownback. She considered it the most important talk of her life.

After the men had listened to Grace tell her story, one asked if it was true that the war in Uganda was inter-tribal. Grace said it wasn't that simple. Another asked her what they could do to help. She said that there were many things, that the United States of America had the power to make the war stop. She told them that if they delayed, an entire segment of the Ugandan population would be wiped out. The men shook their heads and Grace wondered if she had offended them somehow. She stopped talking and waited for them to say something. One thanked her for sharing her experience with them, called her a brave girl, and said that they would do what they could to help her people in Northern Uganda achieve peace.

A short while later these men helped pass through Congress the Northern Uganda Crisis Response Act of 2004. It called on the Bush administration to support a peaceful resolution of the conflict in Northern Uganda. The law signalled U.S. intent to get involved in the crisis, and to work with the Ugandan government to help protect the civilians of the North.

After her talk, Grace Grall felt in her heart that something good was going to happen for Northern Uganda.

That afternoon she visited the museums in Washington. The U.S. Holocaust Memorial Museum, a living memorial to the Jewish Holocaust, overwhelmed her with pain as she realized that a holocaust was happening right now in her own country. She hoped the congressmen she had met understood that.[103]

CHAPTER 35

BANYA'S GROUP, KILAK HILLS, NORTHERN UGANDA

Brigadier-General Kenneth Banya, now second-in-command, was in the Kilak Hills of Northern Uganda trying to figure out how to surrender. Two months earlier, after Kony told the group that the spirit had declared their time in Sudan was over, Banya had crossed into Uganda for the first time in ten years. He'd brought with him his four wives, including Grace Acan and their two children. It was Grace's first time back in Uganda.[104]

Banya was in charge of the women and children. Here in Uganda he saw for himself now how difficult life was, and that the Ugandan military clearly had them outpowered. *We have failed in this war,* he realized. *It is not going to take us anywhere. We are just going to kill civilians.* He'd heard about the amnesty offer over the radio and understood that the international community was involved, so he believed they might truly be able to surrender.

On July 13, 2004, Banya called the station manager of Radio Mega FM and told him that he wanted to come out. The manager responded that he would make arrangements with the military for his surrender. But instead, as Banya waited for a return call, a military airstrike began. A helicopter fired down on his people, mostly unarmed women and children. Behind Banya a bomb fell on his four-year-old son, Grace Acan's child, ripping the boy apart.

Banya knew they would all die. His group numbered just over a hundred, and among them they had only fifteen guns. So he walked into the open field, let his AK-47 drop against his chest, raised his arms in the air, and surrendered. As two gunships fired from above, the military commander walked up to Banya, and surrounded by soldiers, guns drawn, took him into custody. Behind him Grace Acan fled, weeping at the sight of her dead boy, her baby girl strapped to her back.

The Ugandan newspapers were filled with news of the biggest arrest in the history of the war—and reports that Banya had renounced the rebellion and taken the government's offer of amnesty.

A few days later newspapers reported that Banya and other recently returned LRA commanders who had taken amnesty were attending a seminar in Gulu designed to help returning commanders. It was a public relations campaign designed by the Ugandan military and the Acholi religious leaders to prove that any LRA who gave themselves up would be welcomed home. The men were also to undergo the traditional recon-ciliation ceremony in which they would confess their actions, stomp on an egg—to symbolize breaking from the old and opening the new—and then, together with some of their victims, swallow from a bitter root.

Consy Ogwal and Angelina Atyam decided to head to Gulu and welcome the commanders personally. They took the jeep that Oprah had given to the Concerned Parents Association.

Banya arrived with his junior commanders at the Acholi Inn in Gulu. They introduced themselves to the group and were warmly welcomed by the military, religious leaders, and the community at large. When the meetings broke for tea, Angelina grabbed Consy's arm. "Let's go intro-duce ourselves," she whispered. The two women joined the line of well-wishers, shaking hands with the young men who had renounced rebellion. They were all friendly and polite. Banya, who retained his high ranking, was the last in the line. Angelina shook his hand first. "You greet that one," she said to Banya, gesturing to Consy. "Then ask her who she is."

But when Consy saw Banya speaking to Angelina, she approached him herself. "Who are you?" she said without greeting him.

"I am Brigadier Banya." He extended his hand.

She shook it. "I am Consy Ogwal, the mother of Grace." Banya looked into the gentle eyes of his mother-in-law for the first time. His hand began trembling in her grasp. "No, be calm," Consy said, feeling a strength welling up from deep inside.

"Now, where's Grace?" she asked the man who had enslaved her daughter.

"Grace was left behind. She's alive," he said, looking at her warmly. Perhaps he recognized Grace—who was known in the bush to be his favourite wife—in Consy's eyes.

The seminar was beginning again. Banya had to return to his seat, but asked if they could talk again later. During lunch break he sat down to eat with Consy and Angelina. Both were thankful for his polite gestures toward them. He might still hold the key they searched for. As gently as she could, Consy spoke. "Where are the children?"

Banya told her that most of the girls were in Sudan, although some were now in the Ugandan bush. He added that two Aboke Girls were in the bush outside Kitgum and that the others remained behind with Kony. Grace Acan, he said, was now in Vincent Otti's care.

"We heard Grace died," Consy said.

"No," he said.

Consy said that he should call the commanders in the bush and ask them to release the children. She meant all of them, not just Grace. Through the years the parents had prayed for all the children to come home.

Banya nodded and said he would. Consy and Angelina returned to Lira, feeling some hope.

A few days later Banya travelled to Lira and walked into the Radio Wa station to speak on the *Karibu* program. He explained how he'd been arrested, that the Ugandan military was treating him well, that he was tired. And then, addressing Vincent Otti directly, he asked that his women and children be released, as he needed them for himself on this side.

After hearing Banya's appeal, Otti asked Kony, who agreed to the release with one exception: his Aboke Girl wife, Grace Acan, was to be returned to Kony in Sudan.

MEANWHILE, Angelina Atyam's daughter, Charlotte Awino, had been walking for days in the Northern Ugandan bush, following behind her husband, Raska Lukwiya. She carried her youngest boy, a two-year-old, leaving the five-year-old to walk beside her. She was tired and hungry, and her children didn't want to be walking. The youngest one often cried, the older one sulked. And yet they walked. Suddenly, a helicopter gunship attacked them from above.

When the gunfire was over, Charlotte's five-year-old son was gone. Her bodyguard demanded to know what she had done with the boy. Truthfully, she didn't want him. His was a horrible life, and she couldn't bear taking care of him. She must have dropped him in her panic to avoid the hail of gunfire.

The guard claimed that she'd thrown away her child intentionally, that she knew escaping with two children was difficult, and that the UPDF would find the boy and take him home ahead of her.

After that Charlotte was given tighter security. She didn't move without an armed escort, at night she had to sleep in the centre of the group, and she was subject to spot checks to make sure she wasn't missing.

Over the next weeks Charlotte became tormented by thoughts of her son lost in the bush, trying to survive. She may have thought she didn't want him, but now that he was gone, possibly wandering alone in the bush crying for her, she was sick with worry for him. She prayed constantly. And now, after eight years in captivity, her thoughts turned toward escaping—to find her lost son.

And so, almost a month after her boy went missing, during one of the bombings and with her guards all around her and dead bodies everywhere, she simply branched off the path as if going to the bathroom, and with her two-year-old son in her arms, kept walking.

To her it was a miracle: no one followed. And then she ran. After six hours she met another group of rebels, but they ignored her. So she continued walking, and eventually found a village, where a man on a bike agreed to bring her to the army.[105]

It was July 20, 2004. Angelina Atyam and the other Concerned Parents Association executives were at their Lira office for a meeting. At the end of the meeting, just before prayers, the CB radio sounded. "Angelina, stand by for some good news," was the message.

Angelina looked at the five others in the room and smiled. Because they were giving advance notice, she thought it might be a group of children. "Let us stand by and wait," she said to her friends. It didn't cross her mind that it could be an Aboke Girl.

Fifteen minutes later the phone rang and Angelina answered it in her office. "Angelina, your daughter is here," a man said. She went silent, suddenly confused. She put the phone down, walked into the other office, and looked at the vice-chairperson. "You better pick up this phone and listen, because I'm not sure what they're telling me."

He picked up the other extension. On her way back to the phone, Angelina's legs buckled underneath her. She held the wall and picked up the phone again.

The other parents greeted her with hugs and joy, but Angelina felt that her own joy was mixed with guilt and anxiety. She looked at Emmanuel Orongo, the father of Brenda Atoo, an Aboke Girl they'd just heard had died in an aerial bombing. But now Emmanuel was laughing and hugging her.

It was too late to travel on the roads, so it was the next day that Angelina drove the 150 kilometres to Gulu and raced into the army barracks. She saw Charlotte holding a baby. She was skinny, and her legs were all cut up from walking through elephant grass. Charlotte saw her mother, put down her baby, and they ran into each other's arms, crying and screaming. It was the best cry of Angelina's life. Angelina held her thin, bony daughter in her arms, cherishing the feel of the girl she'd lost eight and a half years earlier. Her heart raced and her body trembled as she held her. Their tears fell on each other as they cried together over everything that had happened. Finally—Angelina couldn't tell how long had passed, perhaps two minutes—they both pulled themselves away because Charlotte's little boy, feeling abandoned in this moment of reunion, was now sobbing louder than they were. Angelina scooped him up into her arms and the three of them now continued to hug.

Angelina brought Charlotte and the boy home with her. Two days later, after Charlotte told her mother what had happened to the older boy, Angelina left the house without telling Charlotte what she was doing. Using the vehicle from Oprah, she drove up to Kitgum, to the military barracks not far from where Charlotte's son had gone missing, and asked if they had any lost children.

They did. Kept in the barracks in the back were dozens of children who were lost and unaccounted for. Angelian stepped into the room and soon noticed a skinny, sickly boy who looked a little like Charlotte.

"What's your name?" she asked the boy.

"Vincent," he replied. The boy had been named after Vincent Otti.

This was the name she was looking for. "I'm your grandmother," she said.

She swept the stunned child up in her arms and signed the paperwork to bring him home. When Charlotte saw her little boy she wept. Later that day she changed his name to Miracle.

IN THE BUSH, chaos reigned. The Ugandan military had surrounded rebels in South Sudan and in Northern Uganda and were now attacking. Front-line rebel soldiers tried to hold them off as units raced frantically through the bush amid the gunfire and the bombs from above. Most of the remaining Aboke Girls, and their guards, were running for their lives.

With death all around them, one of the girls, Janet Aber, knelt at the foot of her commander-husband, Sam Kolo. After eight years and two children with him, she begged for an outright release, telling him that if he let her die in the bush without seeing her parents again his guilt would prevent him from ever being happy. One of their children had already been killed. He let her go with their remaining child.

CHAPTER 36

On the morning of August 2, 2004, Florence Lacor, the mother of Angela Atim, woke up feeling uncharacteristically happy. *My goodness, I have a joy,* she thought as she walked to the Gulu World Vision office.

Arriving at the office, she realized that most of the staff were missing. She asked a woman in the office where they were. The woman was surprised that Florence hadn't heard that children were coming today. Then she looked at Florence and recognized an unusually happy glow emanating from her. "Your child is not on the list," she said.

But the joy remained. Florence couldn't stop smiling. The children arrived, and Florence welcomed them, began distributing mattresses and clean clothes, and helped the weak ones to move.

A young woman approached her, recognizing her daughter in Florence's distinctive features. She told Florence that she knew Angela. "I think she's still in the bush," she said. Florence felt so happy for all the children as she went about trying to make them comfortable.

Meanwhile, Angela was 120 kilometres away, across the border in Sudan, carrying the baby of a commander's wife on her back. Ugandan soldiers, still permitted by Khartoum to cross into South Sudan to pursue the LRA rebels, were on their trail, and Angela and other women were on the move in the bushes, evading them. But today Angela had resolved to escape.

When she told the woman whose baby she carried, the woman replied, "Angela, how can you leave when you have my child?" Angela said she'd leave the child behind. The woman began looking for her husband to report Angela's treason, but her husband was busy commanding the defence. Now the woman was afraid to leave her child alone with Angela. "I'm not going to cross the road. If I do, it will mean I'll die in the bush," Angela said. "Please, you might die," the woman pleaded.

Once they reached the road everyone squatted down, but when the sign was given to cross, Angela remained squatting. And because she still carried the other woman's baby, the woman stayed behind with her. An eight-year-old girl noticed them, and she too decided not to cross the road.

Juba was just seven kilometres away, so they started walking in the bush toward town. But when the other woman pointed out that if they were spotted in the bush the soldiers would shoot them, the group walked on the road, pretending to be Sudanese.

Before long a soldier in the Sudanese government forces demanded in Arabic to see their passes. They had no passes. He could tell by looking at them that they were LRA and cocked his gun at them angrily, but just then his fellow-soldiers, Arabs from the North, arrived. They pushed the soldier aside and greeted the women. Angela told them that they were escaped LRA.

The men told the women to come with them to the safety of Juba. One handed the little girl a sweet.

The next day a man Florence Lacor knew from Save the Children called her at the World Vision Centre in Gulu, suggesting she call a colonel to ask about her daughter. The colonel told her that Angela had reported at the UNICEF office in Juba two hours earlier. Florence called the number he gave her. A moment later a frail voice came on the line. It was her daughter at last.

Three weeks later a second planeload of escaped LRA children landed on the Gulu airstrip. Thousands of villagers and dozens of aid workers were there to greet the plane. The runway was covered in flowers that the people had thrown as the plane landed.

There were no stairs for the plane, so the children were told to climb down backward on a construction ladder. But the children, fearing the military, hung back. Angela—as brave as she'd been at the abduction years ago when she wrote out all the names for Sister Rachele—offered to be the first. She climbed down, and Florence opened her arms. Angela, tall, rake-thin, and beautiful, wearing a long African dress given to her by UNICEF in Juba, grabbed hold of her mother.

Streams of tears flowed down their cheeks as they embraced for a long time in silence. Local and international media pushed at each other to take photos of the emotional moment. Finally Florence broke the silence. "You are welcome. I love you. Angela I am sorry for what happened. Forgive me," she said.

Behind her was Janet Akello, now twenty-one, who had returned with her two children. When she stepped up to the plane's door, her father, a Lira-based engineer, started singing, "Jesus, Pray God, Pray God." The Ugandan military had told them to be orderly, but he ran to the plane's door. Janet Akello turned, saw her father standing below her, and collapsed into his arms. "Daddy! Daddy!" she cried. He gave her a long embrace. Her two little sons followed her. "Don't worry," her father said. "Those kids are now mine, they are no longer yours." Her mother then held her as well. Janet cried inconsolably as both her parents carried her away.

As the reunited families struggled to come to terms with the years lost, and the realization that their innocent children were now emotionally wounded adults, the battles in the Northern Ugandan bush continued unabated.

Some parents received news of deaths. The Ugandan military reported to the Concerned Parents Association—now working with Save the Children to help reunite parents with their children—that two more Aboke Girls had died in battle. One of the two, Jessica Anguu—Charlotte's co-wife to Raska Lukwiya—had been found dead in the bush with her five-year-old boy still alive, strapped to her back. The army informed the Concerned Parents Association that they had also rescued a girl who had lived with Jessica.

Hoping to get some news about the others still in captivity, Angelina Atyam and Consy Ogwal went to visit the girl in the Gulu army barracks. Consy introduced herself as Grace Acan's mother. Raska Lukwiya's group had been overlapping with Kenneth Banya's, so Consy thought the girl might be able to tell her where Grace was.

The girl looked at her. "Grace is dead," she said flatly, like a girl who has seen so much death she no longer cared about the living.

Consy couldn't move. "We asked Banya. Banya said Grace was alive," she stuttered.

"No," she said. "There were two attacks. Grace was killed in the afternoon by an airplane bombing by the UPDF."

When a Ugandan soldier joined them, Consy told him that the girl had said Grace Acan was dead. He looked into the files from that day and found the record of the dead. Yes, he said, Grace Acan had been found dead in the battlefield, killed by UPDF fire, with a dead baby girl strapped on her back.

The UPDF had taken photos of all the dead. Rifling through the photos, the officer found the picture showing the blown-up remains of Grace's four-year-old boy, Consy's grandchild. Consy looked at her grandson's remains. "I don't want to see any more pictures," she cried.

Consy went and sat outside in the rain. Banya, who now lived at the Gulu barracks for protection, had just heard word himself that Grace was dead and was also breaking down. In his own way, he cared. She'd been one of his wives for eight years, had borne him two children, and he had recognized her intelligence and ability to work hard in the fields. Banya walked over and sat next to Consy. "So, Mamma," he said to his mother-in-law. "It has come. Grace is dead." The rain poured down on them.

Consy sobbed and screamed over Grace's death. "Don't cry, keep quiet now," Banya said, adding, "I know how you're feeling."

Rage built inside Consy. "I'm not feeling as you're feeling! You're not the mother. Me, I sent Grace to school! Not to be married to anyone. You don't feel as I feel!" she yelled. She was ready to hit him.

Banya chose not to reply, but he continued to sit next to her. Eventually he told her that he wanted to go back into the bush to collect the bodies of Grace and their two children so that they could be properly buried. He checked with the Ugandan military captain on duty, who agreed that military escorts would accompany Banya on this task.

"Now Mamma, you go back home," Banya said. "We'll organize this."

But no word came from Banya or the military, and so Consy's family, along with Father John and Grace Acan's old friends, gathered inside Lira's Martyr's Church for a memorial to the dead girl—and her young boy and baby girl no one had known. The memorial, however, brought no closure. Perhaps because Consy hadn't actually seen her daughter's body, she still held onto hope. She turned to God to pray for Grace one last time. She promised herself that after this she would accept that Grace was gone. Through the night and all the next day she stood at the cross of the Lira Cathedral and spoke to God. When she returned home, exhausted, she felt hollow inside.

Two days later a brief notice appeared in the newspaper: "Banya's wife fled." For eight years, Consy and her neighbour had been spending all their extra money on newspapers. Her neighbour ran across the dirt road between them and showed Consy. *What did it mean? Grace?* Consy ran to another neighbour who had a telephone. The man of the house called the army's Child Protection Unit, where the soldier answering phones confirmed that one of Banya's wives had escaped. "What's the girl's name?" he asked. The soldier wasn't sure, but knew this: she was an Aboke Girl.

Consy sent out the alarm throughout the Concerned Parents Association network. A mother up in Gulu offered to collect Grace and bring her the two hundred kilometres to Lira. But when the woman arrived at the barracks, the soldiers refused to let Grace leave with anyone other than her parents.

A few hours later Consy and her husband arrived at the military barracks. They were shocked by the tortured appearance of their daughter. She was barefoot, had no hair on her head, and was dirty, haggard, and painfully thin. There appeared to be no fat between her bones and skin. She had on only rags, barely enough to cover herself. Scratches and sores covered her arms and legs. She sat with her tiny daughter.

Consy looked at Grace but couldn't recognize her daughter inside this person. The pain of it overwhelmed her. A part of her recognized a similarity in appearance. Although she wanted to be strong at this moment, it was impossible for Consy. She was confused. She cried and looked away from Grace.

Grace Acan looked at her mother crying and felt bad for her. "Mom, don't cry," she said at last. Grace told her mother that it had been hard, but she was now back alive. "You should praise God that I'm back alive, because there are friends of mine who are no longer living, so don't cry."

Then Grace looked down at her young daughter and told Consy that the child's name was Mercy. The little girl was beautiful. Big eyes looked up at Consy and the girl smiled. Consy was a grandmother.

A few days later Grace asked to speak on Radio Wa's *Karibu* program. "Come back, there's nothing they do to you," she said. The rebels had told her that military soldiers kept boxes of condoms in the interrogation rooms so that they could rape without worrying about getting AIDS. Grace had been so convinced that she'd be gang-raped and then imprisoned or killed by the Ugandan military that, after becoming separated from the rebels, she'd hidden for eight days in the bush with her starving daughter before turning herself in to a villager. Now she told the others: "The people accept you. You can come back. It's safe. Please, come back."

Upon her return, she did not seek out Kenneth Banya. That part of her life was over.

KENNETH BANYA was now leading the life of the returned prodigal son. Although he lived in the Ugandan military barracks he went about as he pleased, with bodyguards. He played pool in the local Gulu pool hall and he watched soccer most nights at the Acholi Inn, together and in obvious friendship with older Ugandan military soldiers. After hearing Banya's radio request for his wives to be released to him, the rebels had brought two women from the bush and dropped them off close to a military unit. The two women and their children now willingly lived with him inside the Gulu military barracks.

When Banya walked down the street people greeted him and smiled. He planned business ventures. The international NGO community now suddenly filling the guesthouses in Gulu was shocked, but it was obvious: he was the big man in town.

Museveni named Banya an honorary brigadier general in his own UPDF forces, a ranking equivalent to what Banya had held in the LRA. Rather than leading fighters, though, he began touring the northern regions promoting peace and reconciliation. During his talks, Banya told the people he was ashamed to stand before them because they had suffered so much at LRA hands. He said that it was all Joseph Kony's will, but nonetheless apologized for his own role. He assured people in the southern districts that they could go home, that the rebels were too weak to return.

One October day Banya came to Radio Wa. Deejay Kakaba asked him what it was he wanted to say. "I have come to ask forgiveness from you," Banya said to the civilian population listening. And then he called on his colleagues still in the bush to show mercy on the people. "Chopping off people's arms, cutting their lips, and killing them will not take you anywhere," he said. Banya was accompanied by four top government officials. Dozens of army surrounded the radio station to protect him. Consy and Grace did not visit him while he was in town, and he did not attempt to see his surviving daughter.

Banya moved on to Radio FM Gulu, where he could be heard inside Sudan. He told Kony, Vincent Otti, and Sam Kolo to come out and take the amnesty. "Don't let the amnesty period expire while you are still in the bush," he urged. "Time for rebellion is over. Don't go back to Sudan where you will surely die."[106]

With him was one of Kony's escaped wives, Arach, who also spoke. "We and your children are ashamed. We are treated well, but you continue committing atrocities. Stop killings and mutilations," she said into the microphone.[107]

ABOKE OLD GIRLS ASSOCIATION, KAMPALA

A few weeks later hundreds of professional young women gathered at the Regency Hotel in Kampala to launch a new alumni networking group they called the St. Mary's Aboke Old Girls Association. The women decorated the room in blue and white balloons, matching the school's colours. The Lira district police chief, the district chairman, and five members of Parliament all attended, invited by the women and now supporting their efforts.

As the women entered the room they embraced and wept tears of joy. Some hollered their Acholi tribal call, an old warning call that was now a declaration of the Northern Ugandan spirit of resilience. Some were university students, others had found work at various NGOs or in the government. One had become a member of Parliament, another was a magistrate judge. Among them were Aboke Girls who had been freed that first night because of Sister Rachele, who had escaped in the first year, and the eight girls who had escaped within the last year. These girls, too shy to be made the centre of attention, were the true reason they were all here. The party was in their honour.

The women had brought in an Acholi band. One in the group played a fast drumbeat as the others clacked squash gourds. The young women shook their bodies in energetic dance. Father John accepted a Pilsner beer from one of the women and laughed at the spectacle before him. He may not have had a family or any money of his own, and he had lived so far away from his relatives throughout his life, but he had such reward.

"We are celebrating the spirit of every little girl in the North," said one of the young graduates, a woman who had been among the 109 released on the first night. "War has deprived the North. The worst part is children, especially girls being deprived of education." The Aboke Girls who had recently come out of the bush couldn't help but look at her—her fashionable clothes, a profession, her own apartment in Kampala—with some pain. She made them see what they could have been if all those years had not been taken from them.

The Aboke Old Girls Association announced plans to encourage young girls to stay in school and to offer career counselling in the displaced persons' camps. "It's our way of showing solidarity," the woman said. "The bush has changed their lives. Parents alone can't handle their rehabilitation. We have to help them overcome trauma and pursue their career ambition."[108]

Father John listened with pride. Finally, the young woman introduced him as the patron of the Aboke Old Girls Association. It was through Radio Wa that the group had first conceived of their organization, and it had been in his office that they'd formulated plans for the party. They asked him to give a speech.

Father John stood from his table. "There has been a lot of pain," he said solemnly. He looked at the young women who had just returned and smiled brightly at them. "There is need for holistic healing," he shouted. He raised his hands, motioning for everyone to dance. The women shouted in glee, grabbed the hands of Grace Acan, Charlotte Awino, Agatha Longoria, and the others who'd just come back to them, and pulled them onto the dance floor. The Aboke Girls looked at one another and laughed.[109]

The Aboke Old Girls Association had recently asked Father John to head up their association. Given the intense poverty around them, and, for some, family demands, they wanted him to handle their money. And now his first aim was to get the young women back in school. It was agreed that the women should remain together to support one another, and that they should find a school in Kampala where they were safe from any possibility of re-abduction.

In January 2005 Father John drove the seven girls to Kampala where they toured the schools. When he brought them to a Catholic school established by Father Scalabrini, a wealthy Italian Comboni priest who had been exiled from Gulu in 1989 after speaking out against the military, the girls found a strict Catholic atmosphere similar to what they'd known at St. Mary's, and a school with excellent academic standards. Although some of the parents would have preferred a more liberal school, the girls were united in their calls to attend this religious institution.

Father Scalabrini agreed to pay the tuition for any Aboke Girl who wanted to come to his school. The priests and parents talked it over, and all agreed that keeping the girls together, while encouraging them to interact with others who had never experienced the LRA camps, was probably the girls' best hope for recovery. And so, safe from the rebels and their former husbands, the girls returned to high school.

A FEW WEEKS LATER, tiny Jackie Wagesa, Kony's favourite wife—whom most had given up hope of seeing again because Kony kept her close and well guarded—escaped with her two-year-old daughter.

Returning to Lira, Jackie discovered that, as she had long feared, her mother was dead. The only family she had left was her grandmother, a depressed old woman living alone in a tiny mud hut in a displaced persons' camp inside Lira.

Jackie left her daughter with her grandmother, and just one week after her escape she joined the other Aboke Girls at the school. For ten years she had survived by telling herself that one day she would return to school and that the nightmare would be over. She had an iron will. Four months later, Jackie was the top student in her grade.

CHAPTER 37

NIMULE, SOUTH SUDAN, SEPTEMBER 2005

Bishop Ochola, Archbishop Odama, the Khadi Sheik, and Father Carlos headed out of Gulu, bumping along in a caravan of forty Northern Ugandans heading north along the historic Juba Road across the Sudanese border. For as long as anyone could remember, this fabled trading route that followed the path of the White Nile from Uganda through Sudan had been closed by rebels. Families had been lost to one another, friendships severed. But with peace having at last come to Sudan, the road had reopened only days earlier. Six weeks earlier, John Garang, the leader of the rebel SPLA who had just become the united country's vice-president, died in a mysterious helicopter crash. In spite of that, the south and north, sharing oil revenue equally, were working together for the first time in over fifty years.

The group arrived at the dusty town of Nimule, built along the cascading Nile River. Thousands of Sudanese still lived in displaced persons' camps here as they tried to figure out how to return home.

It was the first week of September 2005.[110] Sudanese villagers welcomed the convoy by throwing flowers on the road. The men climbed out of their trucks and greeted the local Sudanese leaders under the shade of a great tamarind tree. Expectant Sudanese children circled around the elders. One of the Sudanese leaders told them how a lifetime ago, before war and politics had closed them off to one another, the Acholi traditional chiefs, who lived both in South Sudan and Northern Uganda, would meet here, under this mighty tree, to talk and solve problems.

Injustices were resolved here, marriage dowries settled, business arranged.

Young people held up placards outside the circle of elders: RESPECT THE BOUNDARIES, ENCOURAGE THE RELATIONSHIPS. Young Sudanese shouted it out. The elders nodded gravely. Everyone agreed that they'd had enough of war for a lifetime.

Archbishop Odama looked around at the Sudanese crowd. They were Muslim and Christian, old and young, Arab and black, armed forces and farmers, imams and priests. Goodwill and greetings and smiles filled everyone's faces. Father Carlos took notes.

"It is good to visit our grandparents' home," the Archbishop said. "Our grandparents' home is now quiet, and it should help the grandchildren, the Ugandans from the north, to achieve peace too."

Hope was high in Northern Uganda that peace was at hand. Abductions and attacks were down. And Betty Bigombe, the former Ugandan minister whom the Acholi religious leaders had asked to help mediate with the LRA, had left her comfortable job at the World Bank in Washington and for months now, out of a rustic Gulu hotel, had been quietly working on mediation efforts between the LRA and the Ugandan government.

The group soon shifted the conversation to peace. "We never thought we could sit at the same table to talk peace with the Arabs, but we did it," a South Sudan SPLA general said.

Another SPLA general explained to the Ugandans the details of how the Comprehensive Peace Agreement had been reached with North Sudan. How the Machakos Protocol separated religion and state, leaving the South exempt from shariah law. He explained oil-wealth sharing, power sharing, and security details, elaborating that the strategic distribution of troops was key to maintaining peace.

The Ugandans asked about the SPLA's promise to deal with Joseph Kony. But the general explained that right now they needed to be more concerned with their own transformation. The time wasn't right to go on an offensive. Other civil leaders from South Sudan relayed sad tales of recent killings and abductions by the LRA in their own villages. These people were convinced that the LRA still received military support from radical elements inside the Sudanese government.

The South Sudanese leaders reassured Archbishop Odama and Bishop Ochola that the LRA atrocities would not prevent their brotherhood with the Acholi people.

Odama closed the meeting with a funeral prayer for John Garang, whose helicopter had crashed after visiting Museveni just three weeks after becoming the vice-president of a united Sudan. Garang's loyal deputy, Salva Kiir, had assumed his place. "African Sudanese must live in peace as brothers and sisters in this rich country, with a vision of unity and development. This is the message that Dr. Garang left for you. Follow it," the Archbishop said. He pointed to the new flag of Sudan: black for the people, white for peace, red for brotherhood, green for fertility, and the star for the vision.

Then an SPLA general turned to the Ugandans. "Whether you come from Gulu, West Nile, Pader, Kitgum, Lango, or Teso, come back to Sudan to see your ancestors' home."

And with that, the religious party retraced their route back down the Juba Road, believing that peace, prosperity, and justice would soon be at hand in Northern Uganda.

THE WORLD'S EYE had suddenly turned toward the dark continent. Leading the gaze was the musician Bob Geldof, who had organized the Live 8 world concerts of July 2005 dedicated to providing charity to Africa and to pressuring the wealthy G8 leaders into changing their policies toward Africa, including cancelling Africa's crushing debt to the First World. He had enlisted other celebrities, most notably Bono, Pope John Paul II, Tony Blair, and Harvard economist Jeffrey Sachs, in his quest to get people to understand and care. The group travelled the world to rally support for Africa. They did what seemed impossible: they joined the young, the entertainment industry, the religious, the politicians, and the financial types in a common goal. They argued for justice and equality for Africa, and the masses of the West argued along with them.

The World Bank eventually listened, wiping out $50 billion worth of debts to the world's poorest countries. All of Uganda's debt was forgiven.

TWO WEEKS AFTER the religious leaders returned home, the United Nations' International Criminal Court issued the first arrest warrants since its creation in 2003. Indictments for five LRA leaders were transmitted to Uganda, Congo, and Sudan. In theory, Joseph Kony and his top commanders became the world's most wanted criminals.

The warrant for Joseph Kony listed thirty-three counts: twelve counts of crimes against humanity, including murder, enslavement, sexual enslavement, rape, inhumane acts of inflicting serious bodily injury and suffering; and twenty-one counts of war crimes, including murder, cruel treatment of civilians, intentionally directing an attack against a civilian population, pillaging, inducing rape, and the forced enlisting of children.

Vincent Otti's arrest warrant listed thirty-two charges, with eleven counts of crimes against humanity, including murder and sexual enslavement, and twenty-one counts of war crimes. Raska Lukwiya was charged with four counts, including enslavement, intentionally directing an attack against a civilian population, and pillaging. Okot Odiambo was blamed for leading the LRA's massacre at Barlonya camp in February 2004.

Efforts to arrest the men began immediately. Ugandan intelligence reports placed Kony at an LRA camp sixty kilometres north of the red line, the horizontal road a hundred kilometres north of Northern Ugandan border with South Sudan that marked the dividing line up to which, based on a 2002 agreement with Sudan, the Ugandan army was allowed to pursue Kony. With the arrest warrants issued, the Sudanese government gave Uganda a one-month pass to pursue Kony anywhere in South Sudan.

But before Uganda could come for them, the LRA fled South Sudan, floating across the Nile on jerry cans filled with air.[111] The rebels, without food and down to a force of just hundreds, entered the ungoverned jungle of Garamba National Park in the Democratic Republic of Congo.

In December 2005 United Nations peacekeepers staged a daring surprise raid to arrest them. Instead, they were ambushed. The LRA opened fire, leaving eight UN peacekeepers dead before they retreated.

For several months the LRA camped out inside Garamba National

Park, hunting wild game to survive. Their presence in Congo had created an international incident. Emerging from its own war—and after 3.8 million dead—Congo had just democratically elected its first leader since independence in 1960, and President Joseph Kabila did not want warlords controlling swaths of his country. And so, after twenty years of war, the United Nations Security Council addressed the LRA issue for the first time, calling for negotiations and restraint.

Meanwhile Sudan's peace remained fragile, with LRA incursions threatening the development that South Sudan so needed. Almost overnight the LRA went from being a small rebel disturbance in Northern Uganda to the primary problem preventing peace and development in oil-rich South Sudan and a growing threat in resource-rich Congo. South Sudan now understood that the biggest obstacle preventing development and investment in their land was the LRA, and since Uganda could not seem to beat them, it was time for peace talks. And now the international community was watching, and pushing for mediation.

In the spring of 2006 South Sudan's new vice-president, Riek Machar, met with Vincent Otti at the Sudan–Congo border. The two men talked of peace. Pax Christi International, funded by the Swiss government, began to fund these new peace overtures. Before long Machar met with Kony, who agreed to allow Machar to mediate between him and Museveni. Machar sent Museveni a request from Kony for peace talks, and Museveni responded positively. A ceasefire came into effect in July of 2006.

As peace talks gained traction the Ugandan government agreed to send a group that Kony had asked to visit him in Garamba. Included in this group was Kony's mother, whom he had not seen in thirteen years. After the Acholi delegates left Kony's camp in early July 2006, Museveni's government released this statement: "The Ugandan government will grant total amnesty [to Kony] despite the International Criminal Court indictments if he responds positively to the talks with the government in Juba, southern Sudan, and abandons terrorism." Museveni likened Kony to Adolf Hitler, but said he would not bow to international pressure to have the rebel leader arrested. In 2003 Museveni had invited the

International criminal Court to investigate and prosecute LRA crimes, but now the resulting indictments seemed to be preventing the LRA from surrendering. Museveni blamed the United Nations for his current predicament, stating that the "noble cause of trying Kony before the ICC had been betrayed by the failure of the United Nations, which set up the court, to arrest him, despite knowing his location."[112]

The International Criminal Court countered that it was illegal for Museveni, as a signatory of the court, to trade amnesty for peace; that the charges were now beyond Museveni's power to rescind. Kony's was the ICC's first case, and dropping the serious charges against him would open the door for other warlords to use the same tactic.

The peace talks moved forward, albeit uneasily. But Joseph Kony refused to meet the Ugandans in Juba, fearing a trap designed to arrest him and send him off to trial by the International Criminal Court. Meanwhile the Acholi religious leaders, and many others, argued that the ICC was not offering them justice; that such justice would require the additional prosecution of Ugandan government soldiers for their crimes.

In late 2006 the Canadian government donated $1.5 million to the peace process between the LRA and the Ugandan government, making Canada the largest financial supporter of the ongoing peace talks. Yet by December the talks had fallen apart, with the LRA asserting that the Ugandan military were secretly attacking their soldiers in violation of the ceasefire. They threatened a return to war.

But as the months passed, with the Acholi community crying out for Kony to accept peace and the international community pressuring Museveni to accept a mediated settlement, the peace talks progressed. UN Secretary-General Kofi Annan appointed Mozambique's former president, Joaquim Chissano, as the UN envoy to help end what had become Africa's longest war. In April 2007 the two sides were again at the table, with Vincent Otti acting on Kony's behalf.

Optimism for peace was now evident across Northern Uganda. Hundreds of thousands had left the camps, and those who remained felt confident enough to venture out during the daytime to farm their fields. Radio Wa was broadcasting peace messages on the hour, pleading with both sides to come to a solution. Businesses were opening, and trade between Northern Uganda and South Sudan was increasing quickly. The Rachele Rehabilitation Centre for Child Soldiers had been converted into a high school.

CHAPTER 38

Today, in addition to his work as a chaplain, Father John Fraser continues to oversee Radio Wa. In early 2007 the Canadian government donated a significant sum to help the station develop, and with this money Radio Wa expanded its radio signal transmission to include all of Northern Uganda, South Sudan, and Eastern Congo—all the regions where the LRA rebels operate, and collectively, the most conflict-ridden location in the world.

Sister Alba Brulo, the headmistress of St. Mary's school, died of a heart attack in London on April 11, 2006, aged seventy-three. Sister Alba had spent thirty-nine years in Uganda as a nun. The abducted children of Northern Uganda, and especially her Aboke Girls, remained her first thought of the day and last of the night. She had continued to pray for them every day.

Sister Rachele Fassera, the deputy headmistress of St. Mary's, remains in Rome, where she is the Comboni sisters' general secretary. She remains emotionally traumatized by the abduction of the girls and the events that unfolded in subsequent years. However, she expects to be posted back to Northern Uganda one day, and so will see the girls once more.

Eight of the ten Aboke Girls who escaped in 2004 and 2005 continue to study together at the Comboni school in Kampala, where they remain out of the rebels' reach. Their children are being cared for by their parents, or, in the case of Jackie Wagesa, by her grandmother. All intend to become doctors, and most are excelling at school.

Grace Acan, Banya's former wife, is now in Senior 6 and has been elected the school's head girl. Jackie Wagesa, once Kony's prized possession, recently had the highest academic standing of all the students in her grade.

Five of the six Aboke Girls who escaped in the first months of their abduction, before crossing into the hell of life in Sudan, have now graduated from university. One of the girls now reportedly works as a lawyer at the International Criminal Court in The Hague.

Angelina Atyam, as well as raising Charlotte's two boys in Lira, continues her work advocating for the children's release. She publicly met with the mother of Raska Lukwiya, the ICC-indicted commander who had forced upon her daughter two boys, and told the woman that she had forgiven Lukwiya. In a strong gesture of reconciliation, she brought the two boys to meet their paternal grandmother. Raska Lukwiya was killed in a firefight with the Ugandan military on August 12, 2006.

Angelina's daughter, Charlotte Awino, is studying at a private boarding school in Kampala. Agatha Longoria graduated in 2006 from St. Mary's and has returned to her cattle-keeping nomadic people in the Karamoja desert to be with her surviving son and her parents. When she last visited St. Mary's, in 2007, the students said she arrived uncharacteristically happy and glowing; rumours circulated that perhaps she had fallen in love. As there are no phones or outside connections to Karamoja, Agatha seems lost to the outside world.

In contrast, Grace Grall Akallo is on the world's centre stage. After appearing on *Oprah* in 2004 she won an American scholarship and now attends Gordon College in Boston. She intends to enter the field of conflict negotiation and prevention. In April 2006 she testified before the U.S. Congress for the second time, pleading for American help to end the war. She told the panel, "I want to be part of the people struggling day and night to try to bring peace in the world." Today Grace says that although her time among the rebels was a journey through hell, "There's no way you can say that God was not there. God was there. He was watching every step."[113] *Girl Soldier*, a book she co-wrote about her experiences inside the LRA, was published in the summer of 2007.

Consy Ogwal, the mother of Grace Acan, remains in Lira and is raising her younger children as well as Grace's daughter Mercy. After Grace returned home, Consy went back to school herself, and is now a Senior 2-level student. She studies with 120 former child soldiers at the Rachele Rehabilitation Centre high school. Her husband has moved to Kampala.

Isabella, the mother of Louiza Namale, died suddenly in the summer of 2006, and Alfred Olum, suffering from tuberculosis, followed not long after. They leave behind two young orphans.

Teacher John Bosco, who followed the girls with Sister Rachele when they were first abducted, went on to university; he was sponsored by a Canadian journalist who had been impressed by his heroism. After university he had difficulty finding a job, however, and in mid-2006 he was unemployed.

The interfaith Acholi religious leaders remain at the forefront of the latest round of peace talks. In 2006 Father Carlos Rodriguez moved to Kampala to become editor-in-chief of *Leadership,* a Comboni magazine in Uganda. He still travels to the North every other weekend. His mission's founder, Saint Daniel Comboni—the first Archbishop of Sudan—was canonized by Pope John Paul II in 2002, 121 years after his death in Khartoum. His second Vatican-authenticated miracle—saving the life of a Muslim woman who was bleeding to death in childbirth—occurred in a Comboni hospital in Khartoum in 1997 when an interfaith group of Muslims, Catholics, and Coptic Christians prayed together and asked Comboni to save her life. The woman, already without a pulse, reportedly returned to life. Today, she and her family remain devout Muslims. Some Vatican theorists have declared Comboni's Muslim miracle a message from God, foreshadowing what would be the greatest miracle of the third millennium—cooperation between all religions. Comboni's body, interestingly, is buried under the house of the Islamic Khartoum legislature. Over the last forty years the Comboni missionaries of Northern Uganda have been murdered at a higher rate than any other order of Catholic missionaries in the world.

Conflict mediator Ben Hoffman now leads the International Peace and Prosperity Project, a small NGO group of world experts who are testing the concept of preventing mass violence through targeted early intervention. In late 2005 Hoffman was invited to speak at a panel discussion at the University of Ottawa about the prospects for peace in Northern Uganda. He declined, but sent this email to the organizer:

> My experience directly, and deeply with the LRA and Museveni remains a bitterly sad one. I did everything in my power at that time to persuade Museveni to give peace a chance—in effect, to stop playing silly bugger with everyone with all the various "peace initiatives" (religious, his brother, The Carter Center's) and really mean it when he said he was interested in talks. He wasn't then, and I do not believe he is now. As far as the LRA goes I am certain that many of his senior commanders and of course the child soldiers wanted talks.... Kony himself should have been put to the test of talks. Like many guerrillas he may not have been able to be a political actor carrying on appropriately at the table of peace talks. But I argued to Museveni and his Cabinet that Kony should be tested—and that we might be surprised—or indeed, he might have been replaced by commanders who could act politically....

Hoffman went on to write that he'd recommended to Jimmy Carter that they pull out of Northern Uganda and focus on Sudan "rather than bless the hypocrisy and rather than do any harm by staying in." He said that he thought the better path to getting Kony either engaged in talks or out of the way is now through Khartoum. "That is where I would put my effort now if I were able, while leaning on Museveni through the US and others."

Now, nearly two years after Hoffman's email, the peace negotiators are indeed pressuring Sudan while leaning on Museveni. The peace talks look poised to succeed. In May 2007 the two sides signed a comprehensive agreement of principles, although as of August 2007 there is no final agreement. From the LRA perspective, the one outstanding issue is the International Criminal Court indictments against its high command. But as Lloyd Axworthy, a key voice in creating the world court, has stated, there can be no real peace without justice. Bishop Ochola, however, counters that there can be no real justice without forgiveness.

Today, analysts of the North–South Sudan peace agreement recognize that the process was deeply flawed—and in just the same way as Ben Hoffman had perceived before he quit his work with the Carter Center. It is understood that a historic opportunity to solve Sudan's problems in a comprehensive manner was lost when the talks were restricted to the Sudanese government and John Garang's rebels. It meant a silencing of Sudan's other voices. That policy is now known to have been implemented at the insistence of the U.S. government. In hindsight, it looks as though Hoffman was right, and that—just maybe—the genocidal war in Darfur could have been prevented, if only.

St. Mary's Lacor Hospital in Gulu continues to be the pride of Northern Uganda. It treats well over a thousand patients a day. The phenomenon of night-commuting children has ended in Uganda, and after eleven years the displaced persons' camp within the hospital's walls is finally closing down. Twenty years of war, however, have devastated Gulu's infrastructure. Based on Lacor Hospital records, the average life expectancy in Northern Uganda is thirty-nine years for a male and forty-one for a female. Malaria is the primary cause of early death.[114]

Today Yoweri Museveni remains one of Africa's strongest leaders. Western powers continue to support him, although the reality of life in Northern Uganda has damaged his international reputation. Museveni, who says he's committed to building a stronger East African Union, was elected in 2006, amid controversy, to a third term as Uganda's president. He presides over a nation with a median age of just 14.8 years, making Uganda's population the world's youngest.

In November of 2007 the Commonwealth Heads of Government meeting will take place for the first time in Africa—in Uganda. It is the opinion of most insiders that Museveni, concerned for his international reputation, is determined to end the war by the time the leaders of fifty-three countries, and the world's press, descend on his ravaged country.

For the truth remains that Northern Uganda is one of the worst places in the world to be born. By local estimates, the LRA have abducted between 45,000 and 65,000 children during the course of the war. Thousands of those children remain unaccounted for. Hundreds of thousands are dead—mostly as a result of disease resulting from displacement—and as of July 2007 as many as 1.4 million Northern Ugandans remained in displaced persons' camps. One recent study of children in Kitgum reported that 48 percent now suffer stunted development from long-term malnutrition.

But as Grace Grall said recently in a speech she gave in New York City, "The powers of evil won't prevail forever. It will come to an end."

Without a doubt the largest new force is oil. Late last year the Calgary-based Heritage Oil Corporation and the U.K.'s Tullow Oil discovered oil in northwestern Uganda. Initial drilling tests proved so grandly beyond expectations that Uganda is poised to join the ranks of the world's middle-level suppliers of oil. First sales are anticipated for 2009, and Heritage Oil's price on the Toronto Stock Exchange has skyrocketed, rising 2,000 percent in the last few years.

Provided that renewed warfare doesn't break out and corruption doesn't lead to increasing wealth of the few and greater poverty of the many, Uganda should prosper. If peace can hold, the country's future could be as bright as Pope Paul VI had foretold in 1969 when he visited the execution site of the martyred boys of Buganda kingdom. Back then he predicted that a new society, built from those who sacrificed themselves at the foot of the cross and greater than any known in the world, would soon emerge in Uganda. That, of course, is not Uganda's reality, but in this land of interreligious tolerance and forgiveness, where heroism and bravery are known in homes across the land along with the bitter cost of an unending war, it is a conceivable future.

And the returned Aboke Girls, along with their growing children, might be the ones to show the way. Today they are being educated, nurtured, and protected—by their parents, one another, the Combonis, and private sponsors. More than any others they are positioned to help unify and heal their destroyed homeland, to demonstrate that healing and forgiveness are possible, to become the leaders of their new generation.

That is yet to be seen. At the moment, an uneasy peace hovers across this African land. And when oil begins to flow, another story will inevitably begin.

EPILOGUE

In June 2005 Father John Fraser brought me to the Kampala school to meet the eight Aboke Girls who had escaped captivity in the past year. The protective environment of the school meant that students did not leave its grounds during their term and that family visits were limited to every second Saturday afternoon. But the priest who ran the school gave me permission to visit the girls. And although their parents and the school were shielding them from media attention, the girls themselves wanted to talk.

I found them doing their laundry, by hand. Their hair was short, shaved close to their heads, and they wore plain T-shirts, long navy skirts, and flip-flops.

I was immediately struck by the girls' vulnerability, their uncertain gestures, their quiet demeanours. They radiated warmth and solidarity. Yet underneath all that I sensed a big space—a space that had enabled them to bear any torture without its breaking them. For here they sat, together, seemingly moving forward in life again. It felt as though I was meeting the ultimate incarnation of the human spirit, akin to what people feel when they meet the Pope, or, I'm told, how people often react when meeting the Dalai Lama: that they are in the presence of something profound.

We stepped outside the large brown brick building that was their home, and home to hundreds of other students, and pulled white plastic chairs into the shade. I noticed that the girls all had scars on their legs and feet. Although each girl had returned emaciated and malnourished, a few were chubby now. Their enthusiasm for eating, and their resulting "fatness," was for them a source of humour.

They sat in a semicircle around me, and knowing what little I did then, I stumbled, not sure how to begin. "I'm so sorry that this has happened to you," I said. The girls blended in with one another: they dressed the same, kept their hair the same, and their demure manners were that of women uncomfortable with being focused upon.

"Sylvia Alaba came home yesterday," I said, offering news of one more escaped Aboke Girl. I had been in Lira the day before and had witnessed the celebration of her homecoming.

"She escaped?" Their eyes went bright.

"Yes, I met her yesterday. She's at the Rachele Rehabilitation Centre. With a one-year-old baby. She looks okay," I said.

I told them how I'd been sitting in Father John's office at Radio Wa, interviewing the women who'd formed the Aboke Old Girls Association, when Father John's cellphone had rung, delivering the news of twenty-one-year-old Sylvia's escape. Deejay Kakaba had immediately interrupted his announcements for the breaking news. Within five minutes Sylvia's father called the radio station, asking if this could really be true. Three hours later a Ugandan military helicopter delivered Sylvia. The child she carried had been fathered by Joseph Kony. She arrived with twelve other young escapees who had fled to the Rachele Rehabilitation Centre during a battle just that morning. That night Sylvia sent her greetings over Radio Wa to those still in the bush.

A few of the girls jumped up at the news. "We didn't know!" They covered their mouths and laughed with surprise and joy for Sylvia. "Now there's just two more," one of the girls said, referring to Mariam Akello and Catherine Ojok. (Today they are still the only girls who have not yet returned. As of August 2007, they remain with Kony in Garamba National Park.)

Boys were coming close, trying to overhear. The girls leaned in toward me. "Do they know who you are?" I whispered. Although they were eight years older than their classmates, these Aboke Girls somehow still looked like the other thirteen- to sixteen-year-olds around them, not the twenty-one- to twenty-three-year-old women they were.

"Some know who we are."

"Some call us rebel wives. It's hard," said Janet Aber, who had been married to Sam Kolo.

Grace Acan told me that they ignore the comments, and that they have each other to keep them strong.

I looked at shy Jackie Wagesa, smaller and lighter-skinned than the others, and relayed a message to her from her grandmother, whom I'd met the day before. Her grandmother was destitute, and yet had asked me to tell Jackie that both she and Jackie's daughter were healthy and well, and not to worry about them. Jackie smiled and looked down at her hands. "I understand you're doing very well in school," I continued. "Congratulations."

She looked at me, smiled slightly, and looked down again. I knew she had been Joseph Kony's favourite wife, but when I asked the group about Kony, looking at her, she only shuffled her feet and refused to look up.

It was Grace Acan who told me that Kony had spirits that made him do unpredictable things.

"Do you think his spirits are real?" I asked.

The girls allowed a long silence to fill the air. None wanted to answer the question. A month earlier they had been embarrassed by a revealing *New York Times Magazine* feature article about them. The writer had asked about Kony's spirit. "We know he's serving a spirit," Grace Acan had replied. "We just don't know if it's a good or a bad spirit."[115]

"Now I'm feeling he has a bad spirit," said Caroline. "Before, when I was under his captivity, I thought he had a good spirit."

Grace said that they had been confused by him. "When there was a good spirit, he was so friendly and so merciful and so encouraging. When there was a bad spirit, he was very rude and very cruel and gave orders to kill."

At last, Grace summed it up for the group. "He believes, but we don't," she said. Father John had mentioned that Grace was their natural leader; that the rest of the girls deferred to her. They all nodded in agreement, except Jackie, who looked at her feet with a pained expression.

"I understand you are all close now," I said, hoping this would lighten the mood again.

"We are like sisters," Grace Acan said.

"Sometimes sisters argue," I said. That made them laugh, and one assured me that they never argue.

"We're closer than sisters," said Janet. For a while we chatted about the school, their living conditions, their children.

Then I turned the topic back to those previous years. "Can you tell me what happened in the bush?" I said, turning to Grace.

She smiled. A strong, beautiful smile that conveyed such mystery to me. "It was very hard," she began.

THE ABOKE GIRLS

In October 1996, when the girls were abducted, they were all between the ages of eleven and sixteen. What follows is a summary of their subsequent fates, and where they are today.

Rebecca Kia	Given to a rebel commander. Now attending high school in Kampala, in Senior 1. One child.
Jacqueline Wegesa	Joseph Kony's favourite wife. Mother to Rebecca. Currently the second-ranked student at her school in Kampala. Hopes to become a doctor.
Palma Achieng	Given to Nyeko Tolbert; produced two children. Attending school in Kampala.
Grace Grall Akallo	Given to Lieutenant Lakati, who climbed the ranks to major general. No children. Escaped in 1997. Lakati was killed by the UPDF in June 2005. Grace is now attending Boston College on scholarship.
Grace Acan	Given to Brigadier-General Kenneth Banya, with whom she had two children. One died in July 2004. The other, Mercy, lives with Grace's mother, Consy Ogwal. Attending school in Kampala.
Jacqueline Alobo	Daughter of Ben Pere, the first executive director of the Concerned Parents Association, who died in 1998. Married off to ICC-indicted Vincent Otti, LRA's second-in-command. One child. In school in Kampala.
Caroline Anyango	No children. Allowed to leave the LRA after her husband, Major-General Lakati Owor, overheard her friends calling for her on Radio Wa.

Janet Aber	Given to Sam Kolo, with whom she produced two children. Was freed by Kolo in 2004. Kolo has taken amnesty from the government, and lives in Gulu.
Janet Akello	Given to LRA Lieutenant Charles Otim, with whom she had two children. Daughter of a Lira engineer. She is now attending school in Kampala. Otim was captured by the UPDF in 2005, and accepted amnesty. He has reconciled with Janet's father, who now considers Otim as a son.
Victoria Nyanjura	Two children with a rebel commander. Attending school in Kampala.
Susan Ejang	Escaped from the LRA in 2004. Daughter of Ben Pere.
Angela Atim	Co-wife with Louiza Namale. Daughter of Florence Lacor. Given to a commander who died of AIDS in 1999.
Agatha Longoria	Escaped in February 2004 and returned to St. Mary's school in Aboke. One surviving child; the other died while strapped to her back in 2002. She has returned to live with the Karamojong tribe.
Charlotte Awino	Daughter of Angelina Atyam. Escaped in 2004. Attending school in Kampala. Given as a wife to Raska Lukwiya, who was indicted by the International Criminal Court. Has two children from Lukwiya, who are in Angelina's care.
Agnes A.	Escaped in 1999. Graduated from a prominent Kampala high school with the financial assistance of an Irish donor. Preparing to become a doctor.
Caroline Akello	Escaped in late-1996 before entering Sudan. Graduate of university college in Kampala. Recently gave birth to her first child.
Pamela Adokorac	Escaped in 1996, before crossing into Sudan. Completed university.
Barbara Alopo	Escaped in 1996, before crossing into Sudan. Completed university.

Agnes Occiti	Escaped in 1996, before crossing into Sudan. Now a lawyer and activist. Was reportedly recently hired by the International Criminal Court at The Hague.
Josephine Lolem	Escaped before entering Sudan. Has now completed university.
Esther Acio	Escaped before entering Sudan. Has now completed university.
Sandra Everlyn Akot	Escaped before entering Sudan. Has now completed university.
Mariam Akello	Missing. Believed travelling with Kony, likely hiding out in Garamba National Park, Congo. Unknown if she has children.
Catherine Ajok	Missing. Believed travelling with Kony, without children. Probably also in Garamba National Park.
Sylvia Alaba	Returned June 3, 2005, with one baby. Attending school in Kampala.
Judith Enang	RIP. Tortured and murdered December 31, 1997, on Joseph Kony's orders for planning the escape of the Aboke Girls.
Jessica Anguu	RIP. Given to Raska Lukwiya. Killed by UPDF bomb in February 2004. Her child found alive on her back.
Louiza Namele	RIP. Co-wife with Angela Atim. Husband died of AIDS, after which she served as a teacher and slave until her death by a UPDF bomb in February 2004. Daughter of Alfred Olum of Kampala, who solicited the help of Jimmy Carter.
Brenda Atoo	RIP. Killed in 2004 by UPDF bomb, with one child also killed. The daughter of former Kampala banker Emmanuel Orongo.
Grace Oyela	Married.

ACKNOWLEDGMENTS

There are many people, and a few groups, who assisted me either with inspiration or information while I wrote this book. First, thanks to *Reader's Digest* for initially sending me to Africa in 2000. African stories do not often get told in newspapers and rarely in magazine articles, let alone books. By internationally publishing my earlier articles about Northern Uganda, *Reader's Digest* made me believe that, contrary to popular opinion, this book could find an audience.

It was the Toronto-based nongovernmental agency CPAR that first led me to this story by insisting on bringing me to a displaced persons' camp outside Gulu, where they rounded up a group of former LRA soldiers who shared their experiences with me. And when I returned to Uganda in 2005 to begin researching *Stolen Angels,* CPAR-Uganda, whose country manager is a graduate of St. Mary's school, helped me immensely. Thank you to Evelyne Ogwal, Gizaw Shibru, and Pius.

Thanks as well to author Anthony Hyde, who over a long lunch a few years ago encouraged me to write a non-fiction book about an army of children in Northern Uganda. Back then, the story I had intended was not this one, but he began the process that led me to the Aboke Girls.

I hadn't heard of the Comboni missionaries before I began writing this book. To me, they are a testament to the incredible in Catholicism. I am a Protestant by birth, and don't regularly attend church, but, knowing the story of the Combonis as I do now, I am in awe of them. I could not here tell you all their stories, but the heroism that I offer in the depictions of Sister Rachele Fessara, Sister Alba Brulo, Father John Fraser, and Father Carlos Rodriguez is shared by the hundred or so Combonis that now live in Northern Uganda and by the thousands more living in the poorest areas of the world. The Combonis are special. I have never encountered such an order of selfless heroes before, and the world should know more about them.

A heartfelt thanks, as well, to the Stolen Angels of my book: the Aboke Girls. When I first met them I told them that I couldn't think of anything worse happening to a human being, and that I was humbled by their strength to endure. They represent the thousands of others who also suffered, and I hope that these courageous young women will soon become leaders for their wounded generation. I do believe God has nurtured them, and their parents, for this purpose.

Of course, I want to thank all the people in this book who trusted me with their stories. In Uganda, many people assisted me. I don't want to mention them all by name, in part because I want to protect the identities of some.

Els De Temmerman, a Belgian philanthropist, author of the moving and highly recommended book *Aboke Girls,* and founder of the Rachele Rehabilitation Centre in Lira, gave me wonderful access to the people of the Centre, for which I'm grateful. I would also like to thank Ben Hoffman for his time and expertise, and for the efforts he continues to make to end needless violence in the world, especially in Africa. I appreciated the photos from Mike Odongkara and Acholinet.com. I would also like to acknowledge the support of the Canada Council for the Arts.

Stolen Angels was difficult to research, with Northern Uganda's poverty and its ongoing war presenting many impediments. My partner, Mike Blanchfield, who recently became my husband, is the foreign affairs writer at Canwest News. He insisted that I was capable of doing this, went to the Ugandan war zone twice with me, and assisted in the editing. My mother was also a motivational backer from the start, and insisted that I had a duty to write this book regardless of the hurdles involved. Thanks as well to Norman Provencher, and to Penguin Canada—especially to Diane Turbide, Samantha Francis, and Karen Alliston for their editorial advice and their belief in the book.

IF *STOLEN ANGELS* encourages you to want to help, there are many ways to go about it. You may wish to donate to the future of St. Mary's school in Aboke, or more generally, to the Comboni missionaries of Uganda or

Sudan. Most of the recently escaped Aboke Girls are now under the care of the Comboni missionaries and can be directly assisted through their patron, Father John Fraser. Having spoken to the Aboke Girls, I can tell you that what they most want is to know that their own children are being taken care of, and that they and their children can continue in school. They would like sponsors.

St. Mary's Lacor Hospital in Gulu is an amazing institution, with deep Canadian roots, and your donations here would go far. World Vision has also been doing great rehabilitation work in Uganda, and through them you can sponsor a Northern Ugandan child. CPAR-Uganda, focused on water and sanitation, remains one of my favourite agencies. You may also wish to help the chronically underfunded but critically important Acholi Religious Leaders Peace Initiative. If you need help contacting these or other groups, you could also email me at stolenangels@gmail.com.

For my part, I am giving a portion of the proceeds from *Stolen Angels* to Northern Ugandan causes. I remain dedicated to assisting Northern Uganda as much as I can—by actively helping Radio Wa develop and expand, by continuing to assist several of the Aboke Girls, by trying to help the Aboke Old Girls Association to network, by helping launch the Canada Cup soccer league for war-traumatized youth in Northern Uganda, and by recently joining the volunteer executive board of the Canadian International Association of Applied Negotiation. Ultimately, working to prevent anything like this from happening again is the best donation. Your act of reading this book, understanding the issues, and telling others, especially politicians, would be most welcome support. This story didn't have to happen, and public will can help make the next chapter a better one.

ENDNOTES

1. Mahatma Gandhi, *All Men Are Brothers: Life and Thoughts of Mahatma Gandhi as Told in His Own Words,* Krishna Kripalani (ed.), World Without War Publications, 1972. Reprinted by permission of the Gandhi Institute, India.

2. Sam Farmar, "Uganda Rebel Leader Breaks Silence," BBC, June 28, 2006. The report also aired June 28, 2006, on BBC television.

3. Narrative compiled from several direct interviews with the Aboke Girls, John Bosco, the parents, Sister Alba, and secondarily, Sister Rachele. Also from a Comboni missionaries' 1998 unreleased filmed interview with Sister Rachele, by Father John Fraser and Father Provido, assisted by Cathy Metjenyi. Research also from *Aboke Girls* by Els De Temmerman, Kampala: Fountain Publishers, 2001, which was confirmed as accurate by Sister Rachele; and from the taped testimony of Sister Rachele in Paulo Brenna's *Sister, the Rebels Are Here*, Italy: Brest Inc., 2001.

4. www.Comboni.Org, "Comboni Missionaries of the Heart of Jesus, Evangelisers of Justice and Peace," www.comboni.org/index.php?Lingua=EN&ca=10110&CodNews=100041.

5. From the Comboni 2002 beatification ceremony, read at the Comboni House, Kitchener, Ontario.

6. Twenty-three martyrs are remembered at the Mamugongo Pyre site in Kampala. The twenty-third died by fire before these boys. For more details, see J.F. Faupel, *African Holocaust: The Story of the Uganda Martyrs*, Nairobi: St. Paul Publications, 1964.

7. Els De Temmerman, *Aboke Girls*, Kampala: Fountain Press, 2001, p. 36.

8. Letticia Mae, "How I Survived Kony's Hell," *The East African*, December 13, 2004, www.nationmedia.com/eastafrican/13122004/Features/Part2.html.

9. From interviews on June 4, 2005, with the Aboke Girls.

10. Kony's techniques are well documented in Human Rights Watch survivor testimonies as well as in hundreds of other NGO and media reports. This account comes from personal interviews with survivors.

11. Professor Heike Behrend, *Alice Lakwena and the Holy Spirits*, translated by Mark Cohen, Oxford, 1999.

12. No byline, "Kony Will Never Surrender, His Top Commanders Say," *New Vision*, May 17, 2006.

13. Ibid. Testimony of former Brigadier Michael Acellam.

14. Much of this is speculation and recalled years afterward. Some reports say he left with twenty-seven followers.

15. Balam Nyeko and Okello Lucima, "Profiles of the Parties to the Conflict," *Accord,* London: Conciliation Resources, Issue 11, 2002, www.c-r.org/accord/uganda/accord11/profiles.shtml.

16. Deborah Scroggins, *Emma's War,* Vintage Books, 2004, p. 39.

17. There is much controversy here, which is beyond the scope of this book. See "Sudan, Oil, and Human Rights," Human Rights Watch, 2003, www.hrw.org/reports/2003/sudan1103/11.htm.

18. Hundreds of thousands more died in war-related famine and disease caused by displacement.

19. Palma's testimony, *Aboke Girls,* Childsoldiers.net, accessed August 2006 at www.childsoldiers.net/xcms/lang__en/4719/default.aspx.

20. Some of these girls might have transferred to Kony after some time.

21. Henk Rossouw, "An African Tale: First Hell, Then College," *The Chronicle of Higher Education,* Washington, August 8, 2003.

22. "Banya's Story," *Uganda Observer,* September 16, 2004.

23. Quoted from Michelle Rasmussen, "Copenhagen Seminar on Africa Takes Up British Genocide Executive Intelligence Review," October 10, 1997, pp. 50–53. Accessed May 2007 at www.aboutsudan.com/conferences/schiller_institute/copenhagen.htm.

24. "Banya's Story," *Uganda Observer,* September 16, 2004.

25. According to most accounts, Odong Latek, the army commander of the ousted rebels, was not abducted. In fact, it is widely assumed that these men chose to continue fighting after meeting with Kony, although they probably believed they'd be executed if they surrendered. I have here allowed Banya's testimony to tell his truth of the story, for he was there and his facts corroborate well with other testimony, although he does have a motivation to lie.

26. Benon Herbert Oluka, "Kony's Master Planner Spills It," *Uganda Observer,* September 16, 2004, www.ugandaobserver.com/new/archives/2004arch/features/spec/sep/spec200409162.php.

27. *Aboke Girls,* p. 74.

28. *Aboke Girls,* p. 74.

29. "Let My People Go!," Acholi Religious Leaders Peace Initiative, 2001.

30. Grace Grall explained that she saw the bomb explode into the lorry. I have no other accounts that Kony's wives and children died here. It might have been another group that were hit, as I have heard testimony that the wives made it to Juba. No Aboke Girls died in this bombing.

31. Reported in *Aboke Girls,* and from Grace's testimony.

32. Human Rights Watch, "Abducted and Abused, Renewed Conflict in Northern Uganda," July 2003.

33. "From School Girl to Child Soldier, to College," Grace Akallo, www.octeam.com/pdf/newsletter.pdf.

34. Anglican Communion News Service (ACNS) 1127, February 14, 1997.

35. Their modern story of a Protestant Christianity began only in 1948, when Janani Luwum, one of the smartest young men of Acholiland and already a teacher and leader for his people, found God. He became a Protestant minister and swiftly climbed the ranks to become the Anglican Archbishop of the African Great Lakes Region, presiding over all of Uganda, Congo-Zaire, Rwanda, and Burundi. But it came to a brutal end when Idi Amin assassinated him in 1977. The day after he was murdered, Idi Amin's death squad came looking for Ochola, then Luwum's assistant in Kitgum. The Catholic Bishop of Gulu, Bishop Cipriano, smuggled Ochola and his family into exile in Congo-Zaire.

36. *Aboke Girls,* pp. 81–82, starting with this quote and up to "'To avoid any further abductions, the only solution is the military option,' he countered.'"

37. *Aboke Girls,* p. 113.

38. *Aboke Girls,* p. 116. The next quote is from Tina Spencer, *Ottawa Citizen.*

39. "Kony Rebels Massacre 82," *New Vision,* April 22, 1995; "Kony Toll Rises," *New Vision,* April 24, 1995; "Atiak's Longest Day of the Bullet," *Sunday Vision,* April 30, 1995.

40. *Aboke Girls,* p. 127. It also comes together from several other interviews and videotaped testimony of Sister Rachele taken around that time.

41. *Aboke Girls,* p. 128.

42. Simon Simonse, *Steps Towards Peace and Reconciliation in Northern Uganda: An Analysis of Initiatives to End the Armed Conflict Between the Government of Uganda and the Lord's Resistance Army 1987–1998,* Utrecht: Pax Christi Netherlands, 1998.

43. Some of this material is taken from *Aboke Girls,* p. 133, and Elizabeth Rubin, "Our Children Are Killing Us," *The New Yorker,* March 23, 1999, p. 64.

44. Olara Otunnu studied at Oxford University and Harvard Law School, where he was a Fulbright Scholar. From 1980 to 1985 he was Uganda's representative at the United Nations, and between 1985 and 1986, when Museveni took Uganda, he was Uganda's foreign affairs minister and the broker in the failed negotiated settlement between Museveni and the Ugandan government. His uncle, General Tito Okello, who overtook Obote in 1985, was overpowered by Museveni in 1986.

45. www.peacewomen.org/news/January03/Angelina.html.

46. Marc Lacey, "A Mother's Bitter Choice: Telling Kidnappers No," *The New York Times,* January 25, 2003.

47. Comboni Missionaries, unpublished videotape, full conversation between Father John and Angelina.

48. Florence recreated her prayer on camera, and it appeared on *An Unconventional War*, 2007.

49. Anglican Communion News Service (ACNS) 1232, May 9, 1997.

50. Ibid.

51. *Accord*, Conciliation Resources, Northern Uganda, Chronology.

52. Support for the LRA rebels was very low at this point, as Kony had been abducting and killing the Acholi people daily for two years. In my opinion, and that of most analysts, it was not true that the Acholi people supported Joseph Kony, although they did also fear the NRM government of Museveni.

53. The UPDF says that they fired only on suspected LRA-inhabited villages.

54. This version is widely accepted, and detailed in "Let My People Go!" as well as many other accounts and witness testimony of the origins of the camps.

55. "Let My People Go!," Acholi Religious Leaders Peace Initiative, 2001. This allegation is a major ongoing issue in this war.

56. From U.S. government official transcript.

57. History pulled from Deborah Cowley's *Lucille Teasdale: Doctor of Courage*, Toronto: XYZ Publishing, 2005.

58. Sudan Catholic Information Service, Sudan Monthly Report, December 15, 1997.

59. As explained to a crowd of hundreds, and reported in many locations, by Charlotte on October 10, 2004, while at the St. Mary's Memorial in Aboke, as Grace listened and cried.

60. "Kony Will Never Surrender, His Top Commanders Say," *New Vision*, May 17, 2006. Note that the recollection of events from this time is being given years later, in May 2006.

61. Ibid.

62. Helen's Testimony, Church Mission Society. (Alice finally escaped successfully in 2000.)

63. Father Carlos at Makerere Law School, reported in *The Monitor*, "UPDF Killed 30 Children, Says Priest," May 27, 1999.

64. Human Rights Watch, *Hostile to Democracy: The Movement System and Political Repression in Uganda*, New York, 1999.

65. *Emma's War*, p. 348.

66. Bin Laden lived in Sudan from 1991 until the spring of 1996, when he was extradicted as a result of pressure on Sudan from Saudi Arabia and the United States. Reports have surfaced that at this time bin Laden was unofficially offered to the U.S. government, but the U.S. refused. Instead, he relocated to Afghanistan, and in August of 1996 declared jihad with his Al Qaeda army. He declared his intention to force U.S. forces from the Arabian Peninsula, bring down the government of Saudi Arabia, free Muslim holy sites, and support Islamic revolution around the world.

67. David Whitehouse, "What's Behind the Horror in Sudan?," *Socialist Worker,* September 17, 2004, www.socialistworker.org/2004-2/512/512_05_Sudan.shtml.

68. Jimmy Carter, "Have We Forgotten the Path to Peace?," *The New York Times,* May 27, 1999.

69. Joyce Neu, "Protracted Conflict, Elusive Peace Initiatives to End the Violence in Northern Uganda," *Accord,* London: Conciliation Resources, 2002.

70. Whether or not Sudan engaged in slavery is a controversial point. The Comboni priests living in South Sudan did make an international statement that they did not believe these claims, which were being touted and used to collect money in their churches, by mostly American Christian Right groups who had explained to the American populace that the war was about Sudan's desire to Islamize the Christians in the South. The issue is beyond the scope of this book.

71. The LRA say that the Sudanese government never invited them to the talks for their own strategic purposes. The Carter Center, without a direct route to Kony, had relied on the Sudanese government to deliver the invite to the LRA. It is unknown if Kony would have participated in the talks. This statement that he would have is my own opinion.

72. "Greater Horn of Africa, Peacebuilding Project," USAID, 2001.

73. It's relevant to mention here, as an example of the degree of witchcraft and cultism in Uganda, that on March 17, 2000, Uganda became the site of the worst single incident of cult killings in world history, surpassing the previous worst case of 912 dead in the Jonestown mass suicide of 1978. Over a thousand followers of the Movement for the Restoration of the Ten Commandments were found dead in rural Southern Uganda, half in a church that was set on fire, the others in mass graves on the grounds of the cult. They were killed when, after the false prophecy of the world's end failed to materialize, the cult members began asking for their life savings back. The cult, which claimed divine leadership from the Virgin Mary, was led by a former prostitute and an excommunicated Catholic priest.

74. Public testimony of Charlotte.

75. Tamsin Carlisle, "Calgary Oil Firm Talisman Pays Painful Price for Sudan Investment," *The Wall Street Journal,* August 17, 2000.

76. Paul Knox, "Criticism of Sudan Unfair, Ismail Says," *The Globe and Mail,* September 18, 2000.

77. Stephen Lewis, "Canada's Terrible Cross of Dishonour," *The Globe and Mail,* September 14, 2000.

78. The events described surrounding the Ebola virus at Lacor and in Gulu are pulled together from a variety of sources, including direct interviews with several at the hospital. The excellent *New York Times* cover story by Blaine Harden, "Dr. Matthew's Passion," February 18, 2001, and "Dangerous Medicine" by Tom Clynes, *National Geographic Adventure,* May/June 2001, were notable in their help.

79. Tom Clynes, "Dangerous Medicine II," *National Geographic Adventure,* May/June 2001.

80. New Year Peace Message of the Religious Leaders of Acholi, www.arch-dioceseofgulu.org/JPC/ARLPI%20N_YMsg.htm.

81. As reported by Father Carlos Rodriguez Soto.

82. Their letter was dated December 31, 2001, and signed by John Baptist Odama, the Catholic Archbishop of Gulu; Nelson Onono-Onweng, the Protestant Bishop of Northern Uganda; Shiek Musa Khalil, the Muslim Acholi Khadi; and Mcleord Baker Ochola II, the Protestant Bishop of Kitgum.

83. Open Letter to American Ambassador to Uganda from the Acholi Religious Leaders Peace Initiative, Gulu (Uganda), September 22, 2001, to Martin Brennan, American Ambassador in Uganda.

84. Dennis Ojwee, "Kony LRA Rebels Enter Gulu," *New Vision,* June 13, 2002.

85. Human Rights Watch, "Abducted and Abused," p. 36.

86. Yoweri Museveni, "Museveni Responds to Gulu Peace Negotiator on Kony," *The Monitor,* August 28, 2002.

87. "Arrest of the Priests: Peacemakers' Personal Stories: We Were Terrorised That the Soldiers Would Kill Us at Any Moment," Father Giulio Albanese, http://homepage.tinet.ie/~gulufuture/arrest_of_priests%20.htm.

88. Note: That contentious article has been removed from the electronic archives of *The Monitor,* although Museveni's rebuttal remains. There are no records I could find anywhere of that article, and Carlos Rodriguez did not include it in a list of writings he offered to me.

89. *The Monitor,* August 30, 2002.

90. "Priest to Continue Peace Talks," *New Vision,* September 2, 2002.

91. *The Monitor,* September 10, 2002.

92. Henk Rossouw, "First Hell, Then College," *The Chronicle of Higher Education,* Washington, August 8, 2003.

93. This account of Grace beginning life at the Christian University comes from research by Henk Rossouw in his feature, "First Hell, Then College," *The Chronicle of Higher Education,* August 8, 2003.

94. In a 2006 BBC interview, Kony said it was an imposter who called in to radio programs. Although the nature of what was said, and the fact that he was first introduced by Vincent Otti, who was known to make phone calls and whose voice was recognized, makes this questionable, in my opinion.

95. Reproduced and transcribed in various sources, including *The Monitor,* "Uganda: I Want Peace, but Museveni Is the Problem, Says Kony," January 1, 2003, and www.lraproject.com. Transcript copy also given to me by a source.

96. The boy escaped from the rebels several months later, and reunited with Father Carlos.

97. Father Carlos was unaware that a Ugandan soldier had earlier that morning saved his life when he found and removed a land mine planted under the seat of Father Carlos's truck. Jimmy, the boy who'd been abducted, had watched the rebels lay the land mine.

98. This statement is based on unnamed but high-ranking sources who told it to Hoffman.

99. A few weeks later Father Carlos and the Acholi religious leaders sent a report to the United Nations news agency informing them that the Sudanese army was arming the LRA. Father Carlos told IRIN, the journalistic arm of the UN Office for the Coordination of Humanitarian Affairs, when a reporter called: "We always had our suspicions when we kept seeing the LRA with new uniforms and new guns. But we didn't have enough to be sure. Now, with each independent report coming from the bush saying the same thing, we know for a fact that they [the SAF] are doing this." Also see "Khartoum Denies Backing Ugandan Rebels," IRIN, June 19, 2003.

100. Stephanie Nolen, *The Globe and Mail*, June 25, 2003.

101. Compiled from www.rr-bb.com/archive/index.php/t-133278.html.

102. Anonymous, "Museveni Visits Lira, Makes Public Apology," *New Vision*, February 26, 2004.

103. Grace Akallo, *The Chronicle of Higher Education*, October 15, 2004.

104. "Banya's Story," Kenneth Banya, *Uganda Observer*, September 16, 2004.

105. Halima Abdallah, *Uganda Observer*, November 4, 2004. Recordings of the testimonies given by the Aboke Girls on the eighth anniversary of their abduction from St. Mary's.

106. John Muto-Ono P' Lajur, "Stop Killings, Says Kony's Wife," *Monitor*, October 18, 2004.

107. Ibid.

108. Harriette A. Onyalla, "Uganda: After Horror in LRA Camps, Hope Dawns," *New Vision*, December 20, 2004.

109. Ibid.

110. Carlos Rodriguez, "Northern Ugandans, South Sudanese Are One," *New Vision*, September 7, 2005.

111. Another account says that the Khartoum regime provided inflatable rafts for the LRA to travel across the Nile.

112. "Uganda: Gov't, LRA to Hold Talks Despite ICC Indictments," IRIN, July 3, 2006.

113. Spoken at a World Vision headquarters speech in June 2006. Grace was also quoted in the *Washington Post*.

114. St. Mary's Lacor Hospital, *Annual Report*, F/Y 2004/2005.

115. Melanie Thernstrom, "Charlotte, Grace, Janet and Caroline Come Home," *The New York Times Magazine*, May 8, 2005.

SELECTED BIBLIOGRAPHY

Achieng, Palma. *Aboke Girls*. Childsoldiers.net, accessed May 30, 2007, at www.childsoldiers.net/xcms/lang_en/4719/default.aspx.

Acholi Religious Leaders Peace Initiative. *The Forgotten Plight of the People in the Displaced Camps in Acholi: An Assessment Carried Out by the Acholi Religious Leaders' Peace Initiative and the Justice & Peace Commission of Gulu Archdiocese*. Uganda: July 2001.

Akallo, Grace Grall. "An African Tale, Continued: First Hell, Then College, Now a Journey to America," *Chronicle of Higher Learning*. April 9, 2004.

Allafrica.com. AllAfrica Global Media archives, Washington, 1996–2007, accessed June 2007 at allafrica.com.

Archdiocese of Gulu. Reports, statements, and messages accessed in Gulu, June 2005. Also accessed online March 2007 at www.archdioceseofgulu.org.

Axworthy, Lloyd. *Navigating a New World: Canada's Global Future*. Toronto: Alfred A. Knopf, 2003.

Banya, Kenneth. "Banya's Story," *Uganda Observer,* September 16, 2004, www.ugandaobserver.com/new/archives/2004arch/features/spec/sep/spec200409161.php.

Barlow, Maude, and Tony Clarke. *Global Showdown: How the New Activists Are Fighting Global Corporate Rule*. Toronto: Stoddart, 2001.

Behrend, Heike. *Alice Lakwena and the Holy Spirits: War in Northern Uganda 1986–97*. Translated by Mitch Cohen. Oxford: James Currey, 1999.

Brenna, Paolo. Sister, the Rebels Are Here, video documentary and text. Milan, Italy: Brest Inc., 2001. Accessed September 2006 at www.brest.it.

Briggs, Jimmie. *Innocents Lost: When Child Soldiers Go to War*. New York: Basic Books, 2005.

Cirillo, Tescaroli. *Daniel Comboni: A Pioneer of the Church in Africa*. Cincinnati: Comboni Missionaries, undated.

Clynes, Tom. "Dangerous Medicine," *National Geographic Adventure* magazine, May/June 2001. Accessed April 2006 at www.members.authorsguild.net/tomclynes/work2.htm.

Comboni Missionaries. Unpublished video footage, taped May 8–14, 1998, in Lira and St. Mary's Aboke School, Uganda. Accessed from the Comboni Mission House, Kitchener, Ontario, November 2005.

Cowley, Deborah. *Lucille Teasdale: Doctor of Courage.* Toronto: XYZ Publishing, 2005.

De Temmerman, Els. *Aboke Girls.* Kampala: Fountain Publishers, 2001.

East African. Nation Media, archives, 2004–2007.

Farmar, Sam. "Uganda Rebel Leader Breaks Silence," BBC, June 28, 2006.

Geldof, Bob. *Geldof in Africa.* London, U.K.: Century, 2005.

Gifford, Paul. *African Christianity: Its Public Role in Uganda and Other African Countries.* Kampala: Fountain Publishers, 1999.

Harden, Blaine. "Dr. Matthew's Passion," *The New York Times Magazine,* cover story, February 18, 2001.

Human Rights Watch. *Abducted and Abused: Renewed Conflict in Northern Uganda.* New York: July 2003.

Human Rights Watch. *Hostile to Democracy: The Movement System and Political Repression in Uganda.* New York: 1999.

Human Rights Watch. *The Scars of Death: Children Abducted by the Lord's Resistance Army in Uganda.* New York: 1997.

Leadership magazine, articles from issues published between 2001 and 2007. Comboni Missionaries: Mbuya, Uganda.

Mae, Letticia. "How I Survived Kony's Hell," *The East African,* December 13, 2004.

The Monitor. Nation Media Group, article archive, Kampala, Uganda, 1996–2007.

New Vision. Government of Uganda, article archives, Kampala, 1996–2007.

Okello, Lucima, ed. "Protracted Conflict, Elusive Peace Initiatives to End the Violence in Northern Uganda," *Accord,* London: Conciliation Resources, 2002.

Otis, George, Jr. *An Unconventional War* (DVD). Lynnwood, WA: TransformNations Media, 2006.

Rasmussen, Michelle. "Copenhagen Seminar on Africa Takes Up British Genocide," *Executive Intelligence Review,* October 10, 1997, pp. 50–53.

Rossouw, Henk. "An African Tale: First Hell, Then College," *The Chronicle of Higher Education,* Washington, August 8, 2003.

Rubin, Elizabeth. "Our Children Are Killing Us," *The New Yorker,* March 23, 1999, pp. 56–64.

Scroggins, Deborah. *Emma's War.* London: Vintage Books, reprint edition, 2004.

Sewall, Sarah, and Carl Kaysen, eds. *The United States and the International Criminal Court.* New York: American Academy of Arts and Sciences, Rowman & Littlefield Publishers, 2000.

Simmons, Mark, and Peter Dixon, eds. "Peace by Piece: Addressing Sudan's Conflicts," *Accord,* London: Conciliation Resources, 2006.

Simonse, Simon. *Steps Towards Peace and Reconciliation in Northern Uganda: An Analysis of Initiatives to End the Armed Conflict Between the Government of Uganda and the Lord's Resistance Army 1987–1998.* Utrecht, Netherlands: Pax Christi Netherlands, 1998.

Singer, P.W. *Children at War.* Berkeley, CA: University of California Press, 2006.

Soto, Carlos Rodriguez. *Collected Writings* (unpublished), provided to author by Rodriguez. Gulu: June 20, 2005.

Thernstrom, Melanie. "Charlotte, Grace, Janet and Caroline Come Home," *The New York Times Magazine,* May 8, 2005.

United Nations Security Council. *Final Report of the Panel of Experts on the Illegal Exploitation of Natural Resources and Other Forms of Wealth of the Democratic Republic of the Congo.* New York: S/2002/1146, October 16, 2002, and S/2001/357, April 12, 2001.

United Nations Security Council. *Addendum to the Report of the Panel of Experts on the Illegal Exploitation of Natural Resources and Other Forms of Wealth of the Democratic Republic of the Congo.* New York: S/2001/1072.

Van Acker, Frank. *Uganda and the Lord's Resistance Army: The New Order No One Ordered.* Norway: Institute of Development Policy and Management, University of Antwerp, 2003.

Ward, Bernard, mccj. *A Heart for Africa. The Life and Legacy of Saint Daniel Comboni.* Comboni Missionaries, North American Province, second edition, 2003.

"We Were Terrorised That the Soldiers Would Kill Us at Any Moment," Gulufuture.org. Accessed May 17, 2007, webpage title: Arrest of Priests, Peacemakers' Personal Stories, http://homepage.tinet.ie/~gulufuture/arrest_of_priests_20.htm.